The Invisible Republic

Robbie Smyth

The Invisible Republic

The Economics of Socialism and Republicanism in the 21st Century

palgrave
macmillan

Robbie Smyth
Faculty of Journalism and Media Communications
Griffith College
Dublin, Ireland

ISBN 978-3-030-86733-1 ISBN 978-3-030-86734-8 (eBook)
https://doi.org/10.1007/978-3-030-86734-8

This Palgrave Macmillan imprint is published by the registered company Springer Nature Switzerland AG.
The registered company address is: Gewerbestrasse 11, 6330 Cham, Switzerland

Preface

First some harsh words. Ireland today is a flawed society in a failing world. The aspirations of the 1916 revolutionaries have not been met. The promises of the 1916 Proclamation and the 1919 Democratic Programme for Government have been discarded, the UN Declaration of Human Rights is flouted at home and abroad. Our freedom and rights as individuals and communities are subject to a growing number of coercive constraints.

In our world today people are still hungry and homeless, people still go to war and some people still attempt to rule and exploit others and most importantly people still rebel against all of this. It seems that there are some elements of life that are unchanging.

As a republican activist in Sinn Fein and writing in An Phoblacht rebellion was and is the driving force of the republican pulse, the reason we entered the political arena in Ireland. We, I, believe the Ireland of today is not the ideal one, not the perfect one and that there is still a struggle for basic freedoms and justice. The sites and places of that struggle might have changed in the years since the 1994 IRA cessation and the 1998 Good Friday agreement, but the need to take a stand, and to take action, is as necessary, as relevant as ever.

Part of the problem of comprehending this state of coercion is that any attempt to even think about describing or quantifying the scale of economic and political change in the world over the last ten or even 20 years seems an intractable task. The transformations are so vast and so complex.

For example, there are the technological and societal impacts of computer technology, the internet, mobile and now 'smart' phones, the digital communication technologies that drive these products and the accompanying framework of complex networks, as well as information, communication and entertainment products that flow unceasingly from this supposed computopia.

Then there are the mass economic upheavals such as the triumph of the market system over the state capitalism of the soviet bloc, a conquest symbolised so aptly in the fall of the Berlin Wall and the end of the Cold War. Now there are the new wars in the post 9/11 world, and yet another global economic crisis the aftershocks of which are still being felt around the world. But perhaps the most difficult process to quantify is the growing realisation on the planet of the scale of environmental destruction humans have inflicted on this world. These events, these processes are just some of the examples of the profound ways who we are, how we live and how we see ourselves has changed.

In the world of today, the Ireland of today, all of these issues are relevant to the way society takes decisions about how and why it does things, and it is for this reason that this book had to be written. It offers a republican viewpoint of what is the best way to run a society. It is not a blue print, nor a manifesto, it is a series of essays about what I think are important economic issues and problems.

This book was written how I think a lot of us live our lives, full of good intentions, with a lot of false starts, and then periods of diligence, short bursts of 15 or 20 minutes grabbed here and there and so maybe it should be read that way too. I have tried to generate the text that you could just pick any page, begin at a bolded out heading and read to the end of the page. The pieces and the thinking underpinning them are interlocking but they also stand alone, I hope!

It is just another stone thrown in what is an endless battle of ideas about the best way to run a society. I hope the ideas here aren't just relevant to Ireland today, but will also be transferable and understood in other times and other places.

In this book I am attempting two things. The first is to characterise political events as a particular arena of conflict between a path to freedom and ongoing attempts to coerce and exploit the world's citizens. Secondly I want to show that the theories and ideas developed in the eight chapters didn't emerge from a political vacuum, they are the product of not just my musings on the economic society we live in today, but are ideas rooted in the experience of hundreds of years of political conflict.

This book offers a view on the battleground now in the long road to freedom of the people from subjugation, exploitation, whether it was the feudal imperialisms of Europe or the oligopolistic capitalism that sprung from the industrial revolution. It is a road with detours and at present what seems an impasse as a new Dickensian society threatens to emerge.

I felt a need to write this, a compulsion at times. So maybe give it 15 to 20 minutes and if that goes well, maybe another 15.

A start could be to read my conclusions outlined below in the form of nine principles. It might seem foolish or strange to give away the ending! However, this gives an insight into my approach, and how my thinking emerges in the accompanying text. In a small way the opening pages of Wittgenstein's Tractatus Logico-Philosophicus influenced me, and I probably deserve to be made fun of because of this. However, I sincerely believe that we need in this century be able to explain our key ideas simply and clearly, and that is what I have tried to do here.

The Principles of Socialist Republicanism in the Twenty-First Century

1. Individual freedom entails living in a state absent from coercion and exploitation.
2. We cannot be free as individuals unless we can exercise economic and political choices.
3. Republican freedom is conditional on a recognition of social interdependencies and the guarantees of equality of opportunity, access and treatment for citizens.
4. Money is not a neutral benign entity. Too often money is used to enslave and exploit. The renting of money resources should be entirely under the remit of a democratically formed government.
5. Markets will always tend towards oligopolies that seek to profit from their dominance and this is the rationale for market regulation.
6. To underpin the principles of social justice some goods should not be for sale, should not be able to be purchased. The provision and distribution of these goods should be regulated by society's democratically formed institutions.
7. Entrepreneurship is an exercise of republican freedom.

8. We can only understand our society if we measure its activities, processes and outcomes accurately and comprehensively not just in terms of money.
9. Business cannot enjoy rights on a par with an individual citizen. The person is sovereign.

Dublin, Ireland Robbie Smyth

Acknowledgements

This book couldn't have come to me without the road map, the historical trail created by the lineage of republican thinkers, who over the years informed my thinking. Theobald Wolfe Tone, Robert Emmet, Thomas Davis, Fintan Lalor, Padraig Pearse and James Connolly are the giants that deserve acknowledgement and also to be much more widely read today. It was writers and thinkers like Ernie O'Malley, Constance Markievicz, Liam Mellows, Peadar O'Donnell, Sean Cronin, Bernadette Devlin and Gerry Adams who initially introduced these thinkers to me. Any mistakes in my interpretation of these giants is entirely my own responsibility.

On a personal level I want to acknowledge Kevin Gill for support at the earliest of days, Micheal McDonnacha who saw a writer in me and gave me a desk in An Phoblacht. Seosamh MacCarthaigh introduced me to so many ideas and concepts and many more ideas in the years that this book was simmering away.

Lastly to Jane, Sorcha and Diarmuid for unerring support, belief and always thinking that writing while sitting at the kitchen table or on the couch was the most natural thing to do.

Contents

CHAPTER 1

The Invisible Republic: An Introduction

The Battles of Ideas: An Alternative History of Ireland

We are not free in Ireland today. We often have the illusion of freedom, but our guarantees of this are entirely conditional and often arbitrary. Money, status, wealth, social class and power might bestow an illusion of untested freedom on us, a perception of freedom, but in reality we are in an imperfect world and state.

The ideas, propositions and arguments in this book come from a drive to comment on the world as it appears to me today and the concept of seeing that world as a battle of ideas. This is one way to characterise this experience. Viewing Irish history over the past 250 years as a battle of ideas is at first at difficult task. It is easier or perhaps more comfortable to view conflict in Ireland as one of geography, territory or control of resources. This vista creates a history of disagreement and violent clashes where we have the planter in a sixteenth and seventeenth century standoff with the dispossessed natives, or as an eighteenth century competition for arable land in a subsistence based agri-economy or as a twentieth century dispute over partition. In the emerging twenty-first century it is not yet clear where the battle lines are drawn but there are a myriad of areas of disagreement between the political establishment on one hand and those who seek to defy and rebel against it on another. It would not be right to dismiss these aspects of the conflict in Ireland, but what is more important is to site them in another context.

R. Smyth, *The Invisible Republic*,
https://doi.org/10.1007/978-3-030-86734-8_1

That being said it should be noted that perhaps the most annoying perception of the conflict in Ireland over the last 50 years is that of it being a religious one, but this raises the question as to who benefits by having the conflict portrayed in such perpetually antagonistic loaded terms. The *New York Times* in this era stands out as one of the great papers in English, but they still persist in using this twisted viewpoint in its terminology and makes you wonder what hope there is for the other media if this is the standard being set. Have a look at the *Times* in 2006 where Gerry Adams and Martin McGuinness are described as leaders of the "main Roman Catholic party" (Quinn, 2006). Or more recently in 2017 after the death of Sinn Fein's Martin McGuinness, the *New York Times* wrote of "bombings and killings that raged from the 1960s to the 1990s between Protestant and Roman Catholic forces" (McFadden, 2017).

For republicans it is possibly the most exasperating representation of modern Irish culture, particularly as inter religious conflicts are probably the shortest chapter in Irish history and modern Irish society's rush towards secular archetypes in the late twentieth century is unparalleled in the world today. That such a transformation was effected in the Irish psyche undermines any claim that religion was a tangible reason for long term conflict. Yes, there was wholesale sectarianism perpetrated by the British in Ireland and the failed attempt in the twentieth century to create a Catholic theocracy in the 26 Counties showed again an elite in power willing to use religion as a means to maintain influence and control, but in both cases religious issues were fostered by elites, by the political establishment, to hold power unjustly and not because of any deep seated religious beliefs held by the actual population.

There were in fact other more deeply held and believed ideologies in conflict in Ireland and my aim in this text is to look on history for this context as being about these competing, conflicting ideologies and beliefs in an economic context. In this case the perspective proposed is to consider past eras as a battleground of competing ideas and in particular to look on the last 250 years plus from the era of Swift, Grattan and Burke through to the present day.

First there were the British monarchists, with their feudal agricultural oligarchy on one side replaced by a capitalist plutocracy in later years. Alongside this you had the Irish oligarchs and plutocrats of the twentieth and twenty-first centuries who were and still are more than willing to recreate the British capitalist hegemony years later on their own terms.

Then you had those who resisted and at various junctures drove the country to revolution. Central to the resisters' side was and still is the ideology of republicanism; however there was a packed opposition and other political movements many of them republican in nature also filled out the revolutionary ranks particularly as the pace of economic and social change quickened in the late nineteenth century. Not only were republicans resisting but they were also part of a much larger movement campaigning for cultural and national rights, the equality of women and workers, as well as a just democracy on the island. There are also in every era pseudo false revolutionaries, but more on that later.

This process is repeated in many other societies whether it is the USA of the 1770s, the French Revolution, the Levellers and the Chartists in Britain, the Indian National Congress, Cuba in the 1960s, South Africa in the twentieth century, Central and South America in any decade you care to pick, North Africa and parts of the Middle East in the twenty-first century Arab Spring. The drive towards a real process of liberation is part of the base essence of positive humanity.

There was and still is also the reality of people who have been pushed too far, exploited and abused, who rebelled because the harshness of their economic and political reality meant that this course of action could be no worse from the dire circumstances they already found themselves in. The pictures in 2010 of Mohammed Bouazizi, a street vendor in the Tunisian town of Sidi Bouzid, who set himself on fire in a protest at the harassment and exploitation he endured on a daily basis is an apt example for the power of rebellion. His actions were the catalyst for the Arab Spring (Abouzeid, 2011).

In my years as a republican activist I have always taken strength and inspiration from the simple experience of sitting and listening to the struggles and campaigning plans of local groups and their strategies to grow Sinn Fein in their area. There is no glamour to these meetings, the chairs hard, the halls often cold, the time always late and pressing. Yet the people moved on driven to take action again the wrongs and injustices they believed filled the world around them.

Losing the Battle

Victory in this battle of ideas would mean wielding power and the bad news for republicans, especially socialist republicans is that they lost an important round of this conflict in the aftermath of the war of independence and the resulting partitioned Ireland. The good news is that it is also a battle without end, so there is always a chance to return to combat. The battle of ideology was just as important as the physical conflict in the streets and across rural Ireland and though it was fought in these arenas it was also a conflict with widely differing settings.

It was fought in the parliament in Dublin and London, as well as through public meetings, street speeches and other political forums, but also through books, pamphlets and newspapers. In the twentieth century, broadcast radio and TV media were added to these existing avenues and the censorship of this message from radio and television in Britain and Ireland shows how important the channels of communication are to airing struggling conflicting competing ideas and views about what is happening in society. Now in a new century the internet and other new so called 'social' media join the fray as sites of struggle in the competition for whose reality, whose interpretation of what was true and untrue will be believed by the general public and more importantly—who would get to take the important political decisions that give structure and meaning to everyday life.

Victory in the battle of ideas means simple things like deciding what constitutes a crime, who builds the roads and the schools, how do our hospitals work, how will our housing be planned and built, what will our workplace be like, what relationships will our society, our island, forge with the other societies surrounding it, where do the rights of an individual citizen begin and end.

We know republicans lost the battle as the statelets on the island today have few of the characteristics and values that republicans would include in their vision of a free Ireland. The positive interpretation of this state of play is that the republican ideals still endure and despite all attempts to undermine, isolate and dilute these principles, they spring back, as new generations have over the years embraced the core values underpinning what a just equal Ireland would be.

And now republicans on the island are in a stronger position today politically than at any other time since the months after the 1916 rising, their ideological rationale is once again potent and never more relevant to the political and economic environment of the day. Hopefully, if you read this text in 50 or 100 years, you would find republican ideas still active and still relevant to how a society decides how to live. Proving this rationale of the enduring logic of republican struggle is a core theme of this text.

However, there is an element of wishful thinking on my part here, because in the short term focus on the economic downturn since 2008, there have been some gains for Sinn Fein politically, albeit with no guarantee that they are deeply rooted within the 26-County electorate, there has not been a parallel embracing of republican ideals even though there is perhaps increased discussion at an elite level about the rhetoric of a republic. Whether this signals a long term shift in public perceptions or in how elites and key communicators frame social and political debate we don't really know.

In this decade of centenaries, 2013 to 2023, there has been a resuscitated interest and discussion in the actions, motivations, writing and speeches of the republicans involved in the 1916 rising. But as to how long this interest will endure, I for one, can't predict. I never foresaw the scale of the positive interest in the 1916 commemorations and am intrigued at the renewed pride and interest in the Rising and the 1916 Proclamation. In 2019, there is some interest in the 1919 Democratic Programme of the first Dail, but it is unclear if there is a wider public cognisance of the importance of this assembly and how the promises of the January 1919 declarations were not kept.

Controlling the Channels of Communication

One reason for the loss of the battle of ideas that still holds true today was the fact that republicans rarely controlled the arenas and channels of communication. In the time of Henry Grattan, parliament was the premier arena of political communication. The voices and opinions raised here offered more weight than the street radicalism and dissent of the time that was thriving in Dublin and Belfast. Even when events like the Dublin food riots of 1795 took the national attention for a short while, normal service was resumed and ultimately it was the response of the parliament and Dublin Castle that shaped public discourse and determined policy making. Jim Smyth's *the Men of No Property* (1998) is an excellent insight into the street politics of the time.

A way of explaining the importance of perception and how that influences opinion both today and in previous eras is found in the term "Grattan's Parliament". Grattan was but one voice in this parliament and yes he was a dominant figure who managed to effect substantial political change. It was however short lived, ultimately reversed and with the Act of Union, Grattan's parliament was effectively dismantled.

There must have been political voices and opinion opposed to Grattan. It was they who eventually won the battles of the day. He lost. It seems too expedient that their names are not that easily remembered and that in the following decades as the republican struggle evolved we often seem to know more about those who failed than the British elite that vanquished the generations of republican activists.

The Emmet Example

Another example of the importance of the actual forum political discussion is happening in is found in the example of Robert Emmet. Emmet's rebellion pictorially is remembered mostly in a portrait drawing of Emmet and contemporary prints of his speech from the dock and subsequent execution. Again like Grattan Emmet's protagonists are forgotten even though they were the victors at the time.

Emmet's speech from the dock is the other legacy of this time, and is important for two reasons, the first being its enduring legacy and the second being the issue of where and how the speech was made.

Emmet spoke from the dock. He had little control over the setting. Much of his speech is spent defending his actions rather than outlining a vision of the type of Ireland he was fighting for. He was time constrained, limited and interrupted in his oration, there were for many years competing versions of what he said and it is only now that space is given to other revolutionaries of the time such as Anne Devlin. The actual discourse of what Emmet said has been diluted down into the closing sentence where he states, "When my country takes her place among the nations of the earth, then, and not until then, let my epitaph be written" (O'Day & Stevenson, 1992, p. 16). And so for the vast majority of people Emmet has been like Grattan sanitised into a safe relatively uncontroversial historical figure.

There is an equally powerful element of the speech when Emmet responds to the charge that he was an 'emissary of France'. The lines are found in some versions and was reproduced by the OPW in Dublin, according to Wikisource. In this section Emmet addresses Ireland, and says, "Oh, my country! Was it personal ambition that influenced me? Had it been the soul of my actions, could I not, by my education and fortune, by the rank and consideration of my family, have placed myself amongst the proudest of your oppressors? My country was my idol. To it I sacrificed every selfish, every endearing sentiment; and for it I now offer myself" (Wikisource, 2017). Here is the essence of the transcending power of the republican ideal. We want a society where your circumstances of birth, and your perceived social class is a not a constraint or a determinant on your citizenship, this point I return to later.

Though not in the dock today, republican comment and analysis still often has to be heard in the context of an analysis given in the context of responding to allegations and accusations rather than getting to the core of outlining what is a compelling vision of a better society.

Innovative Republicans

Getting access to the means of communication became a priority for republicans in the late eighteenth and nineteenth centuries. They were quick to use the new mediums and the nineteenth century in particular is littered with newspapers, pamphlets and books which were widely read. For example in Tone's time the Belfast based *Northern Star*, 1792 to 1797, had a circulation of 4000 copies (Bigger, 1894) and a cheap abridged version of Paine's rights of man was circulating again by the thousand in book form and in lengthy extracts printed in newspapers of the time (Smyth, 1998, pp. 92–93). It is estimated that the reach of the *Northern Star* was far wider than the circulation as the paper's articles were read aloud at United Irishmen meetings with some putting a figure of at least six readers to every copy sold (Smyth, 1998, p. 29).

The success of *The Nation*, a weekly newspaper founded by Thomas Davis, Charles Gavan Duffy and James Blake Dillon (O'Sullivan, 1944) is another example of early republican media innovators. Its first edition had 12,000 copies printed and at its height had an estimated weekly readership of 250,000 (O'Sullivan, 1944, p. 44). The creation of reading rooms by the Young Irelanders and the Repeal Association was another facet of republican innovation in creating channels of communication to their activist base, along with spinoff publications and imprints such as the Spirit of the Nation, the Library of Ireland and The Voice of Ireland.

In the nineteenth and early twentieth century republicans were prolific writers and printers of news, fiction, literature and a lot of rhetoric. Pearse and some of the other executed 1916 leaders were good examples of these versatile writers whose interests moved from politics to philosophy to literature. One example is that of James Connolly who was not just a political activist but also a writer, a newspaper founder and an orator of renown, but interestingly never in a parliament. His speaking was in public meetings and on the streets, often at the factory gates.

A more recent example of the power and importance of communications infrastructure is shown in the role RTE radio and then later RTE television played in the development of the 26-County state. RTE radio in the early years created through the promotion of live sports and celli dance music a safe identity for the emerging state, this framing was part of a much wider process of sanitising creative output in the new partitioned Ireland (Pettitt, 2000).

The debate within the Dublin government in the 1950s over the development of a state TV service shows the wariness of those in power towards new media. The development of acceptable representations of national culture for radio was only one aspect of the control imposed by the new state administration. The simple truth was that successive governments of different hues censored and tried to ban the production of ideas, of any competing ideologies. Ultimately at some level they were attempting to influence and control creative thought. The school curriculum was similarly sanitised and cleansed. Have a look at Cairns and Richards (1985) Writing Ireland text for an excellent overview of this process.

Film and book censorship became a way of life. Phillip Pettitt writing in Screening Ireland tells how in the first 40 years of operation the new Irish film censor banned approximately 3000 films and "made cuts" in 8000 more (Pettitt, 2000, p. 33). That adds up to more than a film a week being banned. But the effects of this censorship has much deeper implications than banned and censored films. Firstly, there was the huge audience who viewed these films, peaking in 1954 according to Pettit at 54.1 million admissions. That is more than a million people going to the cinema every week and though exposed to a Hollywood worldview, finding that worldview oddly sanitised (Pettitt, 2000, p. 33).

Then there is the second impact of how this culture of censorship affected creative output on the island. Take the example of George Bernard Shaw, a prolific writer across decades. You could buy his books in Ireland, well most of them, and maybe occasionally see his plays, but what of his films? Shaw in the twentieth century receives the Nobel Prize for literature in 1925, a *Time Magazine* cover, an Oscar. There are now 207 entries in the Internet Movie Database for film and TV productions of his work, ranging from My Fair Lady to She's All That, not one of which is made in Ireland (IMDB, 2017). The effect of censorship was to turn our back on

Shaw as a media vehicle, we become spectators to this work. And this is not an isolated case.

What is all the more depressing about the level of social control, censorship and outright coercion applied to Irish society after the end of the civil war was the level of revolutionary fervour and activity in the decades before 1916.

Language, culture, sport, the rights of women, and workers were all part of intertwining campaigns. They were binding together in a new struggle. It was not specifically for Irish freedom in the sense of a national government. This struggle was in the context of demanding that the British state recognise the right of the Irish people to a social and cultural expression of self-determination. Another way of portraying these struggles is in the idea of Pearse's concept of the "spiritual nation", when he wrote that "true political independence requires spiritual and intellectual independence as its basis" (Pearse, 1916, p. 295). The Irish people were emerging out of the travails of the penal laws, the famine and centuries of exploitation. It was a form of cultural apartheid that attempted to destroy not just a people, but also their language, culture and philosophy of life. The Cultural Revolution in Ireland of the late nineteenth and early twentieth century embodied this recovery of a cultural spirit and independence.

The success of the employers in breaking the Dublin workers in the 1913 lockout was also a failure of gargantuan dimensions for the process of national liberation, as it began a decade of violence, resistance and dispute that ultimately weakened the republican cause. As the momentum of the national revolution grew the human casualties severely dissipated those who could articulate the republican case even verbally or in writing. It is no accident that in the aftermath of the Easter Rising, the war of independence and civil war that many of the writers, thinkers and innovative leaders of republicanism were all dead.

In fact in the following decades of the twentieth century it is the voices of other revolutionary minds like Beckett, Joyce, Yeats and O'Casey amongst others who articulate the literary intellectual opposition to the inequitable coercive status quo imposed on the Irish people. O'Casey had been in the Irish Republican Brotherhood and Connolly's Citizen Army but resigned in 1914 (Britannica.com, 2017).

Violent conflict meant that many progressive voices were killed. The incisive intellects that provided the leadership needed to radicalise not just attitudes and opinion but also to get other people to take arms in defence of their ideas were systematically killed, executed, imprisoned and in many cases simply assassinated.

As the war of independence gave way to civil war the politics of grasping power began to take precedence over any ideological underpinning of why the former revolutionaries had been involved in bloody conflict in the first place. And, while another battalion of minds such as Mellows, Lynch, O'Connor and Childers were executed, the newly emerging elite became obsessed not by the ideals of republicanism or building the Ireland envisioned in the 1919 Democratic Programme, but by holding power. Within 15 years some of the remaining progressive voices were dying for their beliefs on the roads outside Jarama in Spain. "Even the olives are bleeding" were the last words of Irish writer and International Brigade commander Charlie Donnelly who was shot in March 1937, and whose revolutionary life is captured so succinctly in Joseph O'Connor's biography (O'Connor, 1992, p. 105).

It seems that, by 1923, the struggle for Irish freedom boiled down to one thing—displacement of British imperialist power and its replacement with a new Irish political class, a new Irish elite. A new simple logic took ascendancy in the battle of ideas. It was that in the context of coping with post colonial exploitation the solution lay not in a social transformation but by the quite hand of an Irishman at the wheel of power, yes Irishman as this new elite in power had decided there was no place for women in policy formation or decision making in this 'reformed' Ireland.

Redefining Irish Freedom

So the parties who eventually took power in the 26-Counties in the 1920s set about redefining Irish freedom, leaving us today in a situation where there are conflicting definitions about what this idea means. This shouldn't surprise us as there has been centuries of conflict, oppression and coercion, resistance and revolution because of this idea, freedom, and what it is perceived to mean. In this decade discussion of freedom and the rights it entails skews from gender orientation, reproductive rights, to housing and water. This is a giant canvas with an array of pressure points signalling clearly the scale of the question today.

What the emerging political elites actually did, firstly Clann na Gaedheal and then Fianna Fail, was to abandon the republican concept of freedom. They refuted a freedom rooted in the ideas of liberty, equality and fraternity, the meanings of which are discussed in detail later. In doing so they were walking away from the core rationale of the previous decades of struggle and conflict. They were governing not with the objective of creating a free society. It was another framework entirely.

Firstly the new governments were ruling in the interests of the economic elites—the business owners, larger retailers, emerging industrial employers, and the now established agricultural property owning farmers who collectively had only a marginal interest in the ideas of Irish self-determination. Self-interest was the dominant philosophy of these groups. Secondly successive governments were swept up in the new technocratic scientific and then in later years Keynesian economics that became the hallmark of the era. Running the economy becomes a tactical mathematic exercise of optimisation and efficiency where values and ideology have no place, unless that can be counted and equated. The economics of counting and aggregating takes charge over the economics of equality! Good government meant merely well planned aggregate spending.

On a third front, internationally a new struggle for hearts and minds of citizens was emerging, it was the rise of fascism. The idea of a paternal corporate state taking charge in a period of unprecedented economic recession was to many an attractive option. You could 'escape from freedom' that seemed so dangerous and threatening into a new corporate comfort zone where someone else was taking the risks. You had a role, with limited responsibilities, and as an exercise of self repression, could live quite comfortably in this new mass society (Fromm, 1941, 1994).

Framing all of this was a fraudulent pseudo political philosophy that Irish freedom had been delivered, signified in universal suffrage and a national or supposedly national parliament. The next challenge was to secure its future through prudent, sound economic management. Such terminology would not be out of place today from Government ministers and in fact it has become part of the core of what makes modern politics so boring and off putting to many people. We won't discuss an economic problem, but we will pound you to silence with prudence.

This task of delivering economic growth and development was all the more difficult because of the constrained resources on the island and then the international recession that the new economy found itself facing. The people had to buckle down, happy in the notion that they were taking the first steps in building a new utopia, a newly polished emerald isle, the Gaelic utopia was coming, just not right now, not this year. Look at W T Cosgrave's speech to the League of Nations in 1923 as an apt example. Cosgrave told the assembly that, "We shall return to our own country to take part with our patriotic people in the enormous work of national construction and consolidation" (DFIP, 2017).

Another take on this idea of a deferred utopia and the ideal Irish nation and the progress that was being made since Independence is found 20 years later in a speech by Fianna Fail Taoiseach Eamon de Valera. The iconic monologue broadcast aptly on St Patrick's Day 1943 is often called 'the Ireland that we dreamed of' speech. Speaking on RTE radio to mark the 50th anniversary of the founding of the Gaelic League de Valera said, "The Ireland that we dreamed of would be the home of a people who valued material wealth only as a basis for right living, of a people who, satisfied with frugal comfort, devoted their leisure to the things of the spirit" (RTE, 2017). The best Ireland is almost within our grasp, just not quite yet.

In order to make this work the orthodoxy of Catholicism was broadened into a political gospel that did not tolerate any questioning of the new political theocracy. Indeed the concept of Catholic sacrifice fitted well into this new Ireland coping with unforeseen economic challenges and little scope for discretionary spending. Ireland was now nominally free and romantic aspirations of the utopian republic had to be tempered with the cold reality of economic management and the complimentary Catholic idea of hardship and suffering now, spiritual salvation later.

It was somehow right that the generation of poets, philosophers, teachers and revolutionaries had died in 1916 or in the bloody conflicts afterwards. They had no place in the new epoch, except of course as silent martyrs, used when needed to endorse the new regime.

Back to Irish Freedom

So it seems we have two separate but intertwined paths through Irish history shaping differing answers to the question of what we mean by political and economic freedom. One path is the evolution and development of republican thought as an ideology and the other is the impact of the last two centuries plus of political and economic development and social change. In the aftermath of the civil war republican thinking hit an impasse. No longer welcome in Ireland, some elements of it migrated as did a number of literary intellectuals who could have set a new tone for the emerging state. And so Ireland lost the already mentioned Beckett, O'Casey, Yeats and Joyce. And I wonder how many other voices, artists, writers that could have made a positive contribution to the developing state were deterred, or left so dispirited, that they decided to forgo a creative life?

Large parts of the remaining progressive republican minds went to Spain with the International Brigades to fight Franco's fascist coup. Other republicans like Ernie O'Malley ended up in Mexico and the USA. O'Malley was the one of the last of the Anti-Treaty prisoners released at the end of the civil war, and within a few years has begun an odyssey that took him walking through Europe and onto the USA and South America rather than live in what John Regan describes as "The Irish Counter Revolution" (Regan, 1999).

O'Malley touches on the lack of depth in the thinking or abilities of those involved in the War of Independence. Writing in the last pages of *the Singing Flame*, his excellent narrative of the period 1921 to 1924, including the civil war and his imprisonment afterward, O'Malley notes that the IRA headquarters staff of what he calls the "Tan time", "did not compare with the Easter Week men" (O'Malley, 1978, p. 285). Indeed he notes that "an element of spirituality and intellect was absent", though "the driving force was there, but no vision or attempt at an economic solution" (O'Malley, 1978, p. 286).

The other path, the establishment narrative, demonstrated the existence of freedom through rising living standards and wider economic choice and indeed the Ireland of the Tiger years and since was commonly heralded both within and outside the island as an example of this path and so the rural electrification programme of the 1930s, house building schemes, school construction linked to catholic parishes and the emergence of other new infrastructure all fit into this trend path. The USA at times follows a similar trail, the widespread union agitation and worker struggles of the early decades of the twentieth century was temporarily salved by the economic boom years begun in World War 2 that rolled into the 1950s.

The USA had the added dimension of its own indigenous apartheid and how it dealt with black civil rights that makes their experience different from Ireland, but what was common in both cases was the emergence of an increasingly homogenous mass society exercising economic consumption choices as a demonstration of political freedom and choice. Howard Zinn's A People's History of the United States is an excellent example of how an informed voice can provide a valid alternative view of the supposedly glorious development of the US from revolution to bastion of democracy (Zinn, 1980).

The living conditions of communities within Ireland today and the island's relationships with the wider world are very different on some levels from those found around Ireland and among its people in the 1780s when the first steps to form a modern government and administration were made. On other levels little has changed, especially when it comes to the issues of economic interdependencies, the relationships between the island economy, the wider Europe and with other dominant international power blocs, as well as how the issues of justice and equality are being dealt with by society. The quality of life, the relationship between the individual and society as well as the issue of national economic sovereignty were all concerns of political society in the late eighteenth century just as they are again today. It is this repetition of dilemmas and the relearning of forgotten ideas and solutions that is recasting republican thought today as a potent ideology to reshape Irish political society.

In the last 90 plus years the second path of economic rationalism and 'aren't we all better off now' has dominated public political discussion. However the need to deal with democratic deficits is never far away and has time and time again come to the surface. Having moved on from dealing with the vagaries and whims of British rule we now face the modern imperialism of the EU that justifies the erosion of democratic choice on the basis of efficiency, or the policies of domestic government that spurn individual rights and overrule whole communities through the creeping centralisation of power in fewer and fewer hands.

There have been occasional spikes and mass exercises of democratic decision making such as the 2018 Repeal the 8th Amendment and 2015 marriage equality referenda, the all Ireland endorsement of the Good Friday Agreement or the rejection of the Nice and Lisbon treaties. However look at the selective central government responses to these mass exercises of democracy. The Nice and Lisbon referenda were rerun because ultimately this exercise in democracy was unacceptable to government and went contrary to their wishes and so it would seem we can have mass exercises of democracy only when the outcome is palatable to government. And when it comes to the Good Friday Agreement the actual implementation and ongoing support of Irish Governments for the agreement has been at best begrudging and often just recalcitrant.

The same arguments that mobilised republicanism in the 1790s, 1840s, 1860s and on and on are still relevant today. Then as now there are those who are not diverted by a few baubles thrown their way and want to challenge government to prove its democratic credentials, and to demand their freedom! Tax cuts are not tax equality, a national children's hospital is not a universal healthcare strategy and a first time buyer's grant won't solve the housing crisis. As long as government fails the basic test of democratic credibility and accountability there will be republicans and others demanding a just society.

The Invisible Republic Uncovered

This repetition of dilemmas and how society responds to them hits to the core of what I see as an Invisible Republic. It is invisible in that for large periods of time it is hard to conceptualise, or people refuse to see, to recognise the links, the connections that bind together the republic of individuals, the republic of households and communities. People refuse at times to recognise the links, connections and interdependencies that underpin our economy.

The fashionable politics of the day may change as may the terminology we use to describe the world we live in, but the traits that drive us, that shape our actions do not, I believe, change that deeply. So when observing human society in its day to day interaction over the years it becomes possible to identify the traits and characteristics that shape it.

For example the powerful lust of acquisitiveness, the concept of success, the idea of being celebrated by your peers, the magnetic desire to have and to exercise power are easily found across not just generations but through millennia, whether it is in themes of the Fianna and Cu Chulainn myths or the wealth obsessed society of today. Indeed the lessons to be learned for today's acquisitive consumer society from the Brown Bull of Cooley saga and the war between Connacht and Ulster that originated in a bedroom tiff between Meabh and Ailill over who had the most possessions has a lot of relevance for the world we live in today. Also strangely relevant to the twenty-first century world is the story of Diarmuid and Grainne and particularly Fionn's obsession with the aging process and the deadly consequences of envy and jealously (Rolleston, 1911, 1986).

These though are the negative traits of society that cross generations. There are positive ones too, that often have a counterbalancing effect and it is in these that I can see the foundations of the Invisible Republic. The positive traits are:

1. The willing republic; a desire to do things better.
2. The idea of a fair go.

3. The belief in a communal society, in that we should all be progressing together in some positive direction, that we must develop positively as a society, and that individual wealth and prosperity is conditional and must be sited within a healthy society and one person's enrichment should not be at the expense of another.

Today we can expand and redefine our definition of communal freedom and include James Lovelock's Gaia concept of recognising that we are only part of a much larger ecosystem and our own activities personal and collective should not imperil that ecosystem (Lovelock, 1982). Communal expands then beyond the relationship of person to person into something much bigger and much more compelling. We need to add environmentalism into our understanding of republicanism.

Where the Invisible Republic becomes the visible one is in those generations where someone or some group of likeminded people show the leadership to cement these strands into the reality of political life. It has been demonstrated time and time again in Ireland over the last two centuries where crisis throws people into situations where they have to act on gut instinct and those instincts are I believe rooted in the precepts outlined here.

The 'Willing Republic': We Can Do Better

The invisible republic can be shown by looking at the writings and political career of republicans like Wolfe Tone, or Thomas Russell, where the starting point of their analysis is rooted in the experience of Henry Grattan's political campaigns. You can see this specially in the writings of Russell through his journals, and the extensive output of Tone both in diary entries, letters, speeches and pamphlets.

Russell for example begins as an interested spectator to the unfolding events of his times, and his early diaries are filled with dinners, drinking and trysts (Russell, 1991, pp. 49–50). But as a political momentum grows in society, it sweeps him up and he moves from revelry to revolt and full time political activism. He despairs at the failure of the parliament in Dublin to administer an efficient management of the island. In 1793 Russell declares that, "These laws are made without our consent" (Russell, 1991, p. 83). Reporting in his journal on a conversation with a miller, Russell writes that the man told him, "I think liberty worth risking life for". Russell wonders "when will a man of fortune in Ireland reason thus.

Our senators and great think of nothing but their own sordid interests. Here was a peasant interested for the freedom of mankind" (Russell, 1991, p. 82).

Tone's contribution to a communal vision of republicanism is seminal. The beginnings are found in documents like the 1790 Review of the Conduct of the Administration of the Last Session of Parliament, in which he states that "The people are now called on to fulfil their duty, by straining every nerve to create an honest House of Commons" (Tone, 1998, p. 247). In the review Tone highlights a number of problems with the work of the Irish parliament including 'impudent prodigality', 'corruption' and 'sale of honours' (Tone, 1998, p. 248). The refusal of the parliament to reform spurs Tone to seek a broader range of allies. In 1791 again proposing parliamentary reform he writes An Argument on Behalf of the Catholics of Ireland asserting that, "The misfortune of Ireland is that we have no national government" (Tone, 1998, p. 279).

When it comes to the founding of the United Irishmen Tone's vision has moved beyond parliamentary reform into the roots of a social and political revolution. The founding declarations of the United Irishmen repeat the claim that Ireland has no national government. He writes "we are ruled by Englishmen, and the servants of Englishmen, whose object is the interest of another country, whose instrument is corruption, and whose strength is the weakness of Ireland" (Tone, 1998, p. 298). Critically Tone's argument is rooted in the principle of equality of treatment. He writes that "No reform is practicable, efficacious, or just, which will not include Irishmen of every religious persuasion" promising "the equal distribution of the rights of man through all sects and denominations of Ireland" (Tone, 1998, p. 299).

In 1796 while leading the first expedition of troops and arms to Ireland Tone writes an address to the people of Ireland asserting that they have to choose between "union or separation", between, "slavery and independence" (Tone, 1998, p. 675).

What Russell and Tone had witnessed was a now all too familiar process. Grattan like many nationalists after him set out with a very basic concept, 'this place could be a lot better run with just a little care and attention'. The application of such care and attention would not be a threat to the status quo, in fact if applied effectively you would end up with a more efficient, productive, happier and therefore more peaceful island. Grattan's legislative achievements were impressive. These include the repeal of Poyning's Law and the passing of a Free Trade bill. However he was involved in a legislature that was representative of fraction of the population, which refused, despite his efforts to emancipate Irish Catholics. The Irish parliament was a rotten institution whose inherent corruption in appointments and elections led to the Act of Union, and disestablishment.

Grattan's logic has been repeated over subsequent centuries. This strategy of the better run Ireland has been espoused by Parnell, Cosgrave and de Valera, as well as the failed promise of reform offered by Clan Na Poblachta in the post-World War 2 Ireland. In the late 1970s and early 1980s Garret Fitzgerald's first years as Fine Gael leader sounded this drum again. They were followed by the more conservative and right wing Progressive Democrats who towards the end of the last century made an initial excursion into politics on a reform platform. In reality they were intent on promoting and protecting the self interests of the upper middle classes, but sold themselves to a wider public as a force of zealous reform out to forge a better state.

Everyone who set out with a reforming zeal has found a willing public anxious to believe in the simple idea that things could be better. It is in this ever present belief that the first signs of the Invisible Republic are found. In the early decades of the twenty-first century, there has been a new phase of political products from the quickly failed Renua, the Independent Alliance and the Social Democrats, who are all in this soft but relevant space.

There is I believe a 'willing republic' on the island. It is manifested in election after election where there have been voters willing to take a punt on those political groupings, usually new ones, or parties under new leadership, who run campaigns making the case for a better managed, more efficient government. There are also the other parties of the Left, whose branding and names have changed but as a socialist grouping or anti austerity alliance they too are proof of the existence section of voters who seek fundamental change on an equality agenda.

A 'Fair Go'

The second pillar of the Invisible Republic is found in the idea of a 'fair go', that everyone should have a chance to advance through life, that everyone has a basic right to equality of opportunity. The 'fair go' concept originated in an Australian miners' strike in 1854, brutally suppressed by the British backed New South Wales militia. The striking miners created their own Southern Cross flag and an oath which read, "We swear by the Southern Cross to stand truly by each other and fight to defend our rights and liberties" (Petersen, 2004). The miners rebellion while brutally put down had huge consequences for Australian politics leading to universal male suffrage in the New South Wales parliament and a series of concessions to basic rights by the ruling rancher and business oligarchy. It paved the way for the emergence of the fair go concept that is all pervasive in Australian society today (MADE, 2017). Search for the terms Eureka Rebellion or 'fair go' and you will see how pervasive this concept still is in Australian society today.

In an Irish context we could more succinctly say that at a basic level the people want to believe in a meritocracy, where hard work, endeavour and discipline yield rewards and wealth, and that inherited wealth and status should not be the reason for your success in life. Perhaps a more contemporary term for this principle is that it is a manifestation of the concept mentioned above of equality of opportunity. This embodies the idea of a 'fair go', but emphasises the principle that this is an opening, a start for the individual, and that this is their inherent, inalienable right. We could extend this idea to encompass issues like the right to educational opportunity, to enter the workforce, to have the potential to own a dwelling, or start a business. It does not guarantee success, only the right to entry, to get to the start line.

The Power of Fraternity

The power of fraternity is the third element of the invisible republic, and there are two driving forces behind the development of fraternity as a concept in Irish politics. One strand is the experiences of those who did show political leadership and forged the bonds that political activism and struggle creates. The period from the United Irishmen to the present day is one where the emergence of fraternal groupings is documented in the writings of those involved. In fact fraternity was a driving force of politics. In the late eighteenth and early nineteenth centuries, political organising involved the development of mass national but locally built political networks. Factors like the need for secrecy, loyalty, mutual dependency and common goals created shared fraternal political bonds which had a much longer term impact on overall society. The first declarations and resolutions of the United Irishmen reflect this. The resolution declared that, "we do pledge ourselves to our country and mutually to each other" and called for the formation of similar societies that would strive "for the promotion of constitutional knowledge, the abolition of bigotry in religion and politics, and the equal distribution of the rights of man through all sects and denominations of Irishmen" (Cronin & Roche, 1973, pp. 128–129).

The second strand driving fraternity was the harshness of the external environment. Political oppression, economic exploitation, famine and wholesale hardship were also powerful forces driving the formation of fraternal bonds, while also giving them a longer term stability and strength.

The dictionary definition of the term fraternity is a brotherhood or a "body of people associated for a common purpose or interest" (FreeDictionary, 2017). In this context I am extending the idea into a recognition that this group also recognises its interdependence in that individual goals can only be fully realised and achieved within a communal sense and that they are diminished without this.

The basic philosophy of the United Irishmen, the organisation set up by Tone and others, is an important stage in the development of fraternal thinking and indeed the articulation of the strands of the invisible republic. This grouping and their philosophy marked the development of a new way of defining Irish freedom. A free Ireland would be a society driven by the principles of liberty, equality and fraternity. While this was a philosophy derived directly from the French and US revolutionary experiences its Irish offshoot became essentially different in character. This was due to the particular nature of the struggle. The scale of British oppression and the development of party politics in Ireland meant that domestic elites emerged who were not advocates of equality, or real democratic structures.

For the United Irishmen, freedom as a tangible article had to be delivered in the context of equality for all the members of that society, qualified with the crucially important concept that it was conditional on a recognition between the members of that free equal society that there was a core strand of interdependence, of what is often termed a "brotherhood". In essence this means a partnership whose basic aim is to deliver the free society but recognises this is only possible if the individuals find some way to mould together to achieve common objectives. It is this fraternity and partnership towards delivering agreed political objectives that underpins republican organisations like the IRA in the past or Sinn Fein today.

It is also found today in the belief held by many in Irish political society and across the social spectrum that there should be a basic minimum standard of living, that collectively we should be able to make ample provision for all the citizens on the island. Examples include the Irish Congress of Trade Unions campaigns for a living wage or fair hours at work (ICTU, 2017) or the work of groups like Barnados on children's rights, Vincent de Paul on poverty and homeslessness.

The experience of the famine and awareness of other experiences of colonial exploitation around the world has created in Ireland a transnational characterisation of this right to equality of treatment and opportunity and is consistently demonstrated by the people in their support for aid, charity and other relief projects, where the per capita contributions from Ireland are often higher than other wealthy states (Griffin, 2016; CAF, 2017).

These are the manifestations of the third strand of the Invisible Republic, the reappearance of which is displayed at crucial periods in Irish history over the past 250 years of support for the concept of equality of treatment and equality of outcome. The civil rights movement in the Six Counties during the 1960s and the second wave of feminist campaigning in the late 1960s and early 1970s are examples of elements of society reacting when there is a justifiable sense of imbalance in how rights and resources are provided for. The PAYE marches of the late 1970s are another demonstration of a public demand for fair play or the 2005 march through Dublin of over 100,000 people in support of the Irish Ferries workers whose jobs were being lost, replaced by international workers whose hourly wage rate would be considerably below the national minimum wage and whose working conditions would be intolerable by any fair standard.

In this decade the growth in support and participation in campaigns against water charges is an example again of how tens of thousands of people can be motivated to march and protest against what they see as a social inequality (Right2Water, 2017).

The overwhelming positive response to the holding of the Special Olympics in 2003 is another example of this as the island north and south participated by hosting teams from around the world and for a while the whole island's focus was on the need to create an inclusive place for people whose needs were often overlooked. Now we use terms like equality of treatment and equality of outcome to better define the fraternity concept in a more contemporary language.

Sinn Fein today has put the equality/fraternity issue at the core of their political project. It has connected with an increasing amount of voters, weary of the establishment political process, its legacy of corruption and failure to tackle the basic quality of life issues of health, education, housing and transport. Voters I believe are willing to interpret the political landscape more and more in terms of a rights perspective and in particular rights that are being denied or diluted.

An example of the acceptance of what Sinn Fein terms a rights based approach to politics over other definitions is the example of how redundant the concept of left and right has become in public life and how meaningless the perceived differences between political parties who define themselves thus is also. This phenomenon is not just confined to Ireland and has been a feature of political party development throughout Europe and North America.

The Challenge of Running the National Economy

So whatever philosophy or ideological outlook you take on there is still going to be that day when you have to formulate a policy, a prescription for dealing with society's ills and what better way to do this than outline how you would run the island economy, it's a big challenge but it is the definitive measure by which any ideology is tested, what decisions will you take, what plans will you make, in whose interest will you act? For republicans the economic issue of how to run a national economy is one of the most important questions we face. Now with the implications of Brexit and a redrawn EU border this critical issue has a new context.

At the beginning of the nineteenth century no-one could have foreseen how the political and economic life of the island would evolve. Grattan's parliament had specifically campaigned against the economic restrictions laid down by the British parliament and won a measure of independence through which the economy grew but with the all too familiar failure to redistribute this wealth. Grattan's reforms still didn't fundamentally change the status quo, even though the slow lifting of the penal laws was returning economic freedoms to the Catholic and Presbyterian communities. Chart's Economic History of Ireland gives a clear and incisive analysis of the economic changes and challenges created by this short period of legislative independence (Chart, 1920).

However the 1803 Act of Union fundamentally altered this process and produced a new challenge in terms of the significant structural inequalities and constraints that were to control economic policy on the island. A possibly conflicting view of the nineteenth century would be to see a series of legislative changes that began to dismantle elements of the economic and social apartheid of the time. These included Catholic Emancipation, land reform, new local government structures and the emergence of universal primary education. However these changes happened within the context of a national economy that was increasingly being absorbed into the British one as just another region, rather than an independent economic entity. This lack of control in the economy was manifest in two fundamental ways.

They were firstly the fact that economic policy making resided in Westminster and any decisions would have to be taken in British interests primarily and secondly that within the economy whatever local economic control remained was exercised in the interests of a small minority of the population. The response to the famine stands out as the high water mark in the inhumanity of such coldly calculated policies that left millions dead or emigrating (BBC, 2011). It also makes the claimed social liberation of the nineteenth century redundant in the absence of a parallel national liberation.

Three groups were significant in the context of the vested interests that did exercise some economic power in nineteenth century Ireland. They were the large land owners, the city and town merchants, the emerging industrialists and large employers. In terms of the issue of economic policy the unequal and exploitative relationship between Ireland and Britain in the eighteenth and nineteenth centuries suited many of these groupings. The writings of Lalor and Connolly stand out in highlighting this reality.

Lalor argued repeatedly in letters and articles that repeal of the Act of Union was pointless without agrarian reform. Lalor's writings show a rights based approach to this analysis. In an 1848 letter to the Irish Confederate and Repeal Clubs published in the Felon newspaper Lalor writes, "no man has the right to assume or claim any species of authority or jurisdiction whatsoever over any other man, against the will, or against the consent of the other" (Lalor, 1975, p. 13). Lalor's was a republican vision. He writes in the Nation in 1847 to the landowners of Ireland telling them what is needed is "a union between all classes of whom the people is composed", the purpose of which is "to organise a new mode and condition of labour—a new industrial system; to frame and order a new society; in a word, to give Ireland a new constitution" (Lalor, 1975, p. 41).

In an 1848 Felon article, titled Rights of Ireland Lalor fully unwraps this idea with his famous phrase, "Ireland her own, and all therein, from the sod to the sky. The soil of Ireland for the people of Ireland" (Lalor, 1975, p. 67).

James Connolly produced a new phase in the development of republican economic thought. In a period of emerging international capitalism and imperialist superpowers the class of factory, mining and industrial workers that had emerged in the eighteenth century had in the nineteenth become a huge section of society, a massively exploited class who were as economically disempowered as the agrarian workers. Connolly asserted in his own writings that these workers, in town and country, held in their own hands the key to political and economic power.

In an echo to the activism of Tone and Davis Connolly appealed to workers to find common cause regardless of religious identity. An example of this argument is found in an article titled "Sweatshops under the Orange Flag" (Connolly, 1988). Connolly attacks both sides of reaction in the pseudo green and orange camps. First he targets the "national freedom orators" of the United Irish League who are "the allies and champion of social reaction, and the enemies of intellectual freedom" (Connolly, 1988, p. 271). Then Connolly highlights the contradictions of the "true blue loyalist leaders", who along with their "unquenchable enthusiasm for the cause of protestant liberty, are the slimiest enemies of the social advancement of the protestant working class" (Connolly, 1988, pp. 271–272). Connolly's final lines in this 1911 article have a resonance today when he writes unless the people realise their common cause they will be "compelled to see Irish Tory employers hiding their sweatshops behind orange flags, and Irish home rule landlords using the green sunburst of Erin to cloak their rack renting in the festering slums of Irish towns" (Connolly, 1988, p. 275).

Connolly worked as a union organiser as the basic starting point for a people's revolution and the creation of an Irish socialist republic. He advocated and continually fought for the creation of inclusive industrial unions that brought workers together in their own interests. He created political parties to advance workers' rights through the councils and institutions of the time. Finally when workers came under armed attack Connolly formed the Irish Citizen Army so that the workers could protect themselves. His actions have an important echo back to Grattan's Parliament and the formation of the Irish Volunteers. These three strands make up the nucleus of Connolly's economic and political theories, summed up in his assertion just weeks before the 1916 Easter Rising that, "The cause of Labour is the cause of Ireland, the cause of Ireland is the cause of Labour, they cannot be disserved. Ireland seeks freedom. Labour seeks that an Ireland free should be the sole mistress of her own destiny, supreme owner of all the things within and on her soil" (Connolly, 1988, p. 175).

The need for a transformed Ireland is found throughout Connolly's work. A nameplate and flag change is not enough. In an 1897 article Connolly warns, "If you remove the English army tomorrow and hoist the green flag over Dublin castle, unless you set about the organisation of the Socialist Republic your efforts will be in vain. England would still rule you. She would rule you through her capitalists, through her landlords, through her financiers, through the whole array of commercial and individualist institutions she has planted in this country" (Connolly, 1987, p. 307).

Two other works stand out here and add significantly to a discussion of Connolly who had few friends in the academic establishment post-independence. A History of the Irish Working Class by Peter Berresford Ellis tracks a communal, social and fraternal Ireland from Celtic times through the recent years of conflict demonstrating the struggles of the working Irish through the centuries against feudal, colonial and economic exploitation and subjugation (Berresford Ellis, 1996). Do read particularly the chapter on Celtic Communism and the attempt by Eoin MacNeill to undermine the Connolly analysis (Berresford Ellis, 1996, pp. 11–13).

Conor Kostick's Revolution in Ireland sheds vital light on the success of Connolly's activism. Looking specifically at the period 1917 to 1923, Kostick reports that public records show 233 strikes in 1920 alone (Kostick, 2009, p. 116). The growth in worker militancy across Ireland and including the Belfast strike of 1919, culminating in a May Day march that year attended by 100,000 people, is also highlighted (Kostick, 2009, p. 72). The creation of the Limerick Soviet and many other soviets, workers' committees and councils in Cork, Galway, Waterford other towns is documented by Kostick, along with a commentary of the widespread success and impact of the 1920 general strike (Kostick, 2009, pp. 129–140). Kostick cites the Manchester Guardian reporting how "It is particularly interesting to note the rise of Worker' Councils in the country towns … which were formed not on a local but on a class basis" (Kostick, 2009, p. 134). The strand of revolutionary fraternity is alive and well in the post 1916 period.

However the stark sad truth of the ending of the War of Independence and the resulting Anglo Irish Treaty was that there was no revolutionary reform. The strikes ended and the emerging new administration took a very different path. “While power changed hands”, writes Francis Costello, “it did not result in a radical transformation of Irish society” (Costello, 2003, p. 285). The reason according to Costello was the failure of Sinn Fein “to advocate a programme of fundamental change” (Costello, 2003, p. 285). The 1919 Democratic Programme “remained a policy statement, not a blueprint for action”, and the “relatively conservative policies embraced by Sinn Fein” were a “key reason for its success in gaining the support of significant sections of the Irish mercantile and middle classes” (Costello, 2003, p. 285). The lessons of Connolly and Lalor had been ignored and the inequitable status quo was replicated by the harp rather than the crown! Connolly’s dire warning of 1897 had come to pass.

From a twenty-first century perspective it is interesting that these exploitative economic relationships are replicated in the current inequalities of world trade and the global economy today. In the world economy multinational firms, the larger states and transnational groups like the EU have the greatest impact and control over the quest for fair trading relationships between the industrial and less developed economies. Exploitative economic relationships are still a feature of the domestic and international economies today.

In fact it was only with the Good Friday Agreement that the idea of attempting to develop an island economy was returned onto the wider political agenda. Until then the idea of policies for island wide economic development were systematically ignored. Proof of this is found in the continual highlighting by Sinn Fein and other progressive parties of the negative impact of partition in the twentieth century. The Sinn Fein view was disregarded. Instead republicans were castigated for participation in a conflict that was inflicting economic costs on the partitioned economies. This is true, the conflict had an economic cost, but so did partition, so did inequality and decades of economic underdevelopment, so did employment discrimination against nationalists, so did the refusal to deal with poverty and social exclusion in unionist and nationalist communities.

It was not until George Quigley, then chairperson of Ulster Bank in 1991 articulated a support for the development of what he termed an “all island economy”, that the political establishment decided to take notice (Quigley, 2015). The banking community decided it was a good idea, so it must be ok then! This episode too reaffirms the importance of the

Connolly and Lalor analysis that it is vested interests of a small group of powerful people and the businesses they represent that has continually set the economic agenda in Ireland. And only a reconquest of Ireland can undo this.

The Radical Response

Republicans addressed these issues in the nineteenth and early twentieth century, most particularly in the period from the 1890s onto 1916. During this era there was a huge output, unmatched since, of considered thought on how a national economy, a republican economy would be run.

Pearse and Connolly stand out now as the core contributors in the early twentieth century. Connolly's contribution and analysis linked the historical lessons on British conquest with the contemporary experience of his day to forge the framework of socialist republicanism. Others such as Davis, Davitt, Lalor and others also made important contributions that I have touched on in this chapter.

In terms of economic thought, the potential of the socialist republic was crystallised in Connolly's writings. His work was both indigenous and internationalist, it drew on the well of what was then over a century of republican struggle.

At the core of Connolly's thesis was a belief in a reconquest of Ireland where a worker's republic could be set up and where there would be a "complete political and economic revolution" (Connolly, 1987, p. 306). The goal of revolution was to free Ireland from the capitalist who is "a parasite on industry" and organise to "destroy their mastership", "to drive them from their hold on upon political life through their political power; organise to wrench from their robber clutch the land and workshops on and in which they enslave us; organise to cleanse our social life from the stain of social cannibalism, from the preying of man upon his fellow man" (Connolly, 1988, p. 212). Connolly sums this up in an 1889 article titled "Let us free Ireland" with the exhortation "organise for a full, free and happy life for all or none" (Connolly, 1988, p. 212).

Connolly also attacks those who "measure a nation's prosperity by the volume of wealth produced in a country, instead of by the distribution of that wealth amongst the inhabitants" (Connolly, 1987, p. 369). His target then was the economic policies of Arthur Griffith's Sinn Fein, but his point is still entirely relevant to the formulation of economic policies in Ireland today. We return to this in Chap. 6 on 'Counting the Republic'.

Wolfe Tone, Individual and National Freedom

The writings of Connolly came out of not just his analysis but that of many other republicans before him beginning with the case made by Tone that Ireland would "never be either free, prosperous or happy until she was independent" (Tone, 1998, p. 30). Tone meant "happy" in the context of the language at the time. The US constitution of 1789 for example talks of 'life, liberty and the pursuit of happiness'. Happiness in this case meaning utility, that humans had a right to seek the greatest value to them from life and the resources around them.

In Grattan's time an emerging commercial middle class was growing more impatient with a parliament run by British stooges and landlords. Grattan secured freedom of trade and legislative independence in 1779 and 1782 respectively. He also saw the wider perspective of the need for a more equal society when he said that the "Irish Protestant could never be free till the Irish Catholic had ceased to be a slave" (Curtis, 2013).

The need for a society underpinned by the principles of equality was developed much further by Tone, who in the United Irishmen was attempting to create "a brotherhood of affection, a communion of rights". It would be a "cordial union, establishing individual and national freedom" (Cronin, 1980, p. 23).

In terms of the changing economic relationships on the island both Tone and Davis had something to add. The competition for scarce resources and the entanglement of religion in that rivalry was one of the driving factors for Tone to realise that his struggle would have to comprise all religions. And when Tone appends in the idea of appealing to 'the men of no property', he gives the extra vital dimension of all social classes, and creates a truly egalitarian basis for building a new Ireland.

Davis: "World Would Be a Factory"

Thomas Davis highlights the negative impacts of the emerging industrial society and he writes in a pointed reference to the work of Adam Smith that "the equal distribution of comfort, education and happiness is the only true wealth of nations" (Davis, 1890, p. 62). Davis expands on this writing that that, "What is it to the English father with an emaciated body that Manchester can sell cheap cottons and Birmingham surpass the fame of Damascus" (Davis, 1890, p. 62).

Davis also addresses albeit briefly the impact of ever greater resources and growing scale in economic activity. He writes that industrialisation was "pampering large capitalists" and "lessening the distribution of wealth even by the very means which increases its production". With some incredible foresight he also writes that "If the economist could the world would be a factory" (Boyce, 1995, p. 155).

Lalor's Reconquest of Ireland

It was Fintan Lalor who first used the term the "Reconquest of Ireland" (Lalor, 1895, p. 94) in an 1847 letter to the editor of the Nation newspaper. Lalor urge the Young Ireland movement to: "Create what has never yet existed in Ireland—an active and affluent husbandry, a secure and independent agricultural peasantry, able to accumulate as well as to produce—do this and you raise a thriving and happy community, a solid social economy, a prosperous people, an effective nation" (Lalor, 1895, p. 31).

In his article the *Rights of Labour* Lalor's detailed analysis of the economic realities of his time and the republican response shows how far republican thinking had developed, especially in terms of the core issues of labour, its productivity in terms of material produced and wealth created and where individual rights lay in these economic relationships.

Lalor writes that "Every man is entitled to an equal share of the land, and all of other things which are the free gifts of nature" (Lalor, 1975, p. 105). Lalor writes of the differences between rich and poor saying that, "great inequalities must exist in every society in relation to wealth; that in fact, there must be rich and poor" (Lalor, 1975, p. 97). However Lalor balances this with the conditional assertion, that "the poor man is entitled to live; in the fullest sense of the word he is entitled to share in all the accumulated advantages of civilisation, not only as regards his physical happiness, but also his moral and intellectual cultivation" (Lalor, 1975, p. 98).

Lalor also highlights that in the Ireland of his day "a few individuals have gotten possession of the whole of the land, which they look upon as theirs absolutely to do with it whatever it may please them" (Lalor, 1895, p. 120). There is Lalor's world no room for the "Landlord Thugs" (Lalor, 1895, p. 121).

Preserving the Status Quo

In the aftermath of the war of independence and then the civil war between the pro and anti-treaty forces, the new administration in Dublin had little of the revolutionary zeal articulated in the years running up to 1916.

In Belfast a twin track economic policy evolved. On one level the new administration mirrored the market capitalist path of the British economy. The second policy platform the unionist government followed was to use what discretionary power it had to favour unionist elites and their supporters over the nationalist and republican population.

In Dublin, despite the divisions of the civil war, it was clear that whoever took power would to some degree start the task of transforming the economic relationships on the island driven by some form of egalitarianism. There was a need for a nominal demonstration of economic independence.

Over the next twenty years what is now Fine Gael and Fianna Fail held power but it was with a conservative ethos at the centre of the government and social life. There was some substantial land reform in the new 26-County state, but at most other levels it was business as usual as the new government was one which retained the existing systems of local government, civil service, law courts and education from the previous British one, albeit with piecemeal changes. Maurice Duverger's seminal work on political parties and pressure groups finds plenty of other examples of this post revolutionary conservatism in the twentieth century (Duverger, 1972).

Added to this was the vastly changed economic situation of an international recession from the late 1920s through into 1930s, that left both economies on the island fighting to contain a collapse in demand, and the knock on impact of significant reductions in economic activity. From an international economic perspective independence could not have come at a worst time.

Alongside these economic challenges was the fact that the new state had other political and economic elites who had come through the revolutionary and conflict periods unscathed. On one side there were the Christian churches, the large farming, banking, and other commercial interests who no doubt would have been opposed to the notion of economic and political revolution. On the other side was a trade union movement that seemed unable to fulfil any real potential as a political or economic force. Kieran Allen's 1997 book on *Fianna Fail and Irish Labour* deals well with the failures of the labour movement in the twentieth century.

So no syndicalist revolution but the new state does take on massive infrastructural projects particularly in housing and electrification, so there was visible delivery of social change, but for many emigration and low living standards remained the norm.

The state though finds a new economic ideology to supplant and gloss over the forgotten revolutionary promises. It was one of who could be the better economic managers. Even today electoral contests in the 26 Counties are still centred on this question. In the Six Counties control of the economy meant not only no new thinking on economic management, the growing economic dependency on Britain was a self fulfilling proof of the overriding political need to protect union with Westminster.

This fact alone would lead to a stymie of economic thought in the north of Ireland. In many ways it led to enforced backwardness as the unionist government when confronted with economic crises sought not to move forward, any modernisation was suspect. Indeed the trinity of agriculture, textiles and heavy industry characterised by the ship building sector would have to be protected at all costs. Anything less would not just be an admission of a failure of economic policy but would cut to the heart of the political raison d'etre of the malformed northern state. Even today such attitudes are still prevalent in institutionalised Six-County economic thinking.

Strangely the institutionalised opposition to economic modernisation in the Six Counties contrasts with the embracement of modernisation in the 26 Counties particularly after the end of World War II. The war generated another economic crisis as the state was forced to introduce rationing for petrol, some foods and imported goods. Combined with the previous decades of failing protectionism the post war economic recession prompted ultimately an openness through desperation to new thinking, albeit new thinking from the free market side of economic thought and analysis.

In the Cold War world it meant adopting the strange position of political neutrality while siding economically with the policies and strategies of the west, principally opening up to the ideas of international investment and industrial lead economic growth. It meant ending an emphasis on co-operative approaches and any economic redistribution would be implemented by means of state transfers and not by any notion of economic reform.

Another paradox was a mass investment in educational resources beginning with the emergence of free second level schooling while an ambitious third level expansion plan was also mooted all with little thought given to the notion that these newly educated students might want to move in a different path, whether it was art, creativity, science or even the most basic of steps where they might want to start their own businesses, they might want to be entrepreneurs. The expanded college intake was merely into existing programmes. There was little new thinking in universities on equipping students with the mental tools for the changing economic relationships of the twentieth century. This was an alumni who would work for government, work for someone else. It was the creation of graduates who would mimic the economic, social and political orthodoxies of the time.

These were all examples of 'social efficiency' in the new Ireland. Some profound economic and social change such as building infrastructure and investing in education was driven not out of a need to create better living conditions for citizens but mostly because of the needs of international firms settling in Ireland and domestic ones growing to export capacity, all of whom required particular services, particular skills and infrastructure built. You could claim that everyone was benefiting here, but it was expediency driving government policy, not equality. For example there were and still are serious questions about how we transformed our education system to facilitate economic need rather than meet social demand or try to create equality of opportunity in education. Pat Clancy highlights the reality of these educational development failures writing in 2015 that there "are a number of distinctive features" in the development of Ireland's third level educational policies (Clancy, 2015). These include, "a failure to develop any serious public and intellectual discourse about higher education policy; the absence of a vibrant research community studying higher education; and a heavy reliance on overseas "experts" to set the agenda for change, to recommend policy options and to legitimate particular changes that have already been decided upon" (Clancy, 2015).

In short the economic strategies of successive Dublin Governments became based on a series of dubious premises. They were:

1. **Expediency:** Being locked into the electoral cycle means sometimes taking short term decisions to invest in a particular strategy or a particular firm, or region when in the long run it doesn't really make sense. The focus on subsidising multinational firms was an aspect of this. Tax cuts in the 1990s to the 2008 recession was another example. Deregulation of the financial sector allowing systemic changes in bank lending is another.

2. **Borrowing other people's ideas:** This is based on the premise of 'let's try this it worked somewhere else'. Examples included privatising public enterprises, jumping on board the emerging computer industry or trying to shore up ailing industrial sectors like the textiles industry. As a strategy the rewards can be great, or the failures damning as resources are squandered with little learning or understanding of what went wrong.
3. **Joining international groups:** Usually this was done without thinking through the all the ramifications and so the 26 Counties state signed up for the EU, the GATT and then WTO, the IMF/World Bank and finally the OECD. The end result of this is that a lot of economic policy becomes part of some Simpsonesque explanation that, "someone else made me do it".

There were two serious fault lines in this approach. The first was the absence of critical thinking on economic issues in the 26-County political establishment. It would be wrong to say that there weren't economists at work pondering and policy making, there were.

What they were actually doing was pondering within the emerging IMF, EU, Private sector neo classical framework of privatisation, fiscal restraint and an active monetary policy. There were a few maverick Keynesians who were either treated as either quaint relics or Trotskyite radicals who would have to be purged.

Equally bad as the vacuum of critical thinking was the attacking and undermining of anyone who opposed this view. The isolation of economists like Raymond Crotty was just one part of this process at the time (Crotty, 1986).

The net result of all of this was and still is a growing misunderstanding of how the economy fits together, what trends are driving it. For example are we undergoing a change as seismic as the industrial revolution in the economy right now? In government they talk information, knowledge and gig economies, but I think that we know less today about the underlying forces driving the economy than we did 30, 50 or even a 100 years ago. We have a lot more information, a lot more data, but a lot less understanding.

This chapter covers a lot of ground, 250 years of history and a battle ground of economic thinking. There are three core themes raised in this chapter that are I believe of value when reading the following chapters they are:

1. The strands of the Invisible Republic.
2. The republican response to the economic dilemmas facing us.
3. The role of the economic establishment post partition to the economic challenges on the island.

The topics I focus on like money and rights, definitions of socialism and free markets, the idea of what we mean by being an entrepreneur, the problems with business theologies, the need for better planning policies and an argument for rethinking how we count and measure things are all part of either the strands of the invisible republic or are examples of the current failures in economic thinking and discourse.

So if you read on, hopefully my choices will make sense to you. The chapters can be read in or out of sequence, they stand alone or can be part of a greater analysis. Even reading one of the short segments in each chapter should make sense!

References

Abouzeid, R. (2011, January 21). Bouazizi: The Man Who Set Himself and Tunisia on Fire. *Time Magazine*.

BBC. (2011). *The Irish Famine by Jim Donnelly*. Retrieved July 24, 2017, from http://www.bbc.co.uk/history/british/victorians/famine_01.shtml

Berresford Ellis, P. (1996). *A History of the Irish Working Class* (3rd ed.). Pluto.

Bigger, F. J. (1894, September). The Northern Star. *Ulster Journal of Archaeology, Second Series, I*(1). Retrieved July 20, 2017, from http://www.libraryireland.com/articles/northernstar/

Boyce, D. G. (1995). *Nationalism in Ireland* (3rd ed.). Routledge.

Britannica.com. (2017). *Sean O'Casey*. Retrieved July 21, 2017, from https://www.britannica.com/biography/Sean-ocasey

CAF. (2017). *CAF World Giving Index 2016*. Retrieved July 24, 2017, from https://www.cafonline.org/about-us/publications/2016-publications/download-the-caf-world-giving-index-2016

Cairns, D., & Richards, S. (1985). *Writing Ireland: Colonialism, Nationalism and Culture*. Manchester University Press.

Chart, D. A. (1920). *An Economic History of Ireland*. Talbot Press.

Clancy, P. (2015, May 26). We Need to Talk About the Future of Third Level. *Irish Times*. Retrieved October 16, 2017, from https://www.irishtimes.com/news/education/we-need-to-talk-about-the-future-of-third-level-1.2221171

Connolly, J. (1987). *James Connolly Collected Works Volume One*. New Books Publications.

Connolly, J. (1988). *James Connolly Collected Works Volume Two*. New Books Publications.

Costello, F. (2003). *The Irish Revolution and Its Aftermath 1916–1923*. Irish Academic Press.

Cronin, S. (1980). *Irish Nationalism: A History of Its Roots and Ideology*. The Academy Press.

Cronin, S., & Roche, R. (1973). *Freedom the Wolfe Tone Way*. Anvil Books.

Crotty, R. (1986). *Ireland in Crisis: A Study in Capitalist Colonial Underdevelopment*. Brandon.

Curtis, E. (2013). *A History of Ireland: From the Earliest Times to 1922*. Routledge.

Davis, T. (1890). *Prose Writings of Thomas Davis* (T. W. Rolleston, Ed.). Walter Scott.

DFIP.ie. (2017). *Speech by William T. Cosgrave to the Assembly of the League of Nations on Ireland's Admission to the League of Nations*. Retrieved July 23, 2017, from http://www.difp.ie/docs/1923/Admission-speech-to-League-of-Nations/454.htm

Duverger, M. (1972). *Party Politics and Pressure Groups: A Comparative Introduction*. Crowell.

FreeDictionary. (2017). *Fraternity*. Retrieved September 24, 2017, from http://www.thefreedictionary.com/fraternity

Fromm, E. (1941, 1994). *Escape from Freedom*. Henry Holt and Company.

Griffin, D. (2016). *Ireland Ninth Most Generous Country in World*. Retrieved July 24, 2017, from https://www.irishtimes.com/news/social-affairs/ireland-ninth-most-generous-country-in-world-1.2425825

ICTU. (2017). *Congress Charter Campaign*. Retrieved July 24, 2017, from https://www.ictu.ie/charter/

IMDB. (2017). *George Bernard Shaw*. Retrieved July 21, 2017, from http://www.imdb.com/name/nm0789737/

Kostick, C. (2009). *Revolution in Ireland: Popular Militancy 1917–23*. Cork University Press.

Lalor, F. (1895). *The Writings of James Fintan Lalor with an Introduction Embodying Personal Recollections by John O'Leary*. T. G. O'Donoghue.

Lalor, F. (1975). *Readings from Fintan Lalor*. Republican Press Centre.

Lovelock, J. (1982). *Gaia: A New Look at Life on Earth*. Oxford Paperbacks.

MADE. (2017). *Museum of Australian Democracy at Eureka*. Retrieved July 24, 2017, from http://made.org/explore/

McFadden, R. (2017, March 21). Martin McGuinness, an I.R.A. Leader Turned Peacemaker, Dies at 66. *New York Times*.

O'Connor, J. (1992). *Even the Olives Are Bleeding*. New Island Books.

O'Day, A., & Stevenson, J. (1992). *Irish Historical Documents since 1800*. Gill & Macmillan.

O'Malley, E. (1978). *The Singing Flame*. Anvil Books.

O'Sullivan, T. F. (1944). *The Young Irelanders*. The Kerryman.
Pearse, P. H. (1916). *Collected Works of Padraic H. Pearse*. Phoenix Publishing Company.
Petersen, E. (2004). *The Eureka Rebellion of 1854 Politics and Culture*. Issue 4.
Pettitt, L. (2000). *Screening Ireland, Film and Television Representation*. Manchester University Press.
Quigley, G. (2015). *A Time to Speak: A Selection of Speeches Made During the Period 1989 to 2013 Reflecting on Economic, Social and Other Issues*. Ulster Bank and Appletree Press.
Quinn, E. (2006, November 26). Protestant Militant Charged in Belfast Attack. *New York Times*.
Regan, J. M. (1999). *The Irish Counter Revolution 1921–36*. Gill and Macmillan.
Right2Water. (2017). *Water Is a Human Right*. Retrieved July 24, 2017, from http://www.right2water.ie/
Rolleston, T. W. (1911, 1986). *Myths and Legends of the Celtic Race*. Bracken Books.
RTE. (2017). *The Ireland That We Dreamed of*. Retrieved September 14, 2017, from http://www.rte.ie/archives/exhibitions/eamon-de-valera/719124-address-by-mr-de-valera/
Russell, T. (1991). *Journals and Memoirs of Thomas Russell* (C. J. Woods, Ed.). Irish Academic Press.
Smyth, J. (1998). *The Men of No Property*. Palgrave Macmillan.
Tone, T. W. (1998). *Life of Theobald Wolfe Tone* (T. Bartlett, Ed.). The Lilliput Press.
Wikisource. (2017). *Speech from the Dock (Emmet)*. Retrieved October 15, 2017, from https://en.wikisource.org/wiki/Speech_from_the_Dock_(Emmet
Zinn, H. (1980). *A People's History of the United States*. Longman.

CHAPTER 2

Rights and Money

Introduction—The Inequalities of Money

Why do we spend most of our lives in debt? Why do we not have enough money? Why do we have to rent money from people or institutions that have money surpluses? This means banks if you're wondering. Why do we then pay them back this money along with extra money as interest? How did it come to be that the process of working and living day to day is governed by money and usually not having enough of it?

It could be argued that the biggest problem in any industrialised economy revolves around money. Why? It begins with the principle that in our economy everything deemed important has to have a monetary value. An endless number of activities and objects are given or denominated in monetary terms. Money is seen not just an objective measure but also as an efficient solution to mediating between the interdependencies that economic activity creates.

If I want a chocolate bar it is much easier to pay with money than offer a lecture or write an article for the cashier, even though these are some of the economic goods I actually produce.

Accepted formal economic theory will tell you that money is a medium of exchange as well as being a measure and a store of value. Turley, Maloney and O'Toole's 2006 *Principles of Economics* takes up this point by quoting the 1972 Nobel Prize winning John Hicks writing that "Money is as money does". It sounds great and money can be these and many

R. Smyth, *The Invisible Republic*,
https://doi.org/10.1007/978-3-030-86734-8_2

other things momentarily but it also has much more potent and important characteristics that transcend the momentary value that currency seems to have in your life right now. The aim of this chapter is to explode some myths about money.

So why the money whine? Well it derives from the republican belief that everyone living in society has rights. This is one of the core ideas in socialist republican political and economic theory. Republicans want to create a society that protects and promotes rights. Not just guaranteeing but also actively promoting rights is a philosophy born out of the separate but linked historical experiences of imperialist, sectarian and institutional discrimination in Ireland. Strengthening this indigenous experience is an analysis stretching back to the United Irishmen in the 1790s where successive generations of republicans witnessed, and at times fought against, the inequalities both in Ireland and internationally that unfettered control of property had. Republicans fundamentally opposed how those property rights empowered those who got to own and control resources in the capital driven economies emerging from the industrial revolution at the expense of the wider population.

This is a consistent theme in republican thought from Tone, Davis, Lalor, Connolly, Markievicz and onto to today. Constance Markievicz, the minister for Labour in the first Dail is vehement on the topic during the 1922 treaty debates attacking people in Ireland who have supported the "English garrison". Markievicz said, "in Ireland they stand for something bigger still and worse, something more malignant; for that class of capitalists who have been more crushing, cruel and grinding on the people of the nation than any class of capitalists of whom I ever read in any other country, while the people were dying on the roadsides" (Oireachtas, 1922, Vol. T No. 10).

The specific argument or proposition here is that money, our supposedly neutral unit of account, can be an impediment to an equal society. Moreover, it is an active element in creating, reproducing and reinforcing inequality.

So what money based impediments and inequalities are blocking a just society? Well some examples are laws that confer extra rights on one individual or group usually to the detriment of another because they hold or control more money resources than another, or the fact that holding money resources privileges one group over another. Most of these cases are about what happens when money impacts how power is exercised.

Inequality of Fiscal Policy

What practical examples are there of rights being denied? One obvious example in the Irish case is the tax law that penalises the average salaried worker, while the self employed and higher earners navigate the tax code in a different and sometimes much more enriching way.

There is in the Irish tax code a tiered system, where access to allowances to avoid tax are skewed in favour of those who have money, the low paid have no saving capacity and little consumer credit. So they can't afford to make contributions to private pensions or healthcare. The next tier up can and do and receive tax breaks in the process. So the price of their healthcare and pensions is cheaper than for other lower paid workers. However this really is small change compared to the tax breaks for the top tiers.

Such a system is common the world over, whether it is the failure in Ireland to take the low paid out of the tax net or deal with a system of reliefs and allowances that allow the super-rich to pay little or no income tax. Such a pattern has been repeated in the US under successive administrations where tax cuts for the higher earners have been portrayed as the cure for all sorts of economic ills. The key issue across tax regimes is the effective tax rate, particularly for workers. It is common for the middle income earners to pay the highest effective tax rates as they do not have the writes offs and other legitimate avoidance loop holes often allowed to businesses and the higher income earners.

Your ability to save or store money is part of the issue here and this applies universally across the globe. The more you can store and not spend immediately but direct into long term investments such as pensions, saving schemes or property the greater the benefits that disproportionately accrue to you compared to someone who cannot save this way. These people have to spend all of their monthly income, perhaps also running into debt. Then they enter that bizarre world of modern commerce, renting money from someone else, because they don't have enough money resources at that point in time. Put simply this money costs more.

Stockpiling money can actually create more money for you, as those who don't have money can borrow your surplus through the banking system. You can make money because of your ability to generate surpluses at the expense of those who have a current money deficit.

The IMF's October 2017 Fiscal Monitor report provides a compelling insight into this money-tax inequality dilemma. The IMF report identifies three areas that are key to addressing inequality. They are the impact of higher taxes on high earners, the idea of a basic income and investment in education and health (IMF, 2017).

Then there are the inequalities in government spending decisions, such as the failure to spend equitably. Ireland has endured many forms of this. One was the discrimination perpetrated by unionist and then British administrations against nationalist communities in the Six Counties. The second is the systematic underdevelopment of the West and North West as resources, infrastructure and consequentially wealth and jobs moved east.

There are many more examples such as subsidies for international business compared with grants on offer to indigenous firms. In education you have the paradox of a seriously underfunded primary school system, with thousands of substandard school buildings, and spending on disadvantage well below the European average, in 2016 the Irish government's educational spend in the primary system was lower than the OECD average. We came 19th out of 34 states (OECD, 2016). Free fees are available to third level students in the Irish education system yet participation of the lower income groups in society is significantly less than participation of students from professional and higher income backgrounds (HEA, 2016). A 2014 HEA report found in Dublin a 99% participation rate of third level students in the Dublin 6 postal district compared to 15% in Dublin 17 and 16% in Dublin 10 (HEA, 2014).

In 2016 the Dublin Government spent €7 million on breakfast clubs for approximately 78,000 deprived children with €42 million spent on the overall school meal programme (Journal.ie, 2017). The Department of Education also spent €115 million in 2014 subsidising fee paying schools. A 2013 Education Department report found that these schools earned €81.3 million in fee income and that each private school had on average an additional €1.48 million to spend annually compared to a school dependent on state funding (Department of Education, 2013). A 2019 Irish Times report put the 2018 figure for subsidies to these 51 schools at €91 million, plus €1 million on infrastructure spending at these schools (O'Brien, 2019). This is just one anomaly, one glaring inequity, in how money creates and intensifies inequality.

So if less state and government money is being spent where you live you are worse off and might have to spend more of your personal income than other similar people or households who benefit from the higher concentration of spending in their area. Worse still the state might actually spend more money on households in better off communities.

An example of this is someone who lives near a state transport system such as rail, road or bus network. Not only are their transport costs lower but often the value of any family held property is higher relative to the concentration of resources.

In short, there are two money questions here. They are how the government in any particular region raises or spends money, what economists call fiscal policy—decisions on spending and taxes.

The Issue of Interdependencies

However there is a much deeper money problem, a more far reaching discrimination that has also generated an institutionalised injustice in our society. It is the interdependencies in our day to day activities that money negates and overrides. Economic interdependencies is a way of characterising the web of connections our day to day activities create. One example would be the power of demand. If more people arrive at the cash register in some supermarkets, they open an extra aisle. If we are the only person in a shop, they might only open a till when we come to pay. Even then there might be a wait. Each individual's money is the same, the scale of multiple people in an economic transaction changes the dynamics of the service delivered.

Economic interdependencies and activities can cause inequality. Money as we know it is an excellent example of this at work. It happens at two levels. The first is one of guilt salving where the price we pay for a good absolves us of any negative effects that might accompany that purchase, our contractual obligations, if there actually are any, end when we hand over the money.

For example just imagine you are buying a cup of coffee. On a basic level you enter into a contract with the shop assistant, who gives you a coffee for a predetermined sum. Usually the cost of the coffee is designated on a menu presented to you upon entry to the shop. You drink the coffee and pay for it. With this monetary transaction you are cleansed of any other responsibilities.

But is it a fair price. How much was the assistant being paid? Do they have sick pay? Is their employer paying social insurance for them? Do they get paid holidays? What about the distributors of the coffee, was the van driver paid a fair wage or the workers in the packaging company? What about the dockers in the port who unloaded the coffee, or the merchant navy workers who shipped it from South America maybe? What about the dockers there or the coffee pickers in the field?

In fact none of these things are worrisome at all because of the protection of money. Money absolves us from worrying about the justness of the interdependencies. It absolves us from having to think about the consequences of our consumption or demand for goods and services. On the other hand money can also bestow a power on those who have it, but how we use that power can be directed and influenced without us thinking about it too deeply. In fact we are more likely to think, 'I worked hard for my money. I was exploited and demeaned for it. Therefore I have to get the best deal I can for me, me, me'!

The argument of the proponents of market economics was that each of the partners in this relationship were willing participants and able to back out any juncture. The shop assistant can chose to search for a better paying or easier job. Similarly the van driver, the docker etc can all choose not to be part of this relationship.

It is up to each of them to negotiate a price for the service they offer. The assumption is that there are multiple labour and economic opportunities available at any given time to each individual involved in this series of market transactions. We the coffee drinker could find another shop too if we didn't like the price, quality of coffee or even ambience of the coffee shop. Ok, so people don't really go around thinking about how they participate in economic relationships but this is still an important point. There is an acceptance here that money creates equality, that money is a neutral part of this economic relationship. It clearly isn't.

For example there are numerous things and economic activities to which we give no monetary value or to which we appropriate monetary values which are so vast and beyond any actual use of benefit from the good or activity.

The work of parents and others in the home is one example. It is possible to figure out the cost of minding children but can you do estimate the monetary value of good parenting? It's close to being nonsense in economic theory because here we have an important societal process for which money cannot measure and so it is overlooked as formal economics ignores that which it can't gauge.

More than once I have been involved in purchases in shops usually or sometimes air travel, where the product cost is a bargain. However why not look more closely at the person delivering the product to you. Can you see the overworked sales staff, the airline stewards on their feet constantly and then obliged to do a 20 minute turnaround and start again, the hotel cleaning staff at work hours before you awake yet still paid the minimum wage. We can see the real costs of our bargains if we look closely enough for them.

Money fails in the first case to be neutral if there are some things to which it cannot give a value or be a medium of exchange. However this is only the first of many flaws in the economic role of money in our daily life.

In terms of its wider role in the economy as a measure money falls to the disease of inflation which simply put is a never ending upward change in prices. It means that because inflation is a creeping thing and like grass growing there is no point when inflation is not a factor in modern economies. This means that at any given time the monetary value allotted to any economic activity is only in that moment.

So what does inflation have to do with inequality? Well it boils down to the question of what control you have in setting or accepting prices. By virtue of living in a relatively large city I could walk with ease between coffee shops until I found the one with the right amount of ambience and quality for a given price. If I don't like a particular establishment it is not a big deal to move one. However if I lived in a rural area, my selection of shops could be limited and maybe be tied to either my access to private transport or dependence on public transport networks.

In this case I am much more a price taker if my local coffee emporium decides to hike up prices. But being a price taker on the cost of a coffee is not that important compared to other products we buy. For most workers and property owners, or private sector renters for that matter, the most likely example of them being a serious price taker is when it comes to paying mortgages and coping with the interest rates levied. In this part of the world the EU Central Bank (ECB) and the US Federal Reserve set interest rates, the prevailing wisdom at work is that they are controlling inflationary forces, and the easiest way to do this is to raise interest rates.

In 2006, ECB rates rose six times, and many households found themselves with considerably less money each month. The rate hikes ate into disposable income. Each household found itself with less purchasing power at the end of the year than the beginning. So was constraining their behaviour really controlling inflation? This was just one of the significant causes of the Great Depression. In the years running up to the 2008 economic collapse money became more expensive. Households and businesses were price takers, locked into their mortgage and loan payments made them easy targets for the international monetary authorities who had no control over higher oil prices or stemming the record profits being made by a range of businesses in the retail, banking and other consumer orientated service providers, that were all the greater contributors to inflation. We, the households ended up paying more. We were paying more for money already borrowed and paying more for the other goods and services that were more expensive. We were at the wrong end of this monetary interdependency.

After the economic collapse, prices fell on many goods, particularly property, but a substantial amount of households were, and many still are, carrying debt, in terms of loans. Many of these households also had property that could not be sold as the owners were all in negative equity.

We mentioned the term purchasing power, which means what tangible goods and services will our money actually buy. In terms of measuring or gauging our purchasing power there is in fact only an approximation between the income of an individual and the goods they buy. The widespread availability of consumer credit and electronic monetary transactions coupled with the ubiquitous bar code means that many consumers only have a general notion of how much they have to pay and how much a basket of goods actually costs them. In this case they are again effectively price takers and are secondary then when it comes to the exercise of economic rights.

Think about this the next time you go shopping for basic groceries and household items. As you approach the cash register, do you actually know how much you have spent or is it an approximation?

Money and Wages

The most important aspect of the relationship between inflation and price setting is in wage negotiation. For example if we analyse the industrial disputes in the Tiger and post 2008 recession eras we find that a lot of disputes fall into two categories.

The first has been the campaign for a minimum wage and fair working conditions, fiercely resisted by employers and given only a nominal symbolic support from the trade union leadership in Ireland. I say nominal because it took a series of union-employer-government negotiations for the minimum wage issue to get on the agenda and then its implementation was staggered over time with an extremely low minimum rate actually chosen. Today in Britain and Ireland there are campaigns focused on the issue that the minimum wage is not a living wage (Living Wage Ireland,

2017; Living Wage Foundation, 2017). The MANDATE union led the campaign against zero hour contracts in Dunnes Stores in the 1990s, yet more than twenty years later it still a significant issue for thousands of workers exacerbated by the emergence of the so-called 'gig' economy and precarious workers.

At the same time of the partnership employer union wage agreements, the rapid economic growth of the 1990s boosted income for those who worked in what was perceived to be key demand engine drivers of the economy. Those working in the lower technology sectors and the less profitable elements of the service industry were often also rans and could only make any headway in negotiations with the argument that they were not seeking a tangible wage increase, rather a minimum threshold against which they could not be paid less. This was the basis for minimum wage campaigns.

Then there are the public sector workers whose monetary demands and subsequent industrial relations conflicts have highlighted the inequalities that permeate money. Take for example Irish secondary school teachers in the early part of the noughties. Their argument for higher wages was an interesting one. Their gripe was that firstly the nature of their job had changed, becoming more demanding, stressful and complex, without a corresponding level of monetary compensation.

Secondly, the teachers' representatives presented themselves as nursing the tiger cubs who were then going into further education and the type of employment, such as IT, financial services and software, where personal financial reward was high. Teachers were not only a key part of the overall economy, they were making a personal financial sacrifice so that others and the economy as a whole would benefit.

Also at work is an aspect of Weber's theory of social class and stratification (Weber, 1964). You could argue that the economic and social status of the teaching profession had been dissipated, diluted during the Tiger years at the same time as their actual role in economic development was becoming more important. It is a strange paradox.

The problem was could government or their appointed arbitrators put a monetary value on the social value that teacher's efforts in the class room were making on the social and economic life of the state?

This conflict between social and monetary values is not peculiar to teaching. Its most common example is to be found in the weekly bin collection. We all expect our bins to be collected. Yet would we pay the bin collector the same hourly wage we receive at work for them to empty our bins?

Maybe we would or not, but this hour of wages lost is in fact one way of measuring the true or real economic cost/benefit we get from having the bins collected so our time can be spent more productively? So how much should we pay the bin collector, the bus driver, web manager, and on through the range of economic activities we interact with daily?

Confused yet? Well you could be forgiven for thinking that there are lots of things money either can't do or does badly alongside what seem like obvious economic efficiencies.

Then there are the issues raised at the start of this section. First was that republicans cannot stress too much how important rights are to them when it comes to putting their political philosophy into practice. Then we went straight into talking about money, why?

The answer is that money undermines the idea of a rights based society. Some examples have been given of the complex web of consumption and production of goods and services that money involves. This web is a conflict between money and rights. Money's importance in mediating the interdependencies in modern economies dissipates and blurs this erosion of rights.

Money carries a lot of baggage. One example we didn't include earlier and could merit a whole chapter on itself is the concept of profit. We do come back to the topic in later chapters. Profit making is often really is a process of impoverishing your neighbour, yet 'profit' is presented often as a much more neutral word.

In terms of alternative economic theory running from the utopian socialists like Hodgkins and Owen to Marx and other communist, anarchist and revolutionary writers this is ground well ploughed so why dwell on it here. From bookshops to Internet chat rooms there is ample comment on some of these ideas. So why bother?

The point and reason is that my analysis concludes that money is the key to the modern economy. If something is wrong with money then the foundation of what we call economics is up for scrutiny and that is the programme of work this book addresses.

We are not quite saying that money is the route of all evil, but it is the route, the infrastructure that holds the modern economy together. It is all pervasive in our media, our culture and individual lives. Celebrity culture often measures value in money terms. How much did your film gross? How many records, books, ticket sales and how much money does this amount to. Why did we watch programmes like MTV Cribs other than to consciously or unconsciously measure how a formerly 'normal like us' person spent their money when wealth and fame are thrust upon them, or is it to measure the difference between us and them in terms of personal wealth?

Consider the disruptive impact of digital technology on the music market. When physical sales dominated the industry performing artists made money from record and then CD sales, along with a share of concert revenue and radio airplay. The physical sales revenue stream collapsed, replaced eventually by cheaper download services like iTunes, which was supplanted again by even cheaper streaming services such as Spotify. Is music as a product worse today, has the quality declined, is the product worth less? Well, it definitely costs less but is more accessible than ever because of streaming and online technologies. Music is still music, we pay less money for it. Here is the key for me. The money value of music has changed in my lifetime. But has the social use value changed? I don't think so.

Consider other areas such as sport. Here across the team based disciplines there is endless comment on the costs of players, their value in money terms, and their wage packages. This is particularly pronounced in the case of the professional soccer leagues. If we look at the British Premier League we can find another good example of the role and the failure of money.

Interest in soccer both in terms of people playing, attending matches, watching on TV and purchasing soccer merchandise has never been greater, though there was some decline in a TV audiences during the 2016–2017 season after years of consecutive growth. In 2018, the 2016–2017 financial reports of 19 of the 20 premiership clubs were published. A Guardian newspaper analysis put the combined revenue of the clubs at £4.5 bn, with Manchester United the most profitable club. They had £581 million in revenue that year and £57 million in profits (Conn, 2018).

The players are bought and sold for ever increasing amounts, with a small tier enjoying lucrative salaries, such as that of Lionel Messi who in the 2017–2018 season earned $646,000 per week, or close to $33.6 million per year (Bonesteel, 2017). In Britain by the end of the 2016 season only two premiership teams, Everton and Chelsea, had agreed to pay all of their workers including contract grounds workers the living wage (Butler, 2016). So with all the TV revenue, merchandise and ticket sales here is an industry with clear interdependencies, yet a significant amount of the people working in the sector earn average or very low salaries.

It's not just football that throws up these inconsistencies, another example is found in the consumption patterns of ordinary retail shoppers who are all trying to beat the money trap of limited income, and buy discounted clothes products in a simple attempt to secure quality without the cost.

When we view our sale purchases we tend to do it in terms of its full price monetary value, which gives the product an intangible quality, deliberately disregarding that it was a sale item, we paid €75, but it was really worth €150, we got three for the price of two. This is not to ignore that some items are clearly better quality than others, they are. What doesn't make sense is the quality that money gives to products. With the growth in the use of brands, and consumer interest in them this trend is only set to continue.

Money's Real Power

We have spent a lot of time here highlighting my perceptions of how money has failed. Yet we must recognise the pressing reality that around the world money is used and plays an important role in day to day economic activity. So it is obvious that the weight is on the opposite side of the argument. I will concede that there are a lot of things money can do, but with the already mentioned caveat that inequalities, glaring and growing, hidden and overlooked, permeate its use and relationships.

The real power of money is to be found in its ability to provide a guide, a forecast, a measure even as to the nature and direction of economic activity. The movement of money through spending and investment provides direction for economic activity.

A way of thinking about this is to consider any economy, the Irish one for example, every day over 2.8 million people go to work and another three million are involved in some form of consumption, non-market production of goods and services or in some form of economic activity.

Individually all these people are making personal choices, some long term like where will I work, what sort of education will I have, where will I live. Will I buy a car and so on?

Most though are involved in very short term decisions revolving around eating, clothing and entertainment. These decisions can be taken on an individual or household basis, such as parents deciding what to buy for their children. These choices create or generate flows of money. It is here that if anywhere the invisible hand spoken of by Adam Smith comes into play.

Money plays a role in directing resources, in shaping economic activity. Here it creates a sort of efficiency in that money becomes a way of allocating investments and other strategic choices, partly because money follows money, whether it is through the paths of following trends or fashions or through more scientific, quantitative strategic investment decisions, always in the pursuit of a return or a profit.

Dublin as a city is a good example of these factors or forces at work. As the income of its inhabitants increases their spending decisions change. This prompts business to react leading to new or changed employment opportunities, new businesses and type of businesses. Nowhere is this more aptly seen than in the retail sector both in the types of shops and the goods on display. It is the flows of spending that signalled the viability of shops that could specialise in mobile phone products or cameras or even coffee. There is also the issue of the actual goods in the shop changing as retailers prioritise one product or set of products over others. How else can we explain how these changes manifest themselves?

Yes there is the argument that big businesses can carry the cost of high street shop rents and that in Britain and Ireland there is a worrying conformity in the nature of high street retailers but there are still many other small businesses starting, old ones closing or changing the scope of their activity in response to the changing volume of sales, and what they perceive as flows of money. Right now one of the most significant challenges facing the high street and mall retailers is the movement of money to online shopping. Here the dominance of significantly powerful businesses has been eroded by the simple movement of aggregate spending flows.

Flows of money also affects longer term decision making, such as the size of shopping units, their location, access to parking etc. This is a crucial point as this is one of the entry points where money can be abused, in that the amount of monetary forces someone can wield can alter these flows of individual consumer choices. We talk about this issue again in the chapters on market systems, business theologies and in the conclusion, as the ability to control or influence the economy, and more importantly the context in which economic choices are made is crucial to the questions of individual freedom and economic rights. How we use money, how we store it is a crucial part of that discussion.

The basic proposition is that: the changing amounts of money spent by the ordinary households or businesses is driving the behaviour and changes of strategy of the total business community. Maybe a better way to explain is to state: it is the changes in aggregate flows of money that are facilitating these changes. Household spending is dictated by a mathematical relationship between monthly/weekly income and its borrowing potential. What interests us here is how we allocate this income into spending decisions. For example, a short term health scare about beef cuts meat consumption but this is just a very small thread in a much larger web.

But how the ongoing range of spending decisions are made is still inconclusive. Formal economic thinking offers us the theory of consumer choice, where the basic concept is that for a given income households or the individuals that they are comprised of seek to maximise the utility, the highest value possible from that spending, especially for that last dollar, euro or pound. This thinking, developed through the nineteenth century by Stanley Jevons, Carl Menger, Leon Walras, Alfred Marshall and others, is called by some the Marginalist School of Economics (Routledge, 2019).

It sounds good but is difficult to measure accurately and conclusively. Another solution is found by considering the type of goods and services being bought and consumed. Again formal economic theory offers a useful angle. Goods are necessities, luxuries or somewhere in between.

So we rationally as consumers allocate our money for a given income between a combination of necessity and luxury goods, with the final allocation being made under the constraint of the force of short and long term factors such as how much disposable income we have right now and how much we can feasibly borrow.

For example we all know that take-aways are more expensive and not as healthy as comparable home cooked options. However at times this rationality is constrained by shorter-term factors such as drunkenness, laziness, pressures of work or maybe the super rational analysis that the time spent at work will yield more income later than the costs saved by home cooking now, so we eat a take away at our desks.

Money is valuable throughout these choice processes, because for each individual their money levels, their disposable income, directs their spending and consumption decisions. At the aggregate level, the sum of these individual short and long term money flows play an even more important role. The aggregate spending flows and changes in the flow direction signal to business, and even government if it's listening, the need to change and hone their operations.

It is true that firms play an important role here because they control the marketing and advertising process investing tens of billions annually to get our attention, but this still doesn't guarantee success. Firms and products are failing all the time.

This then is the power and value of money. Money flows measured properly tell us as a society where to put resources. It is a way of avoiding waste. If you believe that economic activity is an expression of individuality and creativity then how money is spent is part of that individuality and creativity.

Too Much Money

So are we saying no to money? It is an interesting question. They didn't say no in the Soviet Union or in Mao's China, not that either of these state's economic systems have anything to recommend themselves to us. We also have to accept that there are societal forces in how humans interact that have generated the need and support for as well as widespread use and acceptance of money.

A leading criticism of socialism as practised in the twentieth century was that the practitioners tried to ignore economic realities about the role and control of markets and by extension money. We don't want to make that mistake here, if indeed that was what transpired, there are many theories as to the demise of state socialism from conspiracy ones on.

What we do want to do is strip economic theory, especially in its formal sense back to basic principles and at the same time peel back the language and understanding that these principles lie on. Some things we might keep, but everything has to earn its place and who knows, there might even be a place for money.

Postscript: Digital Money

Finally, we need to consider the power of digital technology, the internet and the social media applications that populate it. Much of the information flows in this virtual world are derived from our actual actions, decisions and behaviours, the ubiquity of Amazon, Apple, Facebook, Google and Microsoft in particular means that across many economies these companies have become the repository of our collective choices, decisions and behaviours. However these firms are money hoarders and profitable on a scale never seen before in our economic history. They benefit and exploit for massive profits the complexities and interdependencies of money.

As we move towards the so-called 'Internet of Things' where increasingly aspects of our lives have a connected internet dimension or where a digital record is created of our activities, it is possible that the data from these information flows could take the place of money in mediating our transactions and consumptions. It is possible that the internet knows how much pizza dough is needed in Ireland and can organise the supply of this, can't it? Maybe then the internet can mediate society's supply and demand decisions. Simple isn't it? But I have an inkling that those who make money from money, those who rent it to us might not like this at all.

The abuses of these information flows as demonstrated by the inquiries into the 2016 US elections and the Brexit referendum have shown clearly the challenge of living alongside and at times in a virtual digital rendering of the actual day-to-day world. Information flows are affecting the lived in world, but isn't this what money has done also. In the part of the world where I live, many of us have too many things. We have clothes we never wear, household appliances bought but rarely used, books never read, food not eaten. Yet on the same planet, sometimes in the same region, city or town, there are people who have none of these things. We also have access to money and can accumulate surpluses of things. The people who do not have these surpluses of goods also have constricted access to money or credit.

It is interesting that some of the technology giants like Facebook are proposing their own new digital money products. They are seeking perhaps to join on the bandwagon created by Bitcoin and the other emerging cryptocurrencies. One thing that is clear to me is that the last thing the world needs is another currency aiming to profit from its users.

References

Bonesteel, M. (2017, July 5). Lionel Messi, Barcelona Agree to New Contract Through 2021. *Washington Post*. Retrieved July 30, 2017, from https://www.washingtonpost.com/news/early-lead/wp/2017/07/05/lionel-messi-barcelona-agree-to-new-contract-through-2021/?utm_term=.0222c921b818

Butler, S. (2016, October 31). Everton to Pay Staff Living Wage. *Guardian*. Retrieved July 30, 2017, from https://www.theguardian.com/society/2016/oct/31/everton-to-pay-staff-living-wage

Conn, D. (2018, June 6). Premier League Premier League Clubs Soar into Profit with Record £4.5bn Revenues. *The Guardian*. Retrieved February 13, 2019, from https://www.theguardian.com/football/2018/jun/06/premier-league-clubs-profit-record-revenues-tv-deal

Department of Education. (2013). *Fee Charging Schools, Analysis of Fee Income.* Retrieved October 21, 2017, from https://www.education.ie/en/Publications/Education-Reports/Fee-Paying-Schools-Analysis-of-Fee-Income.pdf

HEA. (2014). *Towards the Development of a New National Plan for Equity of Access to Higher Education.* Retrieved October 20, 2017, from https://static.rasset.ie/documents/news/access-consultation-paper.pdf

HEA. (2016). *HEA Higher Education 2015/16 Key Facts and Figures.* Retrieved October 20, 2017, from http://www.oecd-ilibrary.org/docserver/download/9616041e.pdf?expires=1508510648&id=id&accname=guest&checksum=80AE3B27D238CEA757B7FFB3225EA908

IMF. (2017, October). *IMF Fiscal Monitor: Tackling Inequality.* Retrieved October 20, 2017, from http://www.imf.org/en/Publications/FM/Issues/2017/10/05/fiscal-monitor-october-2017

Journal.ie. (2017). *There Are 78,000 Disadvantaged Schoolchildren Receiving Free Breakfasts.* Retrieved October 20, 2017, from http://www.thejournal.ie/breakfast-clubs-2883544-Jul2016/

Living Wage Foundation. (2017). Living Wage Foundation. Retrieved July 28, 2017, from https://www.livingwage.org.uk/what-is-the-living-wage?gclid=EAIaIQobChMIjtSG97Ws1QIVJ7XtCh1pfAmHEAAYASAAEgIUtfD_BwE

Living Wage Ireland. (2017). Living Wage Ireland. Retrieved July 28, 2017, from https://www.livingwage.ie/

O'Brien, C. (2019, July 30). Private Schools Receive €90 in Public Funding. *Irish Times.* Retrieved August 16, 2019, from https://www.irishtimes.com/news/education/private-schools-receive-90m-in-public-funding-1.3971015

OECD. (2016). *Education at a Glance 2016.* Retrieved October 20, 2017, from http://www.oecd-ilibrary.org/docserver/download/9616041e.pdf?expires=1508510648&id=id&accname=guest&checksum=80AE3B27D238CEA757B7FFB3225EA908

Oireachtas. (1922). *Dáil Éireann Debate on Treaty,* Vol. T No. 10. Retrieved July 26, 2017, from http://oireachtasdebates.oireachtas.ie/debates%20authoring/debateswebpack.nsf/takes/dail1922010300003?opendocument

Routledge. (2019). Marginalist (or Neoclassical) Economics. Retrieved August 16, 2019, from https://www.routledgehistoricalresources.com/economic-thought/essays/marginalist-or-neoclassical-economics

Turley, G., Maloney, M., & O'Toole, F. (2006). *Principles of Economics: An Irish Textbook* (3rd ed.). Gill Education.

Weber, M. (1964). *The Theory of Social and Economic Organisation.* The Free Press, Simon & Schuster.

CHAPTER 3

Market Systems

The Market System an Introduction

A fully working market system is an attractive proposition for anyone interested in economic policy, job creation, tackling poverty or simply wanting to build a better society. The premise of an always efficient use of resources, lowering of prices and increased or optimum production of goods and resources is an appealing one. These are some of the supposed unique selling propositions of 'free' markets.

The Key Questions Are

(1) Where should the market begin and end and where should the state, through regulation, through the activities of national and local government, pitch its tent in the market system?
(2) Should there be limited markets, should the state be the planner of output, what role should there be for local communities?
(3) What do we do about oligopolies?

I don't believe that political parties and governments anywhere on the planet have successfully generated workable solutions to these questions above. Why not? It is because of the power of the status quo in many societies, and how economic elites organise the defence of this power. It is because these elites pander to the interests associated with market failures

R. Smyth, *The Invisible Republic*,
https://doi.org/10.1007/978-3-030-86734-8_3

that profit them as a group. The institutions of state and society defend the way things are because, in my experience, they don't like change they can't control profitably and want to 'guard against unpredictability' (Galbraith, 1967). They do like profit and protection of their wealth no matter where the source of this stems. And so, though it sounds clichéd, it is, but sometimes clichés are true.

These institutional state entities don't like tackling the bigger issues of how society is structured, unless some form of crisis forces them to act. It was Lenin who aptly framed this trait in his assertion that revolutions only happen when "the upper classes cannot carry on in the old way" (Lenin, 1975, pp. 48–51).

These institutions of state are I believe composed of a fluid membership that includes banks, the entire wider financial community from the supposed 'insurers' to their speculator cousins, then there are developers and builders, the larger established business concerns, and those who earn their living from selling services to these groups such as the larger accountancy and legal firms. I have probably left out some entities and maybe I should regularly make a list of those firms that can find a myriad ways to exploit and profit from me.

Even revolutionary parties have difficulties negotiating the market, the critical reason I think is the fear of empty shelves, that any significant market reform or intervention may impact negatively on supply of goods and services. Fixing the market system means ultimately that some goods and services, some market participants would not be in business any more. Some ways of consuming and purchasing would end. This is a scary prospect, intervening in the market could mean periods of unemployment as structural changes transition through the workforce. This has happened and is happening all the time. But for those who want to fix the economy, to reform it, the institutions of state, the mass media would be like vultures waiting to denounce any negative outcome of change or reform.

Take the example of a simple market intervention such as the introduction of a tax on plastic bags in Ireland, which was based on an environmental concern that sought to reduce the waste costs of these bags. The macro economy made the transition easily, and this was the case in other states where the tax was implemented, but in the factories that manufactured these bags people lost their jobs. So imagine market reform on a wider scale. I believe that for many parties and political groupings it has become expedient to accept the belief that market systems and aggregate flows of supply and demand are a natural occurrence, and need prudence and reticence if one is considering interventions. This leads too often to a policy of non intervention unless a system threatening crisis manifests. Then with the threat of massive deathly disruption there is a haste to action, sometimes piecemeal but always reversible. The great recession that began in 2008 is just one example of this process playing out in actuality.

The Great Recession and Ireland

You can move back and forward through history to find examples of how state institutions interact with economic forces, but it is always easier understood to look at the most recent examples of their work in the economy you are from. Take the Irish case of the governmental and institutional response to the Great Recession in Ireland. As economic growth slowed drastically after more than two decades of continual increases, the banking sector suddenly exposed with nonperforming loans and a lack of cash prevailed upon the government to help them. The market had failed, the banking oligopoly in Ireland was insolvent and yet they were able to agree that the government would not only bail out these banks, but would take ownership of them, until the financial markets didn't require anymore government intervention. This agreement was a secretly negotiated deal in which no minutes were kept (Oireachtas, 2016).

It is fascinating that this form of intervention, subsidising of the banking sector and property developers was so readily acceptable. For a period these banks and the billions of euros of developer assets were in state ownership. But for a socialist or left leaning party to suggest a similar scale of intervention in other aspects of the economy such as healthcare or housing would be branded crazy, foolhardy, and time to unleash the 'loony left' attacks. It is worth remembering that in the history of the Irish state it is only right wing conservative parties who have been the leading force in government, a 'loony right' maybe?

The knock on effects of this recession included the creation of massive land and building banks, from unfinished housing estates, undeveloped land, abandoned hotels and office developments across Ireland, even in Britain and beyond. The overreach of greedy Irish speculators was revealed to be impressive in its ambition.

There was an unprecedented opportunity to fundamentally alter how we do business in Ireland, how we plan our housing and our economic decisions around planning the built environment. There was an opportunity to overturn the mistakes of the past. But it ended up being business as usual in a state that had in previous decades been literally held to ransom by property developers and the assorted group of financial and legal parasites who also profit from extortionate house prices, as well as rents for homes and businesses.

In Ireland the refusal of government and the institutional state to face up to the apparent market failure in the property sector was hard to believe. Though they were now bailing out the banking sector and taking ownership in these firms, albeit temporarily, they merely put the building sector in stasis. The state ignored the role of councils who could have been given land and leverage to drive developments that at least had the potential for some democratic input. The state could have created a new development agency taking the lead from the Irish experience of starting semi state businesses in the previous century when the private sector refused or failed to enter markets such as insurance, air flights, shipping or energy.

The Irish government did none of these things. Instead they went lower, auctioning off debt, land and unfinished developments at the bottom of the market cycle to a series of so called vulture funds. Now these prime resources were not even Irish owned and instead were in the hands of international speculators, and as I write this Ireland has rising property process, not enough homes, rising homelessness and the developers are back ready to drip fed housing onto the market while keeping house prices high and rising.

The NAMA Example

Set up in 2009, the National Asset Management Agency (NAMA) was the supposed solution to sort out the multibillion euro property loans pulling Irish banks into a chasm of unmanageable debt. The Irish government and the taxpayer would take over the loans through this new agency.

The business of NAMA was simple. Five banks had lent €74.4 billion in 15,000 loans to 800 debtors. NAMA would sell off whatever assets there were behind these debts, whether it was ghost estates, hotels, development land or unfinished offices. NAMA got a head start when it took over these loans because 57% of the value was written off. So on their balance sheet the loans are only worth €31.8 billion.

Two thirds of the NAMA properties were in the 26 Counties, 6.2% were in Northern Ireland, 20.7% in Britain while other assets were in the USA, Germany and other EU states.

Of the 800 debtors the majority of the debt was held by just 50 individual property developers. This disclosure echoes a claim made by Bertie Ahern in the noughties that the potential development land in Dublin was owned by just 21 developers.

With the stroke of a pen prime real estate and development land all over Ireland was now effectively under control of the Irish government. Yet the years of NAMA's operations coincided with an absence of a government housing strategy.

So as NAMA went to work selling properties, homelessness increased. The number of homeless families increased by 420% between 2008 and 2018 according to Focus Ireland with nearly 10,000 people homeless in the 26 Counties (Focus Ireland, 2019). Rents in 2018 were 31% higher than their 2008 peak according to DAFT.ie (Daft.ie, 2019). CSO house price figures show increases of 6.5% in 2018. House prices fell to 46.7% of their 2007 peak in 2012, they returned to 80.7% of the 2007 figure by the end of 2018 (CSO, 2019). The 2011 to 2016 Fine Gael and Labour government's solution to the housing crisis was Labour deputy leader Alan Kelly's cut in the minimum two bedroom apartment size to 45 square metres, 484 square feet.

The biggest debtor bank was Anglo Irish who had €34.4 billion in loans transferred to NAMA who took them on for €13.4 billion, the largest percentage write down of all the banks. AIB's loans were €20.5 billion, Bank of Ireland €9.9 billion, Irish Nationwide Building Society €8.7 billion, EBS €0.9 billion.

Loans less than €20 million were left on the individual banks' balance sheets. Here is a critical inequality in how debts were treated in the Irish economy after the 2008 economic collapse. Massive portfolio and speculators property loans were effectively halved while the thousands of families and small businesses in debt had no write offs. Going back to our previous chapter, this is a key example of the inequalities of money and how it is treated.

What this second group of homeowners and small business found waiting was a hostile banking sector aggressively following up on debt collection, threatening repossession and sale of properties. These problems were aggravated by negative equity and unemployment of the borrowers. They were unable to pay their mortgages and the loans they borrowed to buy homes were now greater than the houses' sale value.

From inception, NAMA was an accounting exercise where the agency only had to sell off its property portfolio at a profit, which it is on course to do, buoyed in Britain initially by a pre Brexit property speculation bubble and in Ireland by a growing economy.

NAMA had ownership of just under 20,000 completed dwellings, 6,635 of which have been made available to the national Housing Agency, 2000 of which had been transferred by mid 2016. On paper this is positive but it is only a small part of the total NAMA business, the €150 million invested by NAMA in social housing was less than half of 1% of its total property sales by the end of 2016.

For now the vultures have been circling the remaining NAMA assets and for homelessness, house prices and rents it is still the same old cycle of missed opportunities to solve Ireland's housing crisis.

Markets and the Environment

The issue of negative climate change is another example of where we need to recognise the limits to markets and act decisively on where the state should be involved and clarify the responsibilities and the environmental debts, of all economic actors. Firstly we need national and international accounting processes that include figures for our environmental debt. The economic growth and industrialisation of economies across the planet involved investment decisions, monetary transactions, political legislation, wars and occasionally international treaties that made no account of the environmental impact of this economic development.

The costs of environmental degradation were not accounted for in the centuries of economic growth. Now we as an international society still have to fully assess and calculate how the environment is accounted for in our 'free markets'. The negative externalities are only now being partially taken into account and make only some impact on economic activity in the wealthier states. It could be the case that the negative climate change issue is so dangerous and so much of an impediment to humanity's future that all of the world's resources need to be directed to tackling our environmental degradation.

The essential question that is not being fully asked is can the market adapt to include something that it used to disregard as an externality and can a philosophy rooted in a "green theory of value" (Goodin, 1992) be accommodated within the rationale for market driven economic structures in the first place? Can the market take a full account of the real, the true costs of economic activity?

The Consumption Problem

A further complication has been the development over the last century of a consumer driven economy where human activity has been transformed in the context of the amount and frequency of goods consumed by individuals. Any consideration of the role the market system should play in society has to take account of the sheer volume of consumption and the amount of jobs and resources that are tied up in the cycle of consumption and production to meet consumer demand.

More simply put, consumption, through search, purchase and use of goods and services has become the core human activity on the planet today. One small example of this is found in the Irish CSO employment statistics. Out of a workforce of 2.048 million, 283,200, just under 14% worked in the retail or wholesale trade, that's shops to you and me (CSO, 2017).

In the Irish economy today for example literally hundreds of thousands of jobs are dependent on other people's whimsical consumption patterns, whether it is for a new smart phone, sun dried tomatoes or a new moisturising skin cream.

So it would be great if we could live in self-sufficient co-operative communities where money and consumption whims are a thing of the past but we don't. We live in a complex superstructure of consumers and producers where the links between the spending patterns of one group and the production decisions of another are intertwined nationally and internationally.

We must recognise the unsustainability of this consumer economy. There are clearly finite resources and the idea of an economy continually growing through dubious consumption has little merit, not the least for the workers involved in the sector, condemned to a working life of casual hours and low pay. There are also environmental implications arising from this cycle of purchasing and acquisition, which leads to a conclusion that society must think again in terms of economic planning and how we structure economic activity. We are in an unsustainable cycle of production and consumption. Unpicking this with the least negative impacts for the workers and businesses locked into this cycle must become a goal of responsible government.

The Power of the Market

The idea of an interlocking web of markets all busy generating efficient, and to use that still popular buzzword, "competitive" outcomes is worthy of considerable study to see how such a system would work. We need to make a distinction straight away between theory and practice and show the gaps in both processes.

For example the theoretical conditions of perfect competition in a text book sense are unachievable. The notion of the consumers having perfect information or there being homogeneous goods is unachievable in many markets. In fact, a much more likely market structure is oligopoly, where a few large firms dominate a market.

We can see this in abundant examples today, whether it is oligopoly in retail supermarkets, petrol sales, cigarettes, alcohol, media and communications and food producers. A small number of core companies dominates even the market for household domestic and cleansing products. They might seem to be price competitive, but in fact devote a huge amount of their resources to advertising and branding their products. This is not just as a strategy for market share but also as a predatory deterrent to entry by other companies who are attracted to the market by the large profits racked up by Unilever, Procter and Gamble or L'Oreal. Now are our international online and social media markets are dominated by a small number of firms as is the market for the smart phone and mobile technology platforms that these media are used for. Farhad Manjoo writing in the New York Times coined the term "Frightful Five", to describe the dominance of firms like Alphabet, Amazon, Apple, Facebook and Microsoft in our daily lives (Manjoo, 2016).

Indeed the idea of generating supernormal profits in the long and short run underpins a substantial amount of economic activity, even though in the theory of free competitive markets the long-term achievement of such profits should be unattainable. The actual result in the markets we participate in then is that the efficient quantity is never reached and the price of goods produced is higher than it would be in a truly free market regime.

One example of oligopolies in Ireland would be the retail sector. New entrants in the form of Aldi and Lidl have entered the market alongside Tesco, Dunnes and SuperValu and are competing for market share. Therefore, where we have oligopolies in conflict, you might want to call it competition but that would imply that the consumer was a greater beneficiary of this process than is actually the case. In reality, what is happening is an attempt by both the retailers and the producers of the goods sold in these outlets to retain as much profitability on their part surrendering as little value as possible to the consumer.

It is clear that the competition for market share by these firms has constrained prices. However, why is this oligopoly still massively profitable for these firms? The average worker in these companies is not being enriched by this process. For many of them, their working conditions and wages put them in the lowest deciles of income in our society.

The comparative results are not good if we look at simple measures such as: the hourly wage, the living conditions, job security or length of working day for workers involved in the supply chain for many of these companies whether it is food, clothing, manufacturing or technology products. And even here in Ireland and Europe we see low wages, unsocial hours and zero hour contracts in these oligopolistic giants. It could be argued that these low paid workers are being subsidised by the state, through provision of housing and public healthcare that better paid workers would buy for themselves.

Is this really the benefit of competition that consumers get choice, the workers involved get low wages, the owners rack up profits, the state subsidises the process? It is interesting that in Ireland only SuperValu have published annual accounts of their Irish profits. We have no real idea of the scale of profits in this key market that employs so many people and is part of our daily lives as consumers. This is an important flaw in how markets are actually structured, when the companies who participate in the retail market can't or won't tell you how much money they make in it. All of the larger retailers will tell you how many Irish made goods they source or how many Irish jobs they support, but they are mostly silent when it comes to profits made in Ireland.

The Question of Infrastructure

The market economy, any economy really, cannot exist without an infrastructural base. By this I mean the electricity grid, telecommunications networks, the transport hubs, roads, railways, ports, airports, sewage and water systems, the schools, colleges, hospitals, houses and parks. This is by no means an exhaustive list, but I think you get the idea.

Yet economic agents often overlook the infrastructural bedrock that all economies are rooted in. Wealthier, industrialised economies have the fact in common that they have been building infrastructure for centuries. If you look at the oil rich states of the late twentieth century, many of them took the decision to invest their new found wealth in buying and building infrastructure in the form of new cities, ports and airports, hospitals and schools.

The question of who controls the infrastructure, who plans, builds and pays for it has been side-lined, infrastructure is primarily valuable if it can be traded and an income stream created out of it. This has become the norm in the decades since the great monetarist experiments of deregulation and privatisation began in Britain and the US spreading into the EU and across the IMF and World Bank dependent regions. Infrastructural development has to be profitable first, socially useful second. It was this thinking that led to the development and support for private finance initiatives and public private partnerships that have been such a blight on planning and developing infrastructure in recent decades.

A third category of motivation for infrastructural investment is as a form of subsidy, welfare even for the private sector who lobby to be the ones to build the infrastructure and so in many states the capital budget of government is in fact an investment fund for the private sector to profit from.

There has been a systematic running down of the public sector economy, characterised by an ongoing leviathan project to monetise and sell off publicly owned assets. Alongside this there has been either a failure to invest in maintaining, renewing and expanding infrastructure in the mistaken belief that the private sector, the free market economy will provide the needed resources. This hasn't happened.

In Ireland the debacle over the failure to develop a national telecommunications infrastructure is only one example of the failures of the market to invest in infrastructure. You like me may have lost count of the owners and sales of Eircom since the €6.399 billion floatation of the firm in 1999. Then Eircom had debts of €540 million, by 2012, five owners later the firm had debts of €3.8 billion.

According to a 2015 State of the Internet index two-thirds of the 26 Counties has web speeds of 10 Mbps, a rate the EU designates as substandard. By 2017 ComReg, the state telecommunications regulator reported that this figure has risen to 78% (ComReg, 2017). The Irish Government is committed to spending €500 million to improve broadband access but in 2019, we are still waiting for even a contract to be awarded. If Eir was still in state ownership, this might be a very different story.

What the Market System Actually Delivers

In theory perfect competition is an attractive economic scenario, workers, consumers employers, entrepreneurs all integrated into a system where they are perfectly informed, where wages and prices are flexibly integrated, where markets are in equilibrium, where prices and wages are low and where goods are in abundance.

Yet this theoretical idea is not achievable and there are no examples of it across all the markets in the Irish economy or any others for that matter, and I have been looking continually. The conditions of free market entry and exit of perfect competition are unattainable as is the condition of perfect information. In fact the greater access to information created by digital technology, smart phones and social media has not lead to greater market efficiency. Quality information, useful information has a price and in terms of access to information it would seem that this 'marketplace' is flooded with nonsense from dancing cats to social influencers', mere advertisers for bigger brands than them. Advertising is more often about persuasion than information and so must be discounted as a form of reliable information.

The remaining selling point then of the market system is that demand does equal supply across a myriad of markets. The demands created by the self interested behaviour of millions of consumers are fulfilled by the actions of self interested suppliers who produce, distribute and sell the goods and services needed at a given point in time. This was the compelling argument made by Friedrich Hayek in favour of the market economy. Hayek used the term "catallaxy" which is "the special kind of spontaneous order produced by the market" (Hayek, 1982, p. 109). What Hayek doesn't acknowledge is the tendency of this catallaxy, this market equilibrium being constrained and frustrated by the actions of dominant firms and the oligopolies they create.

Indeed it seems that in modern political and business commentaries when the supporters of the market endorse this system, the characteristics they are actually promoting are;

(1) The power of price clearing and in setting equilibrium output levels
(2) A private sector only system, the only suppliers of goods and services are firms, not government.
(3) The idea of deregulating any markets that actually have government involvement, or those that have any form of legislative constraints on their operation like banking or the media.

Threats to Market Efficiency

This leaves us the question of entry and exit, supernormal profits and most importantly information unanswered.

Entry and exit is usually a question of three issues:

(a) **Regulation: Using market entry conditions as a positive force.**

In many markets the numbers of people participating are limited by legislative conditions. For example the 26 Counties has three significant mobile phone companies, two national commercial radio stations, three public ones. There is for now one national bus company. All of this was decided by a national government subject to the constraints of the EU which wants to control state aid and oligopoly.

Control of entry and exit into particular markets is not something limited to the government, the legal and medical professions have lengthy and complicated routes of entry into the profession that can act as a deterrent to those who do not have the resources to withstand the arduous entry process and the depletion of income this creates. What these are all examples of is where market activity is legitimately constrained in the eyes of society.

We don't ask enough who we want in our markets. Maybe I should rephrase that as 'we don't ask enough of the firms who enter our markets'. The entry constraints in terms of working conditions and wages could easily be set as a market entry conditions, and a government could end zero hour contracts. You can enter the market and compete, but you have to meet these requirement first. Why stop here? We could have environmental criteria, social and justice criteria. Some of these market entry requirements already exist, there is for example a minimum wage, there are working conditions laid out in employment law around the world. What is absent is a coherent ongoing thinking of using these criteria as a positive dynamic. For a start, what about a living wage for workers, or a fair price for goods and services. If companies can make profits in the Irish or EU markets, maybe we can set more economic, social and environmental objectives for how they enter and participate in our markets.

(b) **Scale of resources required**

Since the basic principles of the free market were proposed by Adam Smith and others in the eighteenth century the scale of economic activity has exponentially grown. For example launching a mobile phone network, or running even a section of city transport network involves investing huge resources. In Dublin the building of two light rail lines cost over €770 million before even a single passenger was carried. The extensions and linking of the two lines completed in 2017 cost €368 million (Luas Cross City, 2017).

Drilling, refining and selling oil is another example, the manufacture of concrete, the generation of electricity. Other examples are those that have a falsely created scale for market entry. Here we are talking about products like chocolate bars, breakfast cereals, soft drinks or beers. The production of the products is relatively simple, the distribution of them internationally is more complicated, however perhaps the greatest costs are those associated with the development of them as brands, this includes the marketing, advertising. Take away the international branding and advertising costs associated with these products and they can be easily delivered on the smallest hyper local scale.

One of the unforeseen positives of the Great Recession in Ireland was how our retail areas were transformed when the larger companies who in the boom had been outbidding each other for space retreated from the local economy. There were no more British or other international retailer signing extortionate leases in the hope that a growing economy would help meet these costs with higher spend and greater footfall in the more prized retail spaces.

In many cases empty lots were filled with pop up restaurants, galleries, and a range of odd and diverse shops. The emergence in Ireland of new food and drink brands at the same time opens up the question of what was being crowded out of the economy because larger companies with greater resources were able to outbid for property space and maybe get more eye line shelf space in the larger retail stores, or have a larger advertising budget. The firms that have the larger budgets have a predatory power not acknowledged sufficiently when it comes to developing economic policies.

An interesting example of the disruptive and then predictable nature of economic change is the emergence in the international economy today of what the *New York Times* technology writer Farhad Manjoo called in 2016 the "frightening five" (Manjoo, 2016). The previously mentioned five are Amazon, Apple, Facebook, Google and Microsoft. All started, and especially in the case of Facebook and Google, as digital cottage industries.

The others began also on a small scale and the disruptive, transforming impact of the goods and services they produced has been manifest. They and the general computer, internet and creative communications sector they now represent have created a new understanding of economic forces and social relations. They are great examples of what economists call 'new goods'. The products and socially transformative impact they have had on human society is significant.

Isn't it interesting then that these 'new' companies, with manifestoes and positive aspirations characterised in Google's now discarded 'Don't be evil' motto (Basu, 2015) all ran quickly to scale their operations to become dominant in their own often new markets and those of any potential competitor. Just like the retailers, oil companies and the food industry the frightful five and many of their compatriots spurted to become oligopolies in their respective markets. The lesson here in terms of how we expect markets to behave is that the drive to oligopoly is significant among the participants in all markets, new or old.

(c) **Abusing market power**

Here I mean the negatives that can accrue when the participants in a market move beyond oligopoly into forming cartels, price fixing and other predatory regulatory abuses. For the consumer these activities mean that we pay higher prices. We pay extra, they make more profit.

OPEC is probably the world's most well known cartel where participating members agree output levels in order to maintain higher prices. You can visit their website at opec.org. Their objective is simple, they want to keep crude oil prices high, we see the results at the petrol pumps

There are other examples, though the scale and nature of their cartelisation can vary significantly from simple price arrangements to more elaborate forms of price fixing. For example in the European Union a range of mobile phone competitors who aggressively compete for market share in terms of new customers signed up for their services found the time to independently agree to levy all of their customers €1.15 euro a minute for roaming calls received on their respective networks. The EU Commission investigated the allegations of price fixing between these companies and raided the head offices of many of them in the early part of the decade.

In July 2006 EU Commission President Manuel Barrosa proposed a "European Home Markets Approach" after the Commission's investigation in roaming charges found that the €1.15 a minute charge was five times the wholesale cost to the firms. The EU's action has since 2007 reduced roaming charges by 90% and in 2017 EU states ended roaming charges (Temperton, 2017).

The bottom line here is that often free markets are undermined by the more powerful market participants which makes you wonder who really supports a free market after all. Or is the real attraction for firms, especially oligopolies in the advantage they have over consumers, advantages they exploit to make money.

Prices and Demand

My first year college economics textbook had like many others I have seen over the years a series of conditions for what was called a 'perfectly competitive market. There were five criteria among which was the stipulation that all firms are "price takers" and all "buyers have complete information about the product being sold" (Investopedia, 2017).

For the mass of consumers who make up the demand side of any economy a pertinent question is where if ever do they play a role in setting prices and how often do they have 'complete information' about purchases.

In Ireland there are examples such as dentists' visits, medical treatments and purchasing medicine where we don't have accurate information on the prices being charged. Lawyers' costs are not freely available in Ireland and there are many other professions who are not price takers and it is in their interest to frustrate consumers attempts to get compete information. In a simple supermarket setting today it is almost impossible to know the cost of what is in your trolley unless you keep a mental tot on the go. It has become the norm for prices not to be displayed on the actual goods.

Consumers often make decisions about purchasing goods where they are not actually sure of the price being charged, often this can be for relatively small amounts but some of the cases require the expenditure of large sums.

Instances of purchasing products where the exact costs are not known to you even though you have decided to buy the product or have been put into a position where it is a complimentary good and must be purchased include the already mentioned doctor visits, medical tests, purchasing medicines or hiring a solicitor for conveyancing or some other form of representation, or the obligation to have insurance for a car you have purchased.

The quality and accessibility of information has been impacted by two other factors in contemporary society. They are the ubiquitous penetration of advertising across nearly all aspects of modern life and the algorithmic power that the internet and social media use gives the sellers of goods and services. Advertising is all pervasive in our daily lives from the pop up ads on our smart phones to the ongoing renaming of public places with the chosen brands of sponsors. The Point Depot in Dublin became the 02 and is now the 3Arena, just one small example of the depth of campaigning for our attention in today's consumer orientated brand economy.

Alongside this our digital and online engagements happen in an algorithmic context where online businesses are gathering, analysing and distilling an endless stream of information about us as consumers, as buyers and users of goods and services. And this gives these companies tremendous power in not just price setting but designing goods and services for us. The imbalance in power between the consumer, the purchaser and the range of companies they deal with undermines any claim that modern market structures meet the criteria of perfect competition.

The Real Power of Information in the Market System

This is only scratching the surface of the information issue. Information in terms of its flows and its effects on consumers and producers are the really significant but often unscripted examples of market power.

Flows of information and how they affect consumers are central to how the market system works. It is the essence of market coordination and links together the price and supply equilibrium setting characteristics of markets with the most individual and unique of consumers. That this has a massive digital capacity now only makes the information flows more unbalanced in that there are significant packages of information flowing around the economy that could impact on supply and demand for goods and services, but the knowledge and flow of this enhanced information capacity is in the hands of the producers and sellers of goods and services not the purchasers.

An aspect of this digital information is the market dominance of Facebook and Google in selling ads. These platforms have gathered so much information about consumers they are able to commodify this to advertisers. We as individuals are unable to conceptualise our own information flows and are at the receiving of a ceaseless barrage of adverts and other information messages distributed to us individually without the ability to control these flows, other than to turn off our smart phones and digitally disconnect ourselves.

Another good example of market forces and the information aspect to them is found in a brief study of the introduction of mobile phones and how that developed into the ubiquitous smart phone today. Why do we need these devices and why have they become so prevalent, so much of a feature of modern living for old and young? They are not just an example of a consumer good that everyone possesses, they are also an example of how society's behaviour and interaction has been changed by the existence of a product.

Who we are as ordinary people has transformed because of this product. How we write and talk, who our friends are, how we conduct relationships, how we work has changed. So how did so many resources get diverted into this particular economic activity? One answer is that this is an example of market forces at work. Market forces drove technological development and led to industry responding to a growing social demand by consumers for the technology and markets supplied this accordingly.

New providers of services and handsets entered the market as did the companies who created the physical communication network at the same time. Then a second and third wave of new and existing entrants developed the smart phone, the apps and social media networks that dominate its use.

So how did it all start? Was there really a latent unmet demand for this device? Certainly for particular professions such as those trades that are not office based but need to be contactable by customers could benefit hugely from the use of mobile phones. The more well paid professionals may have seen them as a perk, a sign of privilege and indeed in the early days of phone use they were seen as this.

The greater market demand there was, the more the product price fell and this relationship between increases in quantity demanded and falls in the price is a feature of standard market relationships.

However what is unclear is how does the transformation happen between the market meeting what Raymond Williams would have called a "social demand" for a good and that social demand becoming a way of life.

Huge resources have been diverted into the smart phone market, not just in the production of handsets, or the building of the networks, but in the transformation of our high street, where most towns now have outlets selling the phones and other ancillary services. There is it seems no end to the ways the business community has found to develop the smart phone market.

It has not though been all plain sailing. At the end of millennium, telecommunication firms were falling over themselves trying to bid for what is called 3G mobile licences, and firms entered the market with WAP enabled phones. The consumer was not interested. What they were interested in was a bolt on technology that came with mobile phones called SMS, Short Messaging Sending.

Somewhere in the months between the end of the last century and the beginning of the new one, in Ireland as in other mobile markets there was an explosion in SMS use, a market which has now topped off.

What is interesting is that the phone companies played little role in the emergence of this market or the social media networks and app stores that followed it. They certainly exploited these developments, but it was through customer adoption that the information and trend setting emerged that built this market. So it would seem that information flows and how they move from the individual to the aggregate are not always that easily knowable.

It still leaves the question of who, how and why did the smart phone emerge as such a commonly used good. It is clearly not a necessity to survival but has become a must have. People are anxious when their phones are forgotten. They interrupt conversations, meal times and other personal activities just to interact with the device.

What we do know is that here is another market that in nearly all its aspects of use from manufacture of the handsets, their operating systems, their applications, their sale and distribution is a massive economic process that in every market stage has been oligopolised by what have become some of the most profitable firms in the world today.

Conclusions

We don't have functioning free markets, at best we have approximations of them. What we do have are oligopolies, lots of them. When it comes to regulating oligopolies across the world our record is poor. So we have super profitable companies who do compete for market share but only in a limited capacity and not in the way envisaged in free market thinking. When we hear the mantra of the free market being articulated by politicians, financial spokespersons or that vast array of media 'opinionators' that populate our radio, television, newspapers and social media coverage, they need to be challenged. The lie of free markets needs to be exposed and the impacts of oligopoly faced up to.

References

Basu, T. (2015, October 4). New Google Parent Company Drops 'Don't Be Evil' Motto. *Time Magazine*.

Central Statistics Office. (2017). *Persons Aged 15 Years and over in Employment (ILO) (Thousand) by NACE Rev 2 Economic Sector.* Retrieved April 4, 2017, from http://www.cso.ie/multiquicktables/quickTables.aspx?id=qnq03

Central Statistics Office. (2019). *Residential Property Price Index.* Retrieved April 8, 2019, from https://www.cso.ie/en/releasesandpublications/ep/prppi/residentialpropertypriceindexjanuary2019/

ComReg. (2017). *Quarterly Report on the Electronic Communications Market.* Retrieved May 19, 2017, from https://www.comreg.ie/comreg-issues-market-report-q4-2016/

Daft.ie (2019). *Irish Rental Price Report.* Accessed 8th April 2019. Available at: https://www.daft.ie/report/ronan-lyons-2018q4-rental

Focus Ireland. (2019). *Focus Ireland Puts Homelessness through the 10 Year Challenge.* Retrieved February 20, 2019, from https://www.focusireland.ie/press/focus-ireland-puts-homelessness-10yearchallenge-shows-number-families-homeless-dublin-rocketed-420-since-2008/

Galbraith, J. K. (1967). *The New Industrial State.* Houghton-Miflin.

Goodin, R. E. (1992). *Green Political Theory.* Polity Press.

Hayek, F. (1982). *Law, Legislation and Liberty* (Vol. 1 to 3). Routledge.

Investopedia. (2017). *Perfect Competition.* Retrieved June 2, 2017, from http://www.investopedia.com/terms/p/perfectcompetition.asp

Lenin, I. V. (1975). *Selected Works in Three Volumes.* Progress Publishers.

Luas Cross City. (2017). Retrieved May 23, 2017, from http://www.luas-crosscity.ie/

Manjoo, F. (2016, January 20). Tech's 'Frightful 5' Will Dominate Digital Life for Foreseeable Future. *New York Times.*

Oireachtas. (2016). *Report of the Joint Committee of Inquiry into the Banking Crisis.* Retrieved August 5, 2017, from https://inquiries.oireachtas.ie/banking/

Temperton, J. (2017, April 7). Roaming Charges Across the EU will Finally be Scrapped on June 15 (but the UK Could Miss Out). *Wired.*

CHAPTER 4

Socialism: Principles, Practice and Possibilities

What's in a Name?

Every term carries with it history and baggage, often undeserved and unrelated to any actual actions or events. For example there are few people called Doris or Gladice being born today and some of this decades popular names will disappear in the future becoming parodies and mirthful clichés.

Socialism is suffering as a term under the weight of historical baggage. No longer shiny new and full of hope it has become damaged as a term and as an ideology, perhaps terminally by the botched attempts at application of the idea, but mostly from the unrelenting attacks of its enemies. Though, in the United States, in 2019, the term spun into public discourse again as some of the political forces opposed to the Trump presidency and the ever rightward shifts of the Republican Party have used the term as a rallying point. How long lasting this will be remains to be seen. So where does this leave us today? Can we even agree or decide what socialism means? That's before we get to discuss whether it has a value.

Socialism is an economic band-aid, a fix to the excesses of capitalism. What it isn't is an absolute solution. We really don't know whether there is any utopian economy and maybe right now we ought to scotch the notion that a successful economic ideology is a bit like a happy ending in some Dickens novel where Oliver finds a home, enough food and clothing, and a life of unending potential to be enjoyed.

R. Smyth, *The Invisible Republic*,
https://doi.org/10.1007/978-3-030-86734-8_4

Socialism in application is just as unpredictable as capitalism in both its origins and development. Who really understood that capitalism as we know it could emerge from agrarian plutocracies and that it could mutate into parliamentary capitalism and social democratic 'caring' capitalism or the currently dynamic totalitarian but consumer based Chinese hybrid.

We also could not have predicted the paths socialism would take in the nineteenth and twentieth centuries. Now in the twenty-first century the application of socialist theory to economic realities is still primed with the potential to yield desired but still at times uncharted outcomes.

What we do know is that if we believe that the earth's ecosystem and economy cannot sustain another 250 years of economic growth and activity that has transpired since the onset of the industrial revolution then we need an alternative to the short-termist market based consumption driven economy that is increasingly the most common economic system of the new century.

James Connolly describes the socialist republic as "the point of departure" and at the stumbling beginning of the twenty-first century this could be still as true an analysis today (Connolly, 1987, p. 305). Connolly wanted the republic to be "a word to conjure with, a rallying cry for the disaffected, a haven for the oppressed, a point of departure for the Socialist, enthusiastic in the cause of human freedom" (Connolly, 1987, p. 305), We need to move beyond the excesses and crises of capitalism and develop a long term strategy and philosophy to tackle the challenges that await any government.

So what is socialism? Well in the modern world even before you get to the point of defining your ideology you have to spend a lot of your time and policy making responding to the systematic dismantling of even the most minor positive elements of a welfarist or social democratic economy by the Right in government.

Republicans often find themselves in a situation where, rather than defining what they believe in, they have to spend time defending policies and structures that might not have been their first or even second choices.

Examples of this included trying to make the argument for public sector involvement in the economy even though some of the public sector companies owned by the state in Ireland and Europe are badly run, or not delivering the quality of service they could. More likely though is finding yourself arguing against privatisation, against market de-regulation, against welfare cutbacks even though many republicans would have question marks about how the welfare state has evolved and the quality of care it provides, or the real purpose underpinning its existence and provisions.

So socialists and the left in general have found themselves spending the last two decades fighting a rear-guard action defending often imperfect options such as welfarism, the at times inefficient public sector rather than being able to take the initiative and promote real viable socialist alternatives to capitalist excesses.

Some informed voices will tell you socialism means "social ownership of the means of production". This is probably one of the most succinct and accurate definitions you can get. However it suffers terribly from the Doris disease and sounds like the bland clichés of drab patronising politics. But is still a good definition. But how would republicans define socialism.

Themes of Socialist Republicanism

So what is socialist republicanism in its primary form, as social ownership is only is only one aspect of a broader theory? Well one view is to break it down to four themes. They are: (1) A support for social ownership of resources; (2) That in some cases goods should not be for sale; (3) A government needs to have the ability to intervene strategically in economic activity; (4) Equality of outcome with provision of a quality of life for all should be the overriding intent of economic activity.

This might seem like a narrow definition of socialism and in a sense it is. It is though the starting point. Beyond this many republicans believe there is a much greater vista. Travelling such a path means not only a sea change in how an economy does basic things. It means also developing a groundswell of support for such moves, winning public support while generating interest and involvement in a changing economic dynamic. Ultimately this must mean democratic structures of government and decision making that allows real inclusive participation of all in society, but developing that line of thought is another day's work.

Over the years when discussing the idea of socialism I often find myself in conversations which amount to a discussion about fear. Fear that the redistribution themes of socialism would negatively impact the people concerned, that taxes would rise, that there would be political constraints on the individual rights, that there would be a cult of conformity.

People accept I find the idea of arguments about equality and fairness, but never associate this as being a tenet of socialism. There is a fear, a resistance to taking what people perceive as an ideological position, they demand a freedom to sample ideas and move on, and the idea of commitment to a political ideology is alien to many people. There is my world today a culture of wariness about supposed 'big ideas'. People have a rootlessness in this post religion culture in the west, post the cold war and in the midst of the post 9–11 wars and spontaneous terrorist acts they have a fear of those who seem zealots in any matter.

I can see that people have deeply held beliefs and values, usually built on a sense of place, culture and families. They have lifestyles, attitudes and opinions that reflect these beliefs and values. But there is often little room here for political labels. You just don't hear the words neo-liberalism, capitalism or communism in conversation. You did hear the word terrorism, but that's the point. We can think about 'isms' but usually in a negative way.

And so we live in world where people think recycling and conservation is a good idea but they would not consider themselves subscribing to a green ideology. The same way our generation today is taken up with mindfulness and meditation but we are not becoming Buddhists. We want to eat healthier and maybe take personal individual decisions to do this, and we avoid unhealthy foods. But how much thought do we give to the food industry's impact on farming and food quality, and how do we link this to the impacts of capitalism and neo-liberalism. Way too little I think.

Before we expand on our four themes, we have to look at the origins of socialism and explain where the band aid ideology emerged from.

The Origins of Socialism

The articulation of socialism arose out of the economic experience of the early industrial revolution. The arrival of steam driven automated machinery revolutionised the work place resulting in a classic dilemma. Goods were in abundance as never before and workers had never been poorer or more miserable. Socialism as an ideology arises then out of a response to the effects of the industrial revolution.

It centred on one core issue, the social and economic impacts of using huge quantities of workers together in an organised co-ordinated process synchronised with the newly invented power driven machinery, all labouring in the mass production of goods and products.

Control of this process lay with the managers and owners of the factories and companies. Workers were visibly worse off, yet the processes they were collectively involved in were producing not just massive revenue and previously unfathomable levels of output and profit they were also often producing the very goods that would have improved workers living conditions.

How would workers get an equitable share of the wealth that was being created? First they had to develop an understanding of the economic processes of capitalism. It is in this understanding that socialism as an ideology begins and the thread of linked thinking of many socialist, communist, Marxist, anarchist and republican thinkers begins.

Socialism as a philosophy is founded on a shared understanding of the economic realities of capitalism. This shared understanding of the new industrial economy was based on three pillars, the roles of workers, the other factors of production, and the question of who owned them.

Socialist thinkers saw what they believed was the exploitation of workers who had to work long hours for low pay in a dictatorial controlled environment while living at the same time in appalling domestic conditions. At the same time the owners of the non labour factors of production lived in a hugely different environment of wealthy luxury.

Two questions arise here, why if workers controlled one factor of production and capitalists another were there such disparities in the wealth and living standards of either group. How did labour end up the subservient factor?

There are historical examples where through the centuries workers had been treated badly whether this was as slaves, serfs or soldiers, what is clear is that in the pre-industrial times a precedent had been set to value labour less than any other factor of economic activity.

There is also another issue, that of giving personality or character to the non human factors of production. Thomas Hodgkins in his book Labour Defended against the Claims of Capital (1825) describes this process with a very simple example.

He writes of two workers, a fisherman and net maker, the fisherman can only catch a small amount of fish using a traditional line with bait. If he uses a net his catch massively increases. In pure economic terms output has increased. So where is this output generated.

Free market capitalism gives the net a personality, it is the net that produces the extra wealth as this is the different factor in the two fishing expeditions. So whoever owns the net should get the value of the extra fish caught. Hodgkins argues that focusing on the net is an error. It only exists because of the labour of the net maker and yields a result because of the labour of the fisher. So the extra fish caught is totally the result of the mixing of the labour of the two. So it is the people who built and ran the machines that should benefit from its output. An excellent explanation of this is found in Hunt and Sherman's Economics text. (Hunt & Sherman, 1990, p. 55).

This example is the second pillar of socialism's foundations—wealth is the product of labour not of machines and labour. Any machine that seems to be producing wealth is in fact only manifesting the consequences of the original labour used to make it, from the miner deep underground to the foundry worker, the designer the engineer, the fitters and fabricators, the movers, the sellers. The wealth produced is a combination of these efforts of possible hundreds or thousands of individuals. This principle holds as much in the industrial world of the nineteenth century as it does in the digital technology revolution today.

Recognising and rewarding these contributions is a huge task. But I think that it is not just the complexity of how labour and machinery interact that lead early capitalists to reject the ideas of socialism. It is that the emerging capitalists refused to recognise fully and fairly the role of labour in the economy. This also involves acting on a core republican principle of equality of treatment. Capitalists are not and cannot be republicans.

There is also another dimension to the capitalist reluctance to recognise equality of treatment for their workers. It is that the principle of recognising the real role played by workers in producing a good or service would be a recognition of their rights as individuals and would mean recognising that all individuals have economic rights. Capitalists have under duress conceded the political rights of individuals, but recognising economic rights is it seems for them an unacceptable step. It is a much better process to hide and mask the real contributions of workers as having been delivered by machines not people. And so socialism is a response to the denial of rights by capitalism.

The socialist response manifests itself in the belief that the mechanical means of productions should be commonly owned. This would be an acceptable way around the problem of who benefits from wealth production. It is here that slogans about 'abolition of private property' and 'Property is theft' derive. For example Hodgkins had no problem with the idea of a market economy. It was the private ownership of what nineteenth and twentieth century socialists were to call the 'means of production' that was unacceptable.

In the newly industrialised economy of the nineteenth century that was centred around manufacturing this meant workers getting control of the actual plant and machinery. In the new economy of the twenty-first century, it is unclear in some sectors just what it is workers would own, the impacts of their shared intellectual property I think is most likely. But what it is clear is that, through the decades since the 1750s, workers have never been justly rewarded for the economic contribution they were making.

Here then three important outcomes emerge: (1) Social ownership and the idea that some things should not be for sale, (2) Capitalists' rights claims and entrepreneurship arguments, (3) The response of state to dissent. We look at the contested issue of social ownership first.

Social Ownership

So what do we mean by the unwieldy term social ownership of the means of production. In the context of Irish republicanism this is a very important point for two reasons. The first being the colonial experience which meant the indigenous population of Ireland were at various key junctures forced to stand by while the wealth producing elements of the economy were expropriated by the British. They took land, crops and people. Ultimately they created an economy that served their interests rather than those of the Irish people. The famine is the high water mark in this process where millions died and emigrated because of the control the British had over the economy and the wealth producing resources within it, and their unwillingness to redirect these resources to tackling the deprivation and poverty generated by the famine conditions.

You can see in the writings of Wolfe Tone in the 1790s, followed by Davis and then Lalor the outrage these contemporary republicans felt at the deliberate economic mismanagement of vital national and local resources. This is before you add in the issue of exploitation, which was the systematic policy of successive British administrations in Ireland.

The 1916 Proclamation and 1919 Democratic Programme both reflect the lessons of this experience when they state all the resources and wealth producing assets in the state belong to the people of Ireland. This is the essence of the idea of social ownership, that the resources in a society be employed in a manner that benefits all in society, and that no one person or even a minority of persons should have control over those resources and that any profit from them will be used for the benefit of all.

So what sort of resources are we talking about? Well in the nineteenth century this meant principally, the lands and forests, the rivers, the ports, road and rail networks. Also clearly included were whatever fuel and other mineral resources were exploitable. Then as industrial development delivered ever greater technology leaps, it meant the electricity and fixed line communication networks, the power stations and phone exchanges.

Today we are talking about all these things as well as schools, hospitals, websites, intellectual property rights, in fact the list is endless. What is worth noting is that as the list of possible resources grows there has been a parallel decrease in the amount these resources actually still within social ownership in Ireland. Similar trends have been exhibited across the industrialised world and even beyond that.

Ireland is clearly not a colony today, so why is social ownership necessary in today's economy. Where is, to apply an overused business term, the 'added value'. In the chapter on business theologies there is a clear example of added value where because of a failure of the private sector to invest in the developing economy the government had to start their own enterprises dealing in such things as sugar to banking.

The state was able to develop a long term strategy to exploit these resources, private sector firms' strategies are often dominated by the need for short-term return. The state was also able and still is able to develop the resource nationally in way that would have meant incurring substantial financial risks for the private sector, something which is an anathema to most firms.

Then there is the issue of universal access. The phone and electricity networks were rolled out on this basis. Today the issue of broadband roll out is hampered by the failure of the private sector to develop not just a national network but also to take on the idea of access for all.

There is also the issue that when the state uses its financial clout to properly develop a resource, like building a road or phone network, the resulting network has a value created by the universal nature of its access. So why give that away to the private sector?

Then there is the issue of the profits, they can be reinvested by the state in further developing either new resources or building new infrastructure. It is these two simple reasons that make the case for social ownership of resources.

The unresolved question is where should the social ownership stop, or should it be a process without limits. The argument in the nineteenth century by the early socialists and developed further by Marx and others was that the workers as a sovereign people should in fact own everything, all the wealth producing resources and assets in an economy.

In the twentieth century left wing and social democratic governments pulled back from these parameters and found a role for the state in running the enterprises that involved massive investment and could only become profitable in the context of substantial economies of scale. They created what we now call social monopolies usually in areas like road, rail and bus transport, energy generation and distribution and the provision of telecommunications services.

The limits to this social ownership stemmed from the fact that throughout the twentieth century the state showed itself unable to plan the economy in an efficient manner. Or maybe I should refine that and say that were unable to plan and run capitalist market economies and even in the Soviet Union where a form of state capitalism emerged the self proclaimed communists ultimately failed as economic managers.

What we have to ask ourselves today is can we make a case for social ownership of any resources or economic assets in society and if so, can we spell it out simply. Social ownership in European and North American society has had a Jeckyl and Hyde existence going through periods of acceptability and then complete pariah status. Today it is going through a pariah period where social or public ownership of anything road, rail, fixed line phone networks, even hospitals and schools is either downright wrong or undesirable. Social ownership is according to this view stifling, inefficient and unacceptable, though in the great recession the state ended up the owner of a series of private sector institutions. When the market had failed it was now suddenly expediently acceptable for the state to be owner of vital resources.

The prevailing logic is that there has to be a market for everything. The core argument behind this thinking is that an efficient free market will produce more output at a lower price than any other possible market structure or delivery system. In some cases I believe this principle does not hold.

Goods Not for Sale

There are limits to markets, there are examples where the market fails to provide the necessary goods and services. A socialist republican conclusion is that some things, products and services should not be for sale. What I am arguing for here is that in some cases it is clear that there should be no market for these goods. This doesn't mean the banning of goods. It means that the consumer should not be allowed purchase the good, it should and must be available on demand. There is still a need to supply the good. Perhaps the more important message is that an individual's income should not be the determinant of how quickly or what quality of service they get.

The two examples that demonstrate the validity of this proposal are in the areas of education and healthcare. In the free market worldview price setting through an equilibrium of demand and supply are crucial elements in optimising output ensuring that the right amount of a good is produced at the right price.

However in the education and health sectors it is clear that this rule doesn't apply. Is it really possible to put a price on a child's education? This is not to suggest that we cannot determine the right quantity and characteristics of education or health goods to produce. We can, we are just moving away from the fallacy that price of these goods determines how much to produce.

Adopting such a strategy could be the beginning of a much more sophisticated redrawing of the role of markets in macro, national or supra regional economies like the EU.

One of the realities of the market system is that it can produce undesirable outcomes. By undesirable I mean the acknowledgement that society when faced with the total impact of a particular market activity or process would want less negative scenarios.

One example of this is that lots of people recognise the positive impact of the automobile on their life. However, they might not be as positive about the negative environmental impacts, beginning with traffic congestions, accidents, CO_2 outputs, not to mention the environmental consequence of mining for the metals, smelting the ore, drilling for oil, refining it for petrol and building super tankers to transport this.

So how does this turn into an argument for saying that in some cases goods should not be for sale. There are I believe a series of problems with markets that when analysed cumulatively make an effective argument for not selling particular goods.

1. *How is the market created?*

Many markets, particularly in the twenty-first century consumer world, are created from the demands of high-income households. These wealthy families and individuals are most likely to experiment with new goods and have greater disposable income. By being there at the birth of a good it is the demand of these high income groups that initially shape the good or service and in some cases input superfluous characteristics.

2. *Economies of scale*

Some markets have substantial economies of scale and need massive investment to make production of a particular good possible. There is an important question as who will or who should have control over these investments, or this market structure, particularly in the context of point three below.

3. *The idea of universal access*

One of the outcomes of how society has developed is the concept of nations, states, regions and even federal transnational entities. In all cases we are talking about where a governmental, administrative and institutional link is made across a population.

If everyone becomes, or is designated a citizen in a regime where there is some form of taxation and some form of service provision by the governmental administration and its institutions there is usually the belief in a form of equity of access to these services, what we call the principle or the idea of universal access.

Indeed, it is often presented as the defining characteristic of modern democratic society. However, universal access to the state's provision of goods and services is not an easy set of conditions to meet. Its origins in the state today stem back to the idea of a social contract between the individual and society. This emerged in the European enlightenment period. The individual ceases to act like a totally self serving self seeking person and recognises the rights of others. They move away from a state of nature on the basis that signing up for the social contract would confer some benefits on the individual in terms of access to resources or protection from attack

For example in the USA the terms of the social contract are quite explicit in both the 1789 constitution, its amendments and the subsequent Bill of Rights. In our Irish society it means intangible things too like protection under the rule of law but it also means quite tangible measurable effects like access to:

(a) Electricity

(b) The transport infrastructure
(c) Job creation
(d) Telecommunications services, fixed, mobile and broadband
(e) Health services
(f) Education
(g) Information in terms of enriching knowledge and opportunities

The Education Example

In Dublin, the city I currently live in, there are plenty of examples that the principle of universal access is not being met. Across the city, huge disparities exist in terms of educational attainment and disadvantage even though the state is for the most part, through licensed agents, the sole provider of educational services. Children's ability to learn is determined by a complex set of factors including the parents' abilities, the home environment, the wealth of the local community and the strength of its social structures.

In the city the parents of some children have been able to use their wealth to intervene in the educational process through:

(a) Investment in the school
(b) Investment in the child, through grinds and special tutors etc

The level of the quality of school provision is set so low as to make relatively small investments by parents yield large quantities of return. There a series of hybrid educational markets that exist alongside the state provision, where individuals and communities with higher incomes are able to enhance the quality of the product that is provided by the state.

In the Irish education sector it is harder for lower income families to negotiate the educational system as it based on a supposition of:

(a) Family wealth to invest in goods that enhance learning, such a room for study, access to internet resources, funding extra classes and grinds for the student, being able to intervene and skip healthcare waiting lists for children with hearing or sight difficulties.
(b) Parental educational qualifications to augment supplement and enhance school teaching.
(c) Child/parental interest in developing academic skills focused on third level even as the child enters the primary system.

What this means is that from the moment a child enters school, the context and quality of supply of the supposedly standard teaching and quality of the educational product provided is being impacted by a series of other factors. The lower the income and wealth of a family the more negative those factors are.

The Healthcare Example

The healthcare industry is another hybrid market where the state and private sector operate an entwined service. Across the world there is clear evidence that wealthy people live longer. It could be because of less arduous lives, better food and living conditions or it could also be the level of healthcare and the speed with which they can access it.

There are other factors are at play in the education and healthcare examples. It is that because in a situation where you have a relatively high income groups who can pay a higher price for the products and a resource that is relatively scarce the marginal resources are sometimes diverted towards these higher income groups because for the last euro or dollar invested there is a greater potential for financial return even though the marginal benefit for society as a whole would be greater if the last units of health resources were expended on treating the illnesses or teaching the children of low income groups. Have you ever seen for example an advertisement telling you that ten euros can cure a child's blindness? You might also have seen advertisements about laser eye surgery, to enhance the vision of people who can already see. These products live side by side, yet on a basic social justice basis, a Rawlsian 'veil of ignorance' principle, shouldn't we fix everyone's vision before we start offering laser surgery (Rawls, 1971)?

In short where resources are scarce, it is the revenue centres that dominate and pull investment and expenditure towards them. This means that in both cases of education and health the high revenue customers are shaping the products they purchase.

Examples include the case in the health sector where with a finite number of health professionals, some are working in elective cosmetic surgery, or private selective drug rehabilitation, or medical research professionals work in solving and dealing with the diseases of the rich and new ways of guaranteeing longevity.

One example in the medical sector in Ireland today is when you get to see a consultant. In the case of maternity, public sector patients see the available consultant on rotation, without defined appointments, while private sector patients have a designated consultant who they see by appointment, and he or she is expected to attend at the birth. The interesting question is whether we actually need the consultant post in its current format within the medical sector, considering it is the top rung of a medical treatment hierarchy based on exclusion of the low-income customers?

It raises the question as to the structure of service provision across the health service and the differences in skills, responsibilities and ability across the jobs we know as nurses, doctors, registrars, consultants, radiographers. Why do these posts exist as currently constituted? Is it based on an efficiency of service or a false hierarchy of status and exploitation within a workforce that pools income in an elite of consultant doctors? Given the disruption and forced workplace reorganisation in so many professions, isn't it interesting that the medical and legal professions have so far remained impervious to the economic disruption implemented in other industries. I don't think it is because the medical model of service provision is the best of all possible worlds.

State Role

The state is involved in the provision of services in both the education and healthcare markets. It might not be organising these services justly or efficiently, but my argument is that a private sector free market here would aggravate and worsen the existing flawed service provision. The state's flaws I believe in education and healthcare provision stem from two fault lines. The first is the impact of having a hybrid market where the private sector has a parasitic relationship with the state provision which is subsidising profit making in the private provider. It creates at best a two-tier system where higher income individuals can piggy back the general service provision and receive an enhanced service for themselves, while others are denied this quality or speed of service. This is particularly the case in healthcare provision.

The second flaw is the state's failure to adequately democratise the planning of these services. The methods and policies of the departments of health and education and how they engage with citizens needs to be fundamentally changed.

Taking into account the flaws already mentioned there could be a role for the state in running, and organising these markets and others. For example the state could be the sole supplier of the good or could licence, set the terms and conditions for how the good is provided applying maybe the principle of universal access or by setting the parameters of the characteristics of the good.

All of this presupposes that the state can do this fairly, equitably and create the conditions for how a good should be sold in a way that represents the needs of all in society. This is a great challenge. It is the point where politics of the day to day begins, identifying an issue, prioritising the means to tackle it and acting. It is reason we have representative democracies, so that the elected members of a legislature take on this work. Too often though there is a failure, a disconnect between the formulation and implementation of a social policy and the needs of the whole society. The catastrophic systemic failures in housing provision in Ireland are just one example of this.

The reason for picking education and health is that these two goods are critical to the quality of life of individuals, households and the communities they are part of. Education can transform the living conditions and quality of life of any person. So why should the economic status of your parents, or even that of yourself dictate the quality and quantity of the education and healthcare goods you could consume?

Maybe there is only a role for the state in setting the minimum standards for the goods, setting the market entry point such as the minimum level of housing. However I think there is a much wider canvas to be used when it comes to service provision by the state.

Ensuring Economic Equality

If you accept that some market outcomes have negative consequences where does that leave your analysis of the role government policies could or should have in the economy.

Negative Market Outcomes

The negative market outcomes outlined already include;

1. The wrong good being produced because of the disproportionate effects high income consumers can have on the characteristics of a good.

2. Too much supplier control resulting in negative oligopolistic practices, such as not enough output being produced and supernormal profits being earned by firms.
3. Lack of quality in the goods produced.
4. Environmental and other externalities, that the actual price paid for the good does not take account of.

What Action Should We Take?

Is it possible to make markets competitive and fair? There has been in my lifetime much talk among current economic policymakers of the need for competition and to deregulate all aspects of the economy particularly those sections still run by state governments. Indeed the privatisation agenda is at the heart of the EU project.

There is though little time given to the question of are markets fair and are they really competitive? For example in Ireland there are a range of oligopolies active in various market places some even licensed by government.

The private sector oligopolies include petrol stations, household cleansing products, retail supermarkets, alcoholic drink brewers, car sales outlets, mobile phone manufacturers. The ones created by government include mobile phone service providers and electricity generators.

The reason for singling out these markets is that in each case the companies involved have the ability to generate quite substantial profits without any thought given to the question of whether their markets are operating in a fair manner.

Ireland has become one of the most expensive places to live in Europe. This is interesting, as it seems that considerable wealth was created in a period of prolonged economic growth to 2007. This was achieved in an import export orientated open market system. The state had methodically deregulated and privatised state run markets. There was a labour market that was heading towards full capacity. This was despite structural deficiencies such as the impact of an underfunded education system and multigenerational poverty which had left the economy with a relatively high percentage of workers, who were entering the workforce in low wage unskilled posts that existed in this period as a result of the construction boom.

It has also left an economy where the low and middle income workers were not equal beneficiaries in the wealth created. In fact they were effectively being levied through higher accommodation and general product prices for the right to live and work in this economy. Then the economic collapse came in 2008, with a return to growth eventually and guess what, the oligopolies all survived, prices are still high and workers are still being exploited to a higher degree than other EU states.

From a republican point of view this presents a significant problem where the economic activity in your society is clearly generating inequalities. In the context highlighted they are inequalities inflicted on some if not an actual majority of the actual participants in the economy. Can this be fair? And if it isn't what should we do about it?

Courses of Action

In the Irish and international arena there is it seems no political will for the resolution of unfair and inefficient markets. Oligopolies are an accepted fact of the market environment, the focus of competitiveness has been placed in two areas. They are the efficiency of firms and the costs of workers.

For Irish workers this a double slap down. First they are expected to endure high living costs and under resourced economic and social infrastructure. Secondly, they are constricted in seeking any real wage increase as this would damage not just the competitiveness of the firm they actually work in, the knock on effects could affect the competitiveness of the whole economy.

The last decades have seen an all out assault on the wages and working conditions of workers throughout the wealthier economies. Workers have become more flexible on their hours and days of employment, the internet and smart phones have made them permanently connected to their workplace. The qualities of their pensions has been eroded as have the entry level wages of workers. The commitment to tenured contracts has been diluted and now in the so called 'gig economy' workers are pseudo entrepreneurs acting mainly under the terms of Uber, Deliveroo and Airbnb as transport and accommodation logistical support workers.

The general point here is that considerable political will and resources are being inputted in Ireland and internationally into a false idea of what competition should actually be. How can it be that as we enter another century of technological advances that the mass of workers are paid less relatively, work longer hours, in less secure employment, with lower pensions if any?

So what courses of action could a government consider for market intervention with the objective of delivering more equitable and just outcomes?

One option could be the government **intervening as a supplier of a good**. In the Irish economy today and internationally this is less prevalent, though in the Irish case the government owns or has owned and supplied goods and services in the context of airports, airlines, bus and rail services, a range of financial service companies, hospitals, electricity power stations, ports and even peat harvesting, not forgetting the already mentioned cabal of bankrupt banks.

A second option is that of **the state funding the supply of a good** through third parties who would have to meet preset requirements. One example of this in Ireland is the education sector at primary through to third level, where the government funds other suppliers of the good, and who especially in the third level sector actually compete with each other for students.

General practice doctors are funded under a similar mechanism, and the ill patient, who is technically the customer in this case, can choose which doctor to attend.

A third option would be to **licence or franchise** out the right to supply certain services and this also is quite common in Ireland where for example in the mobile phone market we have three major government licensed franchises. For the holders this is a profitable business and there has been ongoing trade between international phone companies buying and selling these licences. They need Irish Government and EU approval for the sales. It seems wrong and a missed opportunity that the government here receives no money when a phone franchise is sold. The 2014 acquisition of O_2 by 3 for €850 million might have earned the Irish government some stamp duty revenue, but surely when a financial asset is being sold that depends on a state licence there should be a future sale payment clause (Taylor, 2017)?

Finally the government could take the role of **providing the safety net** or the supplier of last resort. This is quite common in many economies where the state plays a role in housing, basic healthcare and even media through radio and television stations. However the principle could be applied in many other economic sectors like education, childcare, generic medicines and basic food stuffs. For examples the Mexican government subsidised tortilla production throughout the second half of the twentieth century (Pilcher, 2005).

The Market Intervention Record

There are plenty examples in economies around the world of governments intervening in market activity both domestically and internationally. Some of these are strategic and some are knee jerk reactions to particular economic circumstances.

The Irish case of the semi state companies being formed is an example of strategic intervention, while the US investment and subsidies of arms industry and related companies is another, as is the British investment in developing its own nuclear power generation industry.

More recently the decision of the EU to develop the Airbus plane models is an example of strategic transnational market intervention to provide the EU and its airline companies with an alternative to the Boeing passenger carries.

The Euro Fighter is another example of a transnational collaborative project where four European states have formed alliances through their weapon, aeronautical and engineering firms to produce an alternative to the US based F-16 fighters (Eurofighter.com, 2017).

All of these things are examples of strategic interventions, as would the establishment of the CAP in 1969 or the use of trade subsidies by the more wealthy states during the twentieth century.

Then there are the knee jerk reactions. One Irish example for the 1980s was the government purchase of an ailing coffee house chain, that was deemed to have a cultural historical symbolism that overrode the economic imperative which would have liquidated the company and its assets.

The same government, when faced with the collapse of a major insurance company and the possible insolvency of AIB, one of the state's largest banks, intervened in 1986 to take on the debts of the Insurance Corporation of Ireland, launching a lifeboat for AIB and levying on all banks a special tax on profits for the next seven years to pay for the insolvency costs.

In the Six Counties the British Government intervened repeatedly to invest in the Belfast Shipyards, Shorts, a local aeronautical company and many other related firms. Here economic rationale was deemed secondary to the expediency of saving jobs in the unionist community.

Indeed throughout Ireland and internationally individual governments systematically intervene in the economy through development agencies which fund and subsidise business expansion. Ireland north and south has a range of these development agencies including, Enterprise Ireland, Invest Northern Ireland, the IDA, the Shannon Group and others.

A Socialist Republican Perspective

Socialist Republicans readily accept the argument for government intervention, the question is on what basis, what principles should the intervention be made? On several occasions the principle of universal access to basic infrastructure and services has been mooted in the text. This could be a good starting point for intervention in economic activity, where the state sets the minimum threshold of service delivery whether it is to do with education, health, housing, transport.

A wider definition could include access to things like employment, but this also brings us to another principle for intervention, the idea of equality of opportunity. Could we say that everyone in an economy no matter where they live, or what circumstance they are born into, has the right to employment? This means that their social, personal or geographical circumstance should not be an impediment to them finding work, not just any work but well paid, dignified labour?

Other principles worth considering and which flow from the equality well include the idea of equality of outcome and that everyone has political, civil and economic rights. The protection and promotion of these should be the priority of government.

For example governments have a duty to protect the health of citizens from any negative effects of economic activity. So they intervene in a market setting by licensing pharmaceutical firms subject to conditions that make sure their production processes are not releasing carcinogenic material or other pollutants into the atmosphere or into the workplace.

A government might determine a minimum hourly wage, the right to paid leave, maternity and paternity entitlements etc that employers have to fulfil. These are all examples of interventions based on the recognition of the economic rights of workers.

However, I believe that the definition of economic rights must be set much more broadly. Equality of opportunity and equality of outcome are the cornerstones of a just economy. The equality principle is rooted in a recognition of the consequences of the economic interdependencies we are all linked in through our day to day activities.

Why Equality

The New Right economic philosophers and theorists such as Hayek, Friedman, and Buchanan have always been ready to articulate the argument that inequalities are a natural outcome of economic activity.

In many senses this is true. Some people save now to buy later, some spend quickly, some waste their resources, some people have more ability, more talents, and if they are able to sell these skills or use them in a way that earns income, yes they will be better off. But is this a negative inequality? It is not if their economic success can be obtained without exploiting others. It sounds simple but these are in fact very hard conditions to fulfil.

At the same time socialists must accept that as individuals' make decisions and choices through life there will be different outcomes arising from this. From a republican view, we need to accept that people differ, and that this is the essence of the lived human experience. It is the basis of accepting and promoting individual rights. What the right wing conservative state must be recognise is that within these individual choices are institutionalised embedded inequalities.

For example a male barrister in Ireland might think his well paid legal job was won by the discipline of study, partially it maybe was, but is he not in a profession that is inherently sexist, that treats men better than women and as a male does this not favour him? A 2016 Bar of Ireland survey found that two thirds of women barristers had "experienced discrimination during their careers" (Keena, 2016).

Did he in the Irish case not come through a third level cycle where because of economic conditions not of their making a significant section of the population have impaired chances of entering college (HEA, 2015)? So in terms of the competition to get this job a significant section of the population do not get to the starting post and within his work environment others suffer ongoing discrimination. All of these outcomes privilege the male barrister. Then there is the irony that the prosecution of crime, often from members of the population who are educationally disadvantaged is a source of income for our male barrister when the state prosecutes them through the court system.

The economic interdependencies that have privileged this barrister are significant and complex, yet many barristers would see themselves as hardworking, self motivated driven people, and would not recognise or accept the inequalities that had privileged them in the first place.

For the new right these are spurious notions, inequality in their mind is often desirable. In fact the last decades has generated an emerging school of survivalist Darwinian economists, who have brought the theories of natural selection and survival of the fittest into economic theory.

Conclusions

The interdependency of labour is the key principle of understanding the true nature of economic activity. Socialist ideology is based on the principle that the production of goods and services of all kinds are rooted in the outcomes of shared labour. Control of the means of production, as in who owns and benefits from the profits derived from land, natural resources, machines, technologies, physical and intellectual property, and financial assets blurs this reality. It is people, individuals, and their work, their efforts and creativity that creates wealth. Biased and unfairly privileged economic actors around the world deliberately ignore and deny this reality. We desperately need an economic system that allows people share equitably in the produce of their shared economic activity.

We need our economic actions to have a purpose, in production and consumption. Employment should be meaningful, useful, enriching for the person. The consumption of goods and services should meet this criteria also.

Markets fail and key actors turn to government and ultimately the tax payer and their customers to bail them out. This safety net of last resort is in essence the people. So the people's ownership claim on the resources and the assets of many private sector assets is quite strong.

Some goods should not be for sale. Society is better off, financially and socially by the provision of goods and services. The efficient provision of these services such as healthcare and education enhances and supports the effectiveness of the principles of equality of outcome and equality of opportunity.

Government market intervention can be productive and efficient. Government intervention is a systematic feature of economic policy internationally. The practice of intervention is found repeatedly. Also found repeatedly are untimely, inefficient, useless and wholly negative interventions. Intervention is necessary to prevent oligopoly and cartelisation. It is needed to ensure adequate provision of necessity goods and services particularly in primary markets such as transport, communications and energy where equality of access to a resource is a key requirement of a secondary or complimentary market.

A socialist outlook must be rooted in an equality based approach. Already mentioned are the principles of equality of opportunity, equality of outcome. We need to add equality of access, equality of treatment.

I highlight these equality issues because socialism as a philosophy was a reaction to the negative impacts of the industrial revolution, and at its essence has an equality base. I belief the negative outcomes of the industrial revolution are still prevalent today, but it must also be recognised that there are other negative economic trends arising out of the impact of decades of neoliberalist policies in our domestic economy in Ireland and internationally. A socialist approach rooted in equality principles offers a way of creating an economic environment where useful goods and services are produced, where workers are involved in meaningful work that pays a living wage with acceptable working conditions. Finally, a true socialist approach must have environmental protection and enhancement at its core.

This is the point of departure for socialism in the twenty-first century.

References

Connolly, J. (1987). *James Connolly Collected Works Volume One*. New Books Publications.

Eurofighter. (2017). Eurofighter. Retrieved August 20, 2017, from https://www.eurofighter.com/

HEA. (2015). *National Plan for Equality of Access to Higher Education 2015–2019*. Retrieved August 20, 2017, from http://hea.ie/resources/publications/page/2/

Hodgkins, T. (1825). *Labour Defended against the Claims of Capital*. Knight and Lacey.

Hunt, E. K., & Sherman, H. J. (1990). *Economics an Introduction to Traditional and Radical Views* (6th ed.). Harper and Row.

Keena, C. (2016, April 21). Two in Three Women Barristers Face Discrimination, Study Finds. *Irish Times*. Retrieved August 20, 2017, from https://www.irishtimes.com/news/crime-and-law/two-in-three-women-barristers-face-discrimination-study-finds-1.2618019

Pilcher, J. M. (2005). Industrial Tortillas and Folkloric Pepsi: The Nutritional Consequences of Hybrid Cuisines in Mexico. In J. L. Matson & M. L. Caldwell (Eds.), *The Cultural Politics of Food and Eating*. Blackwell Publishing.

Rawls, J. (1971). *A Theory of Justice*. Harvard University Press. Revised edition, 1999.

Taylor, C. (2017, August 4). Revenue Slips 10% at Mobile Operator Three. *Irish Times*.

CHAPTER 5

The Republican Entrepreneur

The Importance of Entrepreneurship

The ability to take a business idea from conception to completion is in modern economies a prized and valued skill. There is a widespread belief that our diverse market economies need entrepreneurs, people who have the ability to start new projects or ventures. The word has become synonymous with creating new business, but this is only one element of what an entrepreneur is.

Yes entrepreneurs start new businesses or innovate existing ones, but that perhaps is because in the twentieth and twenty-first centuries using the business model as a vehicle for your project, no matter what its actual activity, has become the accepted structure for managing and developing your venture. It could be a coffee shop, a computer software firm, or the activities of an actor, writer, designer, plumber or painter. So you might think of yourself as an inventor but that creativity and research is harnessed and protected in terms of ownership within the form of a firm. Was Da Vinci an artist, inventor, business owner or a combination of all three? He was inspired to think about the world in new ways but he still needed to make money.

The firm and the entrepreneur have become natural bed fellows. In market economies one measure of economic activity is in the number of firms in an economy and the level of growth of that figure.

R. Smyth, *The Invisible Republic*,
https://doi.org/10.1007/978-3-030-86734-8_5

The CSO in Ireland produce an occasional statistical release titled Business Demography and the 2018 release has figures for the number of enterprises in the 26 Counties from 2008 to 2016. In 2008, the year the economy fell into recession there were 244,195 enterprises employing 1,511,920 people. This falls to 238,249 enterprises in 2014 employing 1,334,291 (CSO, 2018, p. 1). Driving these figures annually are the number of enterprise deaths and births. In 2011, 18,076 enterprises 'died' while there were 11,847 enterprise 'births' (CSO, 2014, p. 1). By 2016, the number of enterprises has risen to 250,033 employing 1,478,236 people (CSO, 2018, p. 1).

Other data in this area comes from the annual Global Entrepreneurship Monitor (GEM) reports. The 2015 GEM report for Ireland has data for the years up to 2014 and estimates that 20,400 people were involved in starting a business in 2014 in Ireland, and two thirds of these were the sole owner of the business (Fitzsimons & O'Gorman, 2015, p. 21). In 2018, GEM reported that 26,800 people were involved in starting a business in 2017 (Fitzsimons & O'Gorman, 2018, p. 10). The 2015 GEM report estimates that 6.5% of the 26-County adult population were early stage entrepreneurs, 2.5% had started new businesses and just over 4% were in the planning stages of a new venture (Fitzsimons & O'Gorman, 2015, p. 26).

There is also the question of the size of firms. Some firms are so powerful that they can garner and stockpile entrepreneurial skills within their workforce. This gives them an edge over smaller firms. The combination of buying power in input markets as well as the ability to sell cheaper because of greater scale in their output markets means they have even greater advantages over smaller rivals.

On the other hand large firms are complex organisations and sometimes survival and progress up the ranks of the organisation is the goal of workers rather than take charge of particular projects, ventures or activities within the firm. Any readers who have experience of the larger workplace will no doubt have a lot of examples showing that initiative and excellence are not often requirements for climbing the work career ladder.

The core points though are that the individual entrepreneur should be a valuable asset to any firm and the community they come out of, and that modern market economies need entrepreneurs. However the need for what we now call an entrepreneur is not something limited to a market economy environment.

A Republican Philosophy of Work, Creativity and Entrepreneurship

At a basic level entrepreneurship is about an individual taking control, exercising control over their own economic activity, harnessing their own creativity, and critically determining the value of their own work. Their entrepreneurship is a tangible expression of their own individualism. Entrepreneurship is an exercise of economic freedom.

Freedom to direct your own labour, to plan its deployment and harness your creativity is I believe a critical facility in our world today. It has been important in all the eras that humans have lived and worked in. It is also a unique position that many individuals have never experienced. Slavery, feudalism, castes, professions with controlled entry, assembly line production, the demands of a modern office are all examples of the denial and at best curtailment of an individual's freedom to determine their work choices. So from a republican perspective, the idea of a workplace, a work environment that can demonstrate an absence of coercion is compelling.

At one basic level entrepreneurship can be seen as a form, an expression of creativity. However this individual entrepreneurial activity raises an issue regarding how to deal with shared creativity. Our work environments, our economies are from a micro level upwards rooted in interdependencies. In the digital computerised environment this interlinking and interdependency is even more profound. So for entrepreneurship to be socially and individually valuable we must find a way to discuss and solve the shared and interdependent aspects of work and creativity, who owns and shares ideas in the workplace? Who benefits when there is a monetary, power, or status related profit or return on the efforts invested in the ideas?

What happens when labour is pooled needs discussion. Is it possible to do this in a non-exploitative way? If I have a business idea, if I invent, create or innovate, what criteria impact the shared elements of taking this idea to completion? Do I hire people and agree a price for their labour? Do they become shareholders in my venture, and does that share make them partners in decision making and planning or just a guarantee of a share of future profits?

The link between successful entrepreneurship and the potential for profit and other rewards of social status and power has I believe distorted an important feature of how we work, it is often a shared collaborative environment. However in the uncritical eulogising of entrepreneurship and the individual efforts in creating a business, we fail to recognise the limits of individual effort, and at best too often champion the individual over the collaborative collective effort in economic activity. It is a strange and unjust position to be in, where in order for an individual to freely express themselves in the work environment they need to coerce and exploit others. That cannot be considered a good thing and promoting policies that create or protect that outcome is wrong.

Therefore, the challenge for a republican policy to promote entrepreneurship is how to promote and aid an individual's right to control their own economic activity, without impinging on the similar rights held by others.

Republicans and Entrepreneurs

A common misconception is that republicans don't want to include the business community in their vision of an ideal society or see entrepreneurship as some tainted activity. This is isn't true, if anything republicans understand the role entrepreneurs play in society more than any other political groups.

What republicans do have a problem with is the idea of a free hand for business development without care of the consequences for others. The rights of business cannot supersede that of any other group or any individual for that matter. So entrepreneurs must care about the environment and the impact their venture might have on it. They must care about the rights of workers and the economic interdependencies their business links into. At a basic entry level workers need a living wage and working conditions that are fair and flexible and enhance individual rights.

That being said entrepreneurs have become economic shamans. At their most successful they are celebrated like sports or movie stars, with no-one quite sure just how any particular multi-millionaire developed their successful business ideas. In Ireland and internationally since the nineteenth century entrepreneurs have also been feted as "captains of industry".

In the Ireland of the 1970s and 1980s the seeming can do ability of some private businesses to become successful international profit making ventures was in contrast to the bumbling failures of government especially when it came to the management of state enterprises.

Examples of these so called captains included Michael Smurfit, who with his brothers had inherited a print and packing company that they grew into an international conglomerate, Tony O'Reilly, was a retired sports star who rose through the ranks at Heinz to the position of chief executive, while using his wealth to build an independent empire in the media and home wares sectors in Ireland and again internationally. The Dunne and Quinn families built national retail networks out of small shops.

The family business lineage of many of these entrepreneurs has given sustenance to the belief that these examples are proof of the value of economic Darwinism, implying that success in business is a modern form of survival of the fittest and a positive addition to society.

If true this would explain the importance of entrepreneurs in economic activity but when you actually probe some of the data about entrepreneurship it doesn't quite stack up. Yes there are the super-rich and successful entrepreneurs but they are the exception not the norm.

In fact, the economic collapse in Ireland in the 2008 recession shook out revelations about how the banking sector and government had pampered many of the supposed dazzling entrepreneurial builders, speculators and investors leaving the Irish taxpayer to cover the costs of this laissez faire attitude to entrepreneurial activities. We mentioned this already in the section on NAMA in the markets chapter.

Profits and Entrepreneurs

Then there is the question of profits and there are two issues here. The first is that if we had a perfectly competitive market with the conditions of free entry and exit being met and only normal profits being made what would people's motives for participating in economic activity be? I mention this because core tenet of free market systems is that supernormal profits could not, should not be made. So it couldn't be for extra financial gain as this would only be short term. The concepts of normal and super normal profits are dealt with in the chapter on market systems.

How though does this help us in our search for understanding entrepreneurial motives when profit is not a long term option underpinning market activity? Could it be a creative spirit or a desire to produce for your community? Could it be a prestige factor that enhances your standing in the society or region in that you are an important economic actor?

In today's markets there are tens of thousands of entrepreneurs. What are their motivations? Can all of their actions be boiled down to the pursuit of supernormal profits or public acclaim, because in the majority of examples this is not the case?

The GEM figures used earlier demonstrated that when discussing entrepreneurship we are talking about a significant part of society. It seems that when it comes to engaging in economic activity many people chose to form their own businesses. They want to be free of the constraints of managers, of other people setting their goals or placing limits on them. They want to set their own goals.

So the question today is what is the motivation in terms of economic activity of small businesses that constitute more than 64% of the workforce, when we compare the CSO figures for those working in small businesses with the total workforce as calculated in the CSO Quarterly National Household Survey (CSO, 2016b)?

Today our economy's wellbeing seems to be linked or even dependent to an extent on new business formation and the ongoing growth of existing businesses. We want our existing businesses to grow and develop and new ones to be formed. This activity is a sort of measure of the economic blood supply, how anaemic or iron filled is the economy in any given year.

It is true that our formal media is enthralled with tales of business success feting those who have either built up a business empire or better still got out at the top of market, selling up and realising the multi-million euro value of the business getting to live a life of relaxation and luxury. A fascinating example of this spanning over two decades was the spread of the Apprentice programme and its spinoffs in Britain and Ireland. The original programme featuring Donald Trump spawned Alan Sugar in Britain and Bill Cullen in Ireland as regional spinoffs. You could argue that the profile this programme gave Donald Trump has been a factor in his successful campaign to become US president. Apart from the US version there were 24 other country editions of the Apprentice (Wikipedia, 2016).

However this view of entrepreneurship is only the reality for a very small amount of those involved in business. For the majority of business creators the situation is entirely different. There are no sell offs, no billions to be made. The reality is hard work that can be rewarded financially and creatively. It is hard in that it involves investing long hours and taking financial risks. Yet thousands of people still elect to take this route.

So what should the approach of republicans be to this part of the economy? Why can't we have socialist republican entrepreneurs? We can, and the answer is to focus on entrepreneurship as an example of individual citizens asserting their desire to control and assert independence. It seems often to be a core human desire to be able to highlight your own independent accomplishments.

The Republican Entrepreneur

A republican entrepreneur is driven to want to take greater control of their labour and give shape to their creativity but also are conscious of the rights of other individuals and the communities they belong to or interact with because of their entrepreneurial activity.

The first principles of this republican approach to entrepreneurship would be to redefine what entrepreneurship is or could be. Examples of a more broad definition of entrepreneurship would include:

1. *Community entrepreneurship* where local business projects are set up that at their core do not have an underlying profit motive. It's not that these businesses are designed to be run at a loss. Not so, rather the imperative is to have an efficiently organised project that would not be run on the need to have ever increasing profits or a grand expansion plan.

   Other objectives could be maximising employment opportunities, or providing a complimentary service to other economic activities like a subsidised transport system, a community building project, crèche facilities or after school programmes for working parents. Usually these projects are part of the social economy and what they have in common is the example of people taking control of their local environment determining how they want their community to be structured.

   Given the comprehensive failures of local government throughout the island and the inability to cede any real democratic control of resources to communities this type of entrepreneurship is all the more important in its ability to allow groups of people to take control of projects and ventures that are important to them.

   Too often these community activities are seen as lying outside of formal economic activity, they are an add on, a bolt on, when they are in fact an example of market failure and to an extent a political one also. The institutional market view, and I mean this to mean the normal economic actors in society, particularly the financial sector who have a vital funding role, see these activities as being different because of the lack of supernormal profits.

   Take for example a main street in a small town. The financial assets are the property and the rents that flow from them or the development potential of constructing larger buildings with higher rent yields or maybe they would contain larger businesses with higher levels of turnover.

Empty shops negatively affect the combined activity of the town, yet lowering rent to keep the town more vibrant, or raise the level of economic activity is seen as a last resort. For the town to succeed it needs a hinterland of houses, a transport network whether it is roads, rail or bus. The business potential of the town is the sum of these and other factors. Yet often it is a community activist who acts on the missing elements and this can be anything from a tidy town competition to starting new local community businesses. So the group who form to protect a local post office from closure are making a direct contribution to the economic environment. The open post office will increase footfall in the street, potentially leading to other spending. Groups like this are often not seen as contributing to the local economy, yet they play a vital role. So ensuring the conditions for these groups to succeed and thrive is an important function of government locally and nationally.

2. *Ecopreneurship* where the objectives of this business venture are underpinned not by profit but by environmental objectives. The challenge of negative climate change impacts across the planet make this area worth singling out for two reasons. One, the impact of climate changes necessitates remedial action across all of our social and economic activities. Two, it is a second example where individual effort and creativity is harnessed for a goal that does not have financial return as its core measure of success. Instead it is an activity that specifically deals with an economic outcome that does not have a financial measure and that monetary exchanges have ignored. It is an entrepreneurship that focuses on dealing with the environmental externalities of our economic activity (Schaltegger, 2002).
3. *Intrapreneurship* describes a process where inside large organisations sub groups initiate entrepreneurial activities. The 2015 GEM report has a figure for Intrapreneurship, estimating that 6.7% of the adult Irish population were involved in Intrapreneurship, ranking the 26 Counties 6th across Europe in this category (Fitzsimons & O'Gorman, 2015, p. 27).

   This definition is important as it raises another important question about the individual and work, and how their contributions and efforts are rewarded. As the worker's tasks move into innovation, research and ultimately the creation of new products, processes or services and the sum of these efforts help create something that contributes to increased profits. With this new revenue stream, and increased worth of the company there is a question as to what basis are the intrapreneurs rewarded and how do they share in the increased profitability. They have contributed to the creation of intellectual property in their company, yet often it seems that because the firm had the financial capital to back and underpin the intrapreneurship process it is never questioned as to who owns this newly formed intellectual property.

In Ireland across the island, with its dual administrations and public service structures, it seems that intrapreneurship could be the key for reformatting our public service whether it is the staff at government departments, or state services such as education or health. In both administrations there is ongoing criticism of how the government organises its activities and delivers services to citizens. We have endless angst about the organs of government, and their inefficiencies. This results in an equally endless amount of strategies and consultancy reports and still the problems persist, with the voter wondering where the money is going to and to what effect. Maybe we need an all island policy of intrapreneurship in our state and public services as a way of developing the sector to be more dynamic and self-reliant.

Encouraging and Supporting Entrepreneurship

So how do we direct this entrepreneurial activity to get the best possible use of resources for both the individual or individuals taking on a project? There are two sets of criteria that could be applied. The first set are supportive functions that government at a local or national level could introduce to clear the unnecessary obstacles out of the path of the entrepreneur. The second set are directive and a product of the current economic and social environment. These criteria could and should change over time particularly as economic activity as we know it is changing so quickly particularly in terms of the developing outputs from the so called 'new' information and online communications economy. A visit to the websites of Enterprise Ireland, Invest Northern Ireland, the 26-County enterprise boards and the Six County's Enterprise Northern Ireland network of regional offices shows that all of them offer ground up support to entrepreneurs.

The recession of 2008 created substantial enhancements across the island economy for facilitating business start-ups with in particular a greater focus on entrepreneurship by women and younger adults. In the 26 Counties a one stop approach was finally implemented in enterprise centres to streamline the start up process. Across the island there is still focus on 'high growth' potential businesses, and though access to finance has been made simpler, more can be done to allow all parts of the community start a business.

Finance is the core requirement for an entrepreneur. They need money for business plans to get seed corn funding to start their project, to get money to go into production or to be fully operational. You need to have money to be lent money, so successful ventures begin and end with an ongoing need for finance.

However controlling the use of money is an important part of market economies. You cannot it seems let just anybody get control of money and the banking sector in Ireland up until the emergence of international competition and market liberalisation in early noughties were fastidious in their refusal to invest speculatively in the local economy. What they did invest in speculatively was property which shows a structural imbalance in the economy, in that the perceived profits in the property market were siphoning economic activity into this area away from other sectors.

It is fascinating that even with this prolonged property bubble in Ireland, we still don't have enough houses, or the right fit in office space in terms of the small and large businesses that dominate the Irish economy today and so as I wrote the first draft of this section in 2017 the property bubble began again, drawing resources and focus away from the wider economy into what should be a service industry for the whole economy not its greatest focus.

I suppose the question is how come we don't think about the possible scale of entrepreneurship and the resources that could be invested in this sector in the same way we think about other economic sectors. Ireland's entrepreneurship ranking was 16th out of 25 European states participating in the survey and 6th when it came to intrapreneurship according to the 2014 entrepreneurship report (Fitzsimons & O'Gorman, 2015, p. 21). Even on the formal standard definition of entrepreneurship there is considerable scope for expansion, so if we really want to embrace the entrepreneurship principle there seems to be a business case for investing in this sector. But there is a further distortion to consider. In Ireland and internationally governments regularly get involved in funding, investing in and subsidising business, but there is often significant disparities and inequalities in how this is done.

There is an argument made by the market driven classical liberal economists right up to the Hayek's of today that institutionalised charity such as subsidies, grants or other forms of corporate welfare has no place in the modern economy as it only distorts the real economy from emerging by subsidising needless activity. There are two points to be made here, the first is that government corporate charity, masquerading as investment and grants, or to use a better term 'welfare for business' can massively distort the economy, with resources and effort being concentrated in inefficient activities. However the second point is that even among the most pro free market governments in the world there is a lot of corporate welfare out there.

One example of this is in energy generation. In Britain and the US in particular billions of euro has been invested in subsidising the nuclear industry. Their ongoing plans to build a new nuclear power station at Hinkley in Britain comes with a possible £37 billion price tag in potential subsidies payable to the French energy firm EDF who will build and operate the plant (Macalister, 2016). I wonder what the impact of £37 billion spent on renewable energy would be?

In Ireland and Britain you have the dichotomy of huge spending on incarcerating people from low income backgrounds who commit crime, and at the same time a refusal to spend even a fraction of that sum on investing in either the people or the communities that lower income groups are often ghettoised in. Irish Penal Reform Trust figures estimated that "In 2015, the average cost of an "available, staffed prison space" was €73,802" (Irish Penal Reform Trust, 2019). Again we come up against the importance of who controls how money is used in an economy.

In Ireland across the island there has been long history of economic discrimination In the Six Counties, nationalist communities, full of initiative, but starved of investment have looked on as millions got pumped over the years into lame duck enterprises such as Harland and Wolf, Shorts and others (Hansard, 1975). In the years of the conflict there were a litany of investment failures and examples of discrimination from job opportunities to the availability of investment. The high water mark in this would have to the £80 million invested in the failed De Lorean car plant (BBC, 2005). It was a massive investment all for the creation of 2,000 jobs.

Alongside these massive investment bonanzas we sometimes still have a problem giving the most meagre amounts of funding to prospective entrepreneurs. By 'we', I mean government local and national, as well as employment and economic development agencies.

The Problems of Directing Entrepreneurship

How we see enterprise, how we understand economic processes has changed fundamentally in recent years. Part of the reason is the impact of new technologies, particularly in the communication technology areas and the so called 'internet of things' that have collectively revolutionised how economic activity happens and how and what consumers spend their money on, whether it is online music platforms, personal health and fitness devices or locally brewed craft beers.

There are also factors like rising living standards and a growth in disposable income which has created an increase in consumption and demand for leisure based products.

A simple anecdotal example of the scale of these changes are how, when and why we eat food. I grew up in a society that viewed eating outside the home in a café and restaurant as a rare treat. Eating in the street was bad manners and in fact eating out at all was considered wasteful.

Now with new food technologies, longer and varied work hours, and growing household concerns about food quality how we consume food has changed. We eat out more, food preparation times have fallen drastically because of new technologies like microwaves, and new habits like eating take away food.

When food is prepared within the home often time is of the essence and handy cooking sauce supplements, pre washed, pre chopped vegetables grown organically, corn fed, boned and washed chicken breasts are all elements designed to cut the preparation time.

Someone has to make and sell these goods, the how where and when these goods are produced, marketed and sold is changing how our economy is structured and this is just one type of good.

Irish villages used to be synonymous with the high numbers of public houses. This is still a feature supplemented now by the growing number of cafes and take aways as our food choices change and develop.

Then there is the sourcing of inputs to make this food, as well as the layout and printing of leaflets that will be distributed to thousands of homes, or the design and operation of a delivery app for the goods. Then there are the delivery workers to complete the phone to door service. It is ironic that while some people would dismiss the need for daily bread and milk deliveries to their door, they prize reliable take away services. This is just one example of new forms of economic activity that are increasingly prevalent in Irish society.

The Worker in an Entrepreneurial Economy

The downside of these processes can be the creation of a workhouse economy, as described by Rowthorn and Wayne (1988) in their book on the political economy of conflict in the North. I lived for a while in that society and there was an extraordinary innovation in the amount of services on offer. Some of them were the standard household services that had been in steady decline in the Dublin economy I came from. So Belfast had weekly coal deliveries, daily milk and newspaper services if you wanted. It was also possible to get vegetables delivered, alcohol and cigarettes, even rental videos. Many people also worked as unlicenced taxi drivers. There was little money to be made in these businesses, but there was an absence of other economic opportunities.

The emergence of companies like Uber or Deliveroo has for me an echo back to the Six-County economy and this cycle of low income households attempting to boost their income by selling unique services.

There is a key issue about what people actually work at in our economies today. On my way to work each morning, I see a variety of people, office and retail workers, building site labourers often tired, buying coffees and snacks, blearily resigned to an early start. Then there are people whose job is to give out leaflets to tourists, others stand holding placards all day, or try and get you to sign up and support a charity. Is this the digital economy? Is this the best we can do? It is moments like this that remind me once again that something is badly wrong in how we organise economic resources in society today.

The nineteenth century utopian socialist Charles Fourier was one of the first to discuss this in his book The Theory of the Four Movements (Fourier, 1996). Hunt and Sherman distil Fourier's thinking on 'useful or destructive labour, misdirected work and commerce dominated by middlemen' into a claim that "Fourier believed that in a capitalist economy only one third of people did socially useful work. The other two thirds were directed by the corruption and distortion caused by the market system into useless occupations or were useless wealthy parasites" (Hunt & Sherman, 1990, p. 64). In Fourier's list of useless labour he included the 'army, the idle rich, ne'er do wells, sharpers, prostitutes, magistrates, police, lawyers, philosophical cranks, bureaucrats, spies, priests and clergymen' (Hunt & Sherman, 1990, p. 64).

So I wonder today what would Fourier think of the jobs people have in society today. Many of the occupations he thought were useless in the nineteenth century still exist today. In many shops there are self service tills, the implication of which is that we don't need tellers and wonder did we ever need them. Frontline staff have disappeared from banks, but we have had a growth in so called security jobs, for businesses, transport, entertainment venues. Is this a worthwhile post?

There are so many distortions in our labour market from jobs created by bureaucracy, by elites protecting their interests political and financial. Then there are those who work in industries and sectors of destructive nature or dubious value. Think about where you live inside your dwelling, and consider all the things you might own, have possibly bought and never used. Now think about the people who work in producing, manufacturing m distributing these unused goods and services. Could this be your entry point into contemplating useless work?

Even my job as a lecturer, I wonder how worthwhile it is. If students were brought through a different learning environment would they still need as young adults to sit in classrooms and listen to someone speak? Why do they know so little, why is their ability to learn so impaired after what was in most cases 14 years of schooling? Why have they been trained or conditioned to sit? What does it say about me as the circus master of this performance?

Failure of Understanding

Finally there is another important factor not commonly focused on or admitted. It was that at some basic level we didn't understand economic processes and this is still often the case. By 'we', I mean everybody, government, the media and many political parties just didn't really have a true understanding of economic forces at work.

What we did know was how to mimic what seemed to work, but the why of this was not really known. With hindsight this collective ignorance has in the aftermath of the Cold War and the collapse of the Berlin Wall been rewritten to argue that it was the Left that didn't understand. Now as the digital and information economy grows I wonder who next will be blamed for a lack of understanding, the Great Recession of 2008 being the latest instalment in this never ending farce.

If true, that the Left were to blame, this would be great, but substantial sections of the academic community were victims of this ignorance shown for example by the support and admiration bestowed on Alban Phillips in 1958 for his inflation/unemployment trade off curve. In 1976 the monetarist Milton Friedman received his Nobel Prize for economics and used the lecture to offer a compelling treatise debunking the Phillips Curve theory (Friedman, 1976). At this stage Phillips thinking was well into its second decade of implementation as the core plank of many European, US and other industrialised nations' economic policies.

In my lifetime I have witnessed a series of economic fads, some more potent and enduring than others and they again point to an at times deliberate misunderstanding of economic theories. The one that never goes away is the need for 'competitiveness' in the economy. Nothing must interfere with the competitiveness of the firm, yet when you looked at the obstacles to competitiveness especially through a news media frame it often seemed that encouraging competitiveness often meant attacking workers, their wages and working conditions as the core reason for this loss of so called competitiveness. Next in line is so called red tape, otherwise known to you and me as 'health and safety regulations'.

Economic Mimicry and Other Policy Failures

Examples of economic mimicry in Ireland were the failed attempts to create an industrial base in the 26 Counties. Ship construction, car manufacture and steel smelting were just some of the flawed projects that soaked up scarce resources.

This scenario has been repeated across the world where failed flagship projects meant massive job losses in the host communities. When the host enterprise finally failed the result was often utter misery through the unemployment and negative multiplier effects as the small local businesses all dependent on the disposable income from the wage packets of the neighbouring factory also felt the knock on effects, many closing down or severely curtailing their activities.

This scenario was repeated again and again not just in Ireland, but across Europe and North America. The last great example and most recent failure of economic mimicry is the deregulation of financial services that internationally sparked the 'Great Recession' of 2008.

The problem of economic policy failures in Ireland is not just in the failure of mimicry projects. There are other observable traits.

1. Uneven development of supporting infrastructure.
2. Ignorance of indigenous resources.
3. Side lining of the co-operative principle.
4. Stifling initiative, creating a fear of failure culture and an enterprise bureaucracy.

Lessons Learnt

So what have we learnt about economic processes to think we can direct entrepreneurship today? Well for starters we should be in a position where we cannot repeat the mistakes of the past and a lot of entrepreneurship can begin with the Samuel Beckett principle of "Ever tried, ever failed, try again, fail better" (Beckett, 1983).

The four sets of failures outlined above are also examples of the denial of republican ideals and the economic rights of Irish citizens and are a serious deterrent to those wanting to expand businesses or those wanting to start new ventures.

Geographical discrimination was a feature of both economies and in the Six Counties was a tool of Unionist discrimination. What excuse did successive 26-County governments have who were systematically discriminating against their own voters, creating in both cases, a situation where political and economic power became mainly centred in cities and some other population centres. Large parts of the west and midlands, the border regions, the unchecked urban and suburban slums were ignored. The 2005 Combat Poverty Agency report is just one of a series of academic studies that highlights these imbalances (Watson et al., 2005).

So when it comes to starting a business venture equality of opportunity was not guaranteed. Then there was an added tier of discrimination drawn from the growing belief developed in the 1950s and still prevalent at times to this day that the Irish economy's problem was missing elements. Protectionism had failed to grow indigenous enterprise, so the solution was to transplant enterprise from abroad, particularly the USA. For aspiring Irish business you were clearly second class.

Our successes in the food industry are patchy at best as mass production became under the CAP the focus of agricultural activity to the detriment of developing new products and processes. It is amazing to me that it has been the recent recession that has driven innovation in small food manufacturers. Did it really take massive indebtedness for the state, the tax payer and many homeowners for us to wake up to new quality foods?

Similarly in terms of forestry, developing renewable energy or exploiting fossil fuels the activity was uneven and lacks a long term focus.

Take the example of exploiting gas and oil resources. The search for oil and gas has at various periods over recent decades caught the national attention. In Norway at the beginning of the 1960s there were no skills in the exploration sector resident in the country; now with Statoil the Norwegians are able to develop Irish natural resources for the enrichment of Norwegian citizens. This happened because successive Norwegian governments took an active interest in developing skills, knowledge and ultimately ownership of their domestic resources (Norsk Petroleum, 2016).

Successive Irish governments were wary of getting involved in oil exploration, didn't have a long term view and let international oil and gas companies not only set the agenda but also formulate exploration policy in Ireland leading to a situation where Ireland has the lowest levies on revenue from oil exploration in the world today. Conor McCabe has the most succinct summary of the Irish national resource give away beginning in 1958 with the sale of exploration rights to 27,000 miles for £500 (McCabe, 2011).

Then there was the question of business structure. Formal partnerships, and the share ownership structure of multinational firms was considered superior to co-operative approaches. According to the Irish Co-operative Society today there are 12,000 people in the 26 Counties employed in co-ops out of a total workforce of nearly 2 million (ICOS, 2016; CSO, 2016a). The decline in agricultural co-ops and the failure of the structure to spread into other economic areas is I believe a critical mistake in the development of entrepreneurship in Ireland. It also meant that unconsciously the concept of fraternity in an economic sense has been undermined, another blow to the republican ideal. I do believe that entrepreneurship is a key aspect of the republican philosophy, but it is clear when you consider the question of shared ownership of ideas and effort that the co-operative approach offers another viable avenue to organise an economic venture when there are multiple people involved.

Bureaucracy of Enterprise Development

Finally there was and at times still is the bureaucracy of enterprise development. Ireland today has not one or even two enterprise agencies, but the number runs to double figures.

In the Six Counties there has been some work done on streamlining agencies into the Invest Northern Ireland banner, but what is still questionable is the productivity, efficiency and philosophical outlook of this and other agencies.

In the 26 Counties the divisions between agencies are a mix of the political and logistical. Its logistical in that the IDA deal with Foreign Direct Investment (FDI), Enterprise Ireland have the remit for indigenous firms that have what they term "export potential" and county enterprise boards promote micro and small business, not in the export arena.

Then comes in the politics with Údarás for economic development in the Gaeltacht area and previously Shannon Development in the South West now part of Enterprise Ireland. What doesn't make sense is that having empowered two such bodies not rolling out regional development agencies across the island, particularly as the regional imbalances in the Irish economy are so pronounced.

A second issue is that despite the plethora of development agencies there are still thousands of firms who operate without any agency input. Those that do have contact have to at times jump through a series of bureaucratic hoops, such as have they more than 50 employees, Are they "export ready"? Do they fit into the agency profile? One example of this is the growing media and communications industry which are employment intensive and growing sectors, yet Enterprise Ireland used to not fund certain media companies. County enterprise boards will, but the growth in organisations such as Fumbally Exchange, which has grown from one site in Dublin City to three, shows significant gaps in the Enterprise development environment (Fumbally Exchange, 2016).

Two things jump out for me, one is that the economic collapse of 2008 highlighted challenges and opportunities that the Irish enterprise bureaucracy was not up to dealing with. The second issue is that maybe we need a more flexible institutional approach to enterprise development, enterprise strategies life span should be time limited and always open to change. There are examples of this thinking within the enterprise agencies where they focus on a particular sector such as games in the early part of this decade.

Then there is the fact the IDA, Enterprise Ireland and county enterprise boards perform better in periods of economic growth. In the recession they could do nothing to stall the collapse of construction industry employment or the failures of retail outlets that were dependent on construction industry multiplier effects. When tens of thousands of new households are being formed that means a lot of couches, carpets, TVs, crockery, beds and the other endless domestic products are also being bought. When the number of new homes falls so does demand for these complimentary products.

In the Ireland of 2016 and 17, the IDA, Enterprise Ireland and enterprise boards had a banner year, but so did the economy as a whole. So do we really need these enterprise agencies in their current forms and structures?

An article in the June 2005 Economic and Social Review by Helena Lenihan, Mark Hart and Stephen Roger addresses this issue. They found that approximately €5.5 billion had been spent on direct assistance to firms by the IDA, Enterprise Ireland, Shannon Development and Udaras in the years 1980 to 2003. The authors also found that evaluation of this spending has rarely moved beyond ensuring the money was spent as planned rather than how effective were the investments made.

This comes as no surprise, Sinn Fein's then Enterprise and Employment spokesperson Arthur Morgan asked a Dail question in November 2002 as to whether any audit had been done of the 19 employment taskforces created in 1997 by the Fianna Fail/Progressive Democrat government. The task forces were formed in each case after massive job losses were announced in particular areas like Fruit of the Loom in Donegal.

Sinn Fein were told that no evaluation had been done and as the spending was across different departments it was not feasible to gauge the effectiveness of the taskforces. The ESRI reports authors found a "poor evaluation culture in Ireland" and that nearly 50% of Irish firms given grants to create jobs would have generated the jobs anyway. It leaves the question as to whether we have wasted over €5 billion.

What about the Six Counties and the record of Invest Northern Ireland? The 2004 INI annual report showed huge imbalances in how the agency's money is spent. The largest amount of INI funding was spent in the Belfast region, with substantially more funds being pumped into south and east Belfast, which are more likely to have unionist workers in them.

A council-by-council breakdown of Invest NI funding shows that Belfast gets the lion's share of INI support receiving over 45% of all assistance in 2003–2004 and was set for nearly 47% of all planned investment in 2005, Within Belfast it is South and East Belfast that gets the majority of that support.

In comparison the then seven border council areas (Armagh, Omagh, Newry & Mourne, Dungannon, Fermanagh, Strabane and Derry) received just over 20% of planned investment.

These figures provide proof that investment was not being directed to border areas despite well-documented evidence that these are severely disadvantaged. A calculation of the financial assistance per head of population showed that the six council areas together received £5,752 per person living in those council areas compared to £27,054 or nearly five times this amount, for each person living in South Belfast. The then seven councils West of the Bann received £20 million less than Belfast in 2003–2004 and the planned investment is £92 million less.

In terms of INI's total spending, they spent £71 million in the 12 months to the end of March 2004. £12 million went on supporting new inward investment with a forecasted 1,099 jobs. In terms of locally owned companies INI offered £59.82 million in assistance to 2,970 projects 254 of which were actually new start ups. The INI annual report did not give details of the jobs associated with these projects.

A 2011 report by Hart and Bonner which evaluated INI investments from 2001 to 2008 found that though there was growth in sales there was no impact on employment (Hart & Bonner, 2011, p. 3). A 2018 report from the Northern Ireland Assembly Research and Information Service found that Belfast South received the most INI funding followed by East Belfast and Lagan Valley. In the least funded constituencies came a mix or areas including Strangford, East Derry, North Belfast and South Down (NIARIS, 2018). The imbalance in funding still continues.

In 2015, the Department of Jobs, Enterprise and Innovation published an evaluation report which covered the IDA, Enterprise Ireland and the county enterprise boards, renamed as local enterprise offices in 2014. It is broadly positive of the three agencies but still recommends strengthening of their evaluation processes (DJEI, 2015, pp. 31–32). One way of doing this is to compare the performance of agency backed firms with those who received no aid and compare their growth and performance. My reading of the 2015 report would be that this is not done.

The most recent assessment of the efficiency of enterprise agencies in Ireland was published in 2017. It found that Enterprise Ireland policy is in line with best practices, however "the level and composition of expenditure may need to be refocussed", and "EI appears to have become a more efficient agency in recent years" (Reidy, 2017).

No matter how well the agencies report on their evaluations there is still a need to rethink the role that the agency community plays in enterprise particularly in the context of who formulates the long term policy and who has day to day control of the running of the agencies.

The Next Decades of Jobs

Where will the next decades of jobs come from? How will the Irish economy secure its long term viability as an economic unit? The reason for posing these questions is that there is a tendency today among media and academic commentators to analyse the Irish economy in a very narrow way. Their analysis is divided into before and during the Celtic Tiger Boom and then after the 2008 recession. Analysis of the Six-County economy is even more simplified into why its economic performance is not more like the Celtic Tiger experience, or more like a region of Britain. Which British region the North should be compared to is unclear, because here the economic divisions and inequalities are more pronounced than in Ireland.

What would be more refreshing and valuable is to take a long term view. When you do this it becomes clear very quickly that the Celtic Tiger period is a small spike in the long term progression of the Irish economy. We don't know for example whether that period is a temporary shift or the movement towards a new long term trend path. The economic collapse of 2008 has clearly show the difficulty of predicting future economic trends?

In recent decades we have seen employers and industries rise and fall or sometimes merely stagnate. Take for example what is seen as a traditionally Irish enterprise—Guinness. Output levels have increased at the Dublin plant, especially since the parent company Diageo decided in 2004 to close the Park Royal plant in London and increase investment in the Dublin St James Gate brewery. However employment levels are historically low at the company and operations have been shut in Dundalk, Waterford and other facilities as the company rationalises its operations. In the nineteenth and twentieth century Guinness acquired a range of competitor breweries, ultimately shutting them and relocating the operations to Dublin. At an aggregate level the value of the output has risen, but in terms of other economic impacts the company's contribution to local and domestic economy has decreased. Many other industries have played out this scenario of conglomeration and employment shedding.

However in the brewing sector another trend has emerged—micro brewing. Here output has increased by 550% in the three years to the end of 2015, as a series of new entrants, new entrepreneurs, enter the market (IBA, 2016; Taylor, 2016). A similar transformation is underway in the whiskey market. Yet the new beer entrants, 63 microbreweries according to a 2015 local enterprise report (Feeney, 2015), shows two things. One, the importance of market entry and two the power of entrepreneurial trends. These new businesses are a tiny share of the total beer market, 2% of the total beer market in 2015, and 2.9% by the end of 2017 (Taylor, 2016; IBA, 2018). Yet they are the dynamic element. This trend of the small entrepreneur is the key to driving the economy forward in the coming decades.

Yet our economic commentary is too often just solely on the macro scale and we wonder how long will the comparative advantages we have now in export markets persist? We have seen in recent years the macro economic impact of Guinness supplanted by pharmaceutical firms and the then it was Coke, Intel and Dell. Now our island is home to Microsoft, Apple, Google, Amazon, Facebook, a cross section of the new economic giants. The distorted relationship these firms have with the Irish economy was exposed in the revised CSO figures for the Irish GDP (Burke Kennedy, 2016) and by Dennis O'Hearn in 1998.

A mix of pharmaceutical and technology companies account for a significant proportion of Irish exports (IEA, 2015). How will we secure the comparative advantages that keep these companies here now into the medium and long term future? Do we even want to, there may be a need to move on to the next generation of transnational firms rather that repeat the mistakes of the past subsidising enterprises that are no longer viable.

Our comparative advantage now stems from a favourable international location being inside the EU, with the basic power, transport and telecommunications infrastructure in place. Alongside this we have relatively lax regulation in terms of corporate governance, environmental protections, low tax on business profits and payroll, a helpful government and a well educated, flexible pliable workforce.

These are not unique characteristics and many of the lower income new EU entrants have realised that they can replicate large elements of the Irish model in their own economies. Then there are other factors like the product cycle where first world economies develop and produce the early versions of new technology products. Just look around the modern home, workplace or even your pocket and consider the amount of technologies that have arrived in the last century. In the technology driven consumerism of the twenty-first century this is a very important process. As the production process of the new technology becomes more stable and demand for the product grows particularly as its relative price drops the production of the good moves from the region where it was invented and developed to other lower cost manufacturing locations.

Historical examples would include the colour television, invented in the USA but world production is now sited in South East Asia. Then there is the semi conductor also invented in the USA and made in a range of low cost locations usually outside of the US like Ireland. Similar examples can be found in the pharmaceutical markets and in other ICT sectors as well as the smart phone and tablet devices so much a part of our lives now.

In Ireland we are caught between two stools and it is this that cuts to the heart of our enterprise entrepreneurial challenge. We are not a site for the development of new products. We have in the last 20 years emerged as a location for the initial stages of a new product's life cycle. How long we can sustain this position is very unclear. There are three options.

1. Keep on the path we are on now, nestling between the host firms with new products and the lower cost production locations. This has its risks. Take the example of the iMac which developed in the USA was initially produced in Apple's Cork facility. As demand for the new product soared, the Irish lost out to cheaper larger production locations. Ireland's Apple plant has been in production since 1980 which is unique for both Apple and the tech industry (O'Dwyer, 2015).
2. Cuts costs and try to compete with the lower cost locations. This is difficult as in Ireland as living costs particularly in terms of housing and childcare have soared in recent years as the economy has grown, and even after the collapse this is still an expensive place to live (Eurostat, 2016). For the firm the rise in energy and other costs has also been substantial, so it is hard to see how Ireland could take a path other than the already existing one of controlling costs while increasing productivity. This process has left us as one of the lower wage, high productivity locations in the OECD, but still higher cost wise than many of the new EU entrants and unable to compete with many other low wage locations.
3. Begin a process where the Irish economy emerges as an innovative location for the development of new products. If taken we could

also attempt to go a step further and redefine what we mean and understand to be economic activity in the modern economy. All of this is constrained by the fact that having thrown in our lot with the EU, the Irish economy north and south has surrendered key elements of economic sovereignty and has to operate within very tight parameters in some areas, particularly when it comes to the input of the state to this process.

Knowledge of the Twenty-first Century Economy

If we think back to the previous points about the failure of economic mimicry we need to set some constraints of our own. It is that any economic strategy or policy package must be viewed in the context of developing an understanding of the massive shifts underway today in how our economy operates and interacts.

For example the jumping of investors onto the dot-com bandwagon at the end of 1990s and the speculative property bubble of the next decade is just one example that mimicry is alive and well.

Now we have the 'internet of things', before this briefly it was anything with the word 'bio' or 'nano' in it. In previous decades the words digital and turbo has similar effects, but perhaps the most unabashed is the still unfulfilled, but still lobbying, nuclear power interests who would portray themselves as a lovable Fagan who can regularly it seems pilfer the pockets of unwitting governments ready to finance their unviable schemes.

So what is different about the economic processes households, firms and governments are interacting in today? There are a number of areas where tangible change is visible. They are:

1. *The growth of new goods* and the effect they are having on society. In Ireland like many other developing economies there has been an extraordinary impact on consumption and culture through the introduction of new goods and services. The impact of the television on family behaviour in the household is one example; the sale of food technologies like the microwave and complimentary food products is another. The game changing role of the mobile and then smart phone technology in terms of the behaviour of users and the growing range of associated products is in contemporary Irish life perhaps the best example of the new economy in international and indigenous terms.

The growth of mobile/smart phone usage across the developed economies is significant and in many cases is greater than fixed line ownership. In Ireland young and old, rich and poor have embraced the mobile phone and its more advanced offspring the smart phone which fuelled the growth in social media usage. Texting might have created a new form of communication but the impact of social media has created a whole new generation and culture of communication. The collective impact of these technologies is to fundamentally change how we live, in terms of work, relationships and family dynamics, so understanding the impact of these new goods on society is vital.

2. *Internationalisation of consumption and production.* Initially the first draft of this piece was written on a Dell PC assembled in Ireland from parts imported from other Dell plants around the world. It has an Intel Celeron chip, also made in Ireland, but users all over Europe could have the same machine in front of them. The Microsoft operating system is also made here, but the profits revert to Microsoft HQ in Seattle through a firm based in the Irish Financial Services Centre called Round Island One, as do the revenue ultimately from the diet coke bottle open on the desk. My clothes come from destinations as remote as Indonesia, Turkey and Malta. Most of us, myself included, are unaware of the where and how the products we purchase come from, just as we are unaware of the uniformity behind these purchases, whether it's a coke, a burger, a pair of jeans or the simple act of purchasing a coffee and croissant, these are choices being made in the same way by people all over the richer economies on the globe.
3. *The information economy.* It has been a feature of economic activity particularly in the second half of the twentieth century that more and more people are working in some aspect of the information economy. This covers not just the media, but teaching, telecommunications, computer and software sectors, the job of delivering post or working in a call centre. These are all aspects of the information economy. Processing storing distributing, analysing and generating information are all aspects of this information economy. Associated with it is the concept of what people now call the digital revolution where new communication and computer technologies were linked

up to formerly standalone media and communication platforms like radio, TV, recorded music, PCs, newspapers, the internet and mobile phones. In terms of our first factor above this is a major growth area for new products and in terms of entrepreneurship in Ireland could be an area worth focusing on in terms of breaking into the product cycle and generating new employment opportunities. However, the reality of this economic sector is that like so many other industries it rapidly became dominated by a small number of major firms, and another series of oligopolies has been born. A quick example of this is found by categorising the apps on my smart phone. The only Irish ones are to do with news, weather or sport. The vast majority of the other apps originated in the USA.

4. *Other new technologies.* Apart from changes in the computing, communication and media sectors there are widespread parallel technological shifts in biotechnology and pharmaceuticals. In recent decades in the Irish economy anything to do with these two areas was officially designated "a good thing" with little debate on whether this is actually the case. We need to conduct at national level a cost benefit analysis into these new technologies in terms of the full economic impact including the true environmental costs. A 2017 Silicon Republic report found that there were 300 of what they called 'life sciences' companies and of the top 25 firms in this area, 24 of them were based in Ireland (Burke, 2017).
5. *How we work.* The agricultural and industrial revolutions were just that, a revolution in economic processes that fundamentally altered society. Are we in the process of another revolution now with the combined impacts of new technologies in the information, communication and science sectors? There have been significant changes in the Irish workplace. They fall into two areas. The first is the impact of technology on the workplace and the second is in how the office or work environment is organised. In terms of technology computer information systems are everywhere, not just in the PC on your desk, but in the workplace intranet and bespoke software technologies that underpin your work. In the college where I work now, the library is run through computer and information technology. So I can access borrowing data, assess what books are in the library and connect with a range of online resources linking not just other libraries but some mass virtual information warehouses holding electronic versions of books and articles as diverse as the journal of

media economics or a downloadable version of Edith Wharton's Ethan Fromme.

In the Spar across the road stock control is controlled through the cash registers using product bar codes meaning that little or no extra stock is carried in the actual shop. But daily sales prompt deliveries from wholesalers to maintain the fully stocked shelves. These are just two small examples which have built up in changed workplaces for nearly everybody in employment. What opportunities and threats is this opening up for the Irish economy?

The changes in how the workplace is organised is characterised most by the emergence of teams and intricate management structures in even the smallest workplaces. Veblen in his 1899 Theory of the Leisure Class and 1904 Theory of the Business Enterprise outlined excellently the emergence of this managerial class along with a society of middle class consumers (Veblen, 2012).

The idea and purpose of entrepreneurship has been undermined and blunted by the emergence of a managerial culture. This happened through the emergence of large institutions of government in the nineteenth and twentieth century and large private firms. They created within them substantial opportunities for career advancement and financial enrichment for people who could find employment safe from the vicissitudes of negative market forces. They didn't have to conceptualise work as a place of competitive productivity, they wanted a more stable working career. The problem for business enterprise is that the managerial classes become an interest group in their own right and ultimately can have a detrimental effect on economic activity and social equity.

We can see this managerial class at work in society today whether it is the hospital consultants presiding over their medical hierarchy of exploitation and personal financial enrichment, or the overpaid executives who ensure their own shareholdings and pension funds while casting the actual productive workers aside. A 2017 Equality Trust study found that CEOs of the top quoted companies on the FTSE had annual remuneration packages 386 times those earning the British annual living wage of £13,662 (Equality Trust, 2017).

6. *Economic links.* The disparities between CEO salaries and average workers is part of an ongoing trend in economic processes particularly since the end of World War II and demonstrates a detachment

between the labour activities of literally hundreds of thousands of workers and the wealth of the economy they live in. For example a 100 workers in Dublin's financial services sector can create more wealth in a year than thousands of restaurant workers in the same city, but who has made the greater contribution to the Irish economy? It leads us to a question of what should be the core goals of economic activity. Is it wealth creation or employment maximisation and are the two goals compatible or not.

What Sort of Workplace?

So where do all of these developments leave the Irish economy. We have lots of new economy activity here but not a lot of control over the processes and no ownership of a lot of the knowledge created in the economy, and in a world where the information economy is an ever growing sector, a lack of control over the core resources is an important issue to be addressed.

We also need to find a method that maximises the benefits of this new work and economic environment in a way that is not just focused on revenue generation and profits, as it has become clear that in the Celtic Tiger years business in Ireland has generated more revenue and more profits while other important quality of life issues deteriorated. For example the travel to work time, the cost of housing, the availability and cost of childcare, the quality of employment. In the years since the economy has grown again, but the working conditions have deteriorated further.

In Ireland today there are ever more people working but some important dichotomies are emerging. As Dublin for example becomes more multi ethnic it is clear that a lot of the lower paid, unsocial hours employment is being filled by the new Irish, who are often serving, cleaning, cooking, doing security or delivering food for the rest of us. Is this the social community environment we want?

My local Spar like many others is a busy shop. The old Irish workers tend to be behind the salad counter or get to be managers, there is CCTV all around the shop focusing not just on the shelving to stop customer theft, but also on every till and counter to monitor employees. Is this the workplace we want to be the model for the future? It is time to reconsider the ideas of Fourier on useless and destructive labour.

Multiple Economies

What we have in Ireland today are multiple economies or maybe a better analogy would be a series of economic pillars holding the edifice of the national economy together. The pillars are:

1. *The partitioned national economy* with its two pointless distinct units, with separate tax, currency and administrative environments, which culminates into a serious distortion of how the island economy should operate.
2. *The international FDI economy*, which is still growing and has investment levels unrivalled within the EU and internationally.
3. *Indigenous exporters.* In terms of the Irish economy these were the most underperforming group all through the Tiger years, yet in many cities and towns they are a vital cog in the overall economic environment.
4. *Small and micro businesses.* In terms of employment these are the life blood of the economy, some exist to sell services onto the FDI and indigenous economy or the general business to business market but the vast majority of small businesses are selling goods and services to households and it is available disposable income that drives demand in this sector. In the Great Recession the growth and ingenuity demonstrated in new start ups showed the resilience and importance of this sector.
5. *The public sector.* Often this is the most overlooked part of the economy but the public sector has a vital role to play in the provision of goods and services that the private sector is either unwilling or unable to efficiently provide. Transport, energy, education, health and telecommunications all stand out as sectors that could more efficiently and equitably supply goods and services to wider economy.
6. *The local regional economies* from Dublin, Belfast, Cork, Galway and Limerick to the next tier of towns are critical economic hubs. Their critical mass creates its own eco-environment. Even small towns can generate eco-environments. One feature of the larger towns and cities is higher retail rents and property prices as the economy grows. The disparity between local economies and their relative sizes can sometimes be detrimental for the smaller economies as the larger cities and towns act like economic magnets pulling available resources to the centre.

7. *The administrative bureaucratic economy.* The government itself is an economic actor not just through its employment levels but through its buildings and offices, at national and local level, through its investments and spending in the national economy.
8. *The agricultural economy* from its multinational producers to local micro businesses is a key part of economic activity economically and culturally across the island. In the great recession agriculture was one of the few sectors that continued to grow. The level of entrepreneurship across the sector is another example of economic resilience that is often overlooked.

Entrepreneurship Across the Multiple Economies

We need entrepreneurship strategies that focus on all the multiple economies that build into the island economy. A disproportionate focus has been encouraging entrepreneurship in developing new exporters, getting small firms to become larger ones. How much focus though is there on the smaller scale entrepreneurship? Yes in Ireland like in other developed economies there is a bureaucracy of support for small business through the county and city enterprise boards in the 26 Counties and Enterprise Northern Ireland in the Six Counties.

What is needed is a broader commitment to the concept first postulated in 1973 by the economist Ernest Schumacher that “Small is beautiful”. Schumacher’s vision of smaller local environmentally sustainable economies not driven by the growth mantra is within our grasp.

We can do it by:

1. *Ensuring access to market* and providing a conduit for entrepreneurs to get their goods to customers The farmers market idea is now fashionable again in Ireland but it needs active government support through simple legislative acts such as making planning permission for new retail parks subject to the condition of building small low rent markets within or alongside the proposed structure.
2. *Reclaiming the manufacturing process.* What is wrong with producing goods within your own local economy with resources gathered locally? In Ireland and internationally the concept of manufacturing is one of huge scale and low cost. Is this the only method of production possible?

Higher income households are interested in quality products, especially in terms of food and other areas. We are also talking about healthy, safe products. When you buy a chocolate bar the wrapper tells how many calories, carbohydrates etc there are within it. It doesn't tell you where the products were sourced or the working conditions it was made within. Surely there is room for this information.

This isn't just a proposal of import substitution repackaged. It is a proposal to rethink what is possible in the local economy, whether it's a locally made beer, bread, furniture, website, software package or even TV or radio programme. The success of French wines or German beer shows the power of local brands and at times their global reach. The point is the technological developments are rewriting how economic activity evolves, the question is, are we on board to benefit from the untapped potential.

References

BBC. (2005). *DeLorean's Dream of Belfast Car Empire*. Retrieved August 4, 2016, from http://news.bbc.co.uk/2/hi/uk_news/northern_ireland/4367473.stm

Beckett, S. (1983). *Worstward Ho*. Calder.

Burke, E. (2017, May 29). Ireland is a Home for 24 of the World's Largest Top Biotech and Pharma Companies. *Silicon Republic*. Retrieved April 6, 2019, from https://www.siliconrepublic.com/careers/biotech-pharma-companies-ireland

Burke Kennedy, E. (2016, July 12). Handful of Multinationals behind 26.3% Growth in GDP. *Irish Times*.

Central Statistics Office. (2014). *Business Demography*. Retrieved June 29, 2016, from http://www.cso.ie/en/releasesandpublications/er/bd/businessdemography2012/

Central Statistics Office. (2016a). *Business Demography*. Retrieved September 4, 2017, from http://www.cso.ie/en/releasesandpublications/er/bd/businessdemography2014/

Central Statistics Office. (2016b). *Quarterly National Household Survey, Quarter 1 2016*. Retrieved July 5, 2016, from http://www.cso.ie/en/releasesandpublications/er/qnhs/quarterlynationalhouseholdsurveyquarter12016/

Central Statistics Office. (2018). *Business Demography*. Retrieved March 6, 2019, from https://www.cso.ie/en/releasesandpublications/er/bd/businessdemography2016/

Department of Jobs, Enterprise and Innovation. (2015). *Evaluation of State Supports for Enterprise*. Government Publications.
Equality Trust. (2017). *Pay Tracker: Comparing Chief Executive Officer Pay in the FTSE 100 with Average Pay and Low Pay in the UK*. Retrieved August 27, 2017, from https://www.equalitytrust.org.uk/sites/default/files/Pay%20Tracker%20%28March%202017%29_1.pdf
Eurostat. (2016). *Comparative Price Levels of Consumer Goods and Services*. Retrieved September 9, 2016, from http://ec.europa.eu/eurostat/statistics-explained/index.php/Comparative_price_levels_of_consumer_goods_and_services
Feeney, B. (2015). *Craft Beer and Microbreweries in Ireland 2015*. Retrieved September 6, 2016, from https://www.localenterprise.ie/DLR/Publications-Resources/Enterprise-Reports/Reports-Library/Report-for-the-Independent-Craft-Brewers-of-Ireland-2015.pdf
Fitzsimons, P., & O'Gorman, C. (2015). *Entrepreneurship in Ireland 2014, Global Entrepreneurship Monitor, the Annual Report for Ireland*. Department of Jobs, Enterprise and Innovation.
Fitzsimons, P., & O'Gorman, C. (2018). *Entrepreneurship in Ireland 2017, Global Entrepreneurship Monitor, the Annual Report for Ireland*. Department of Jobs, Enterprise and Innovation.
Fourier, C. (1996). *The Theory of the Four Movements*. Cambridge University Press.
Friedman M. (1976). *Inflation and Unemployment*. Nobel Memorial Lecture. http://www.nobelprize.org/nobel_prizes/economic-sciences/laureates/1976/friedman-lecture.pdf.
Fumbally Exchange. (2016). *About Us*. Retrieved August 24, 2016, from http://www.fumballyexchange.com/
Hansard. (1975). *Northern Ireland (Harland and Wolff)*. Retrieved August 3, 2016, from http://hansard.millbanksystems.com/commons/1975/aug/01/northern-ireland-harland-and-wolff
Hart, M., & Bonner, K. (2011). *Data-Linking and Impact Evaluation in Northern Ireland*. Aston University.
Hunt, E. K., & Sherman, H. J. (1990). *Economics An Introduction to Traditional and Radical Views* (6th ed.). Harper and Row.
IBA. (2016). *Beer Exports up in 2015 as Production Increases for the First Time in Five Years*. Retrieved September 6, 2016, from http://www.abfi.ie/Sectors/ABFI/ABFI.nsf/vPagesBeer/Media~Newsroom~beer-exports-up-in-2015-as-production-increases-for-the-first-time-in-five-years!OpenDocument
IBA. (2018). *The Irish Beer Market 2017*. Retrieved March 18, 2019, from https://www.abfi.ie/Sectors/ABFI/ABFI.nsf/vPagesBeer/Home/$File/IBA+Beer+Market+Report+2017+-+web.pdf
ICOS. (2016) *Our Members*. Retrieved August 23, 2016, from http://www.icos.ie/members/introduction-2/

IEA. (2015). *Top 250 Exporters—An Analysis of the Leading Exporters by Turnover on the Island of Ireland.* Irish Exporters Association.

IPRT. (2019). *Facts and Figures.* Retrieved August 21, 2019, from http://www.iprt.ie/prison-facts-2

Macalister, T. (2016, July 7). Estimated cost of Hinkley Point C Nuclear Plant Rises to £37bn. *Guardian.* Retrieved August 21, 2019, from https://www.theguardian.com/uk-news/2016/jul/07/hinkley-point-c-nuclear-plant-costs-up-to-37bn

McCabe, C. (2011). Sale of the Century: the £500 Deal for Ireland's Gas and Oi. *History Ireland*, 19 (4).

NIARIS. (2018). *Where and Why Does Invest NI Invest in the North?* Retrieved March 18, 2019, from https://www.assemblyresearchmatters.org/2018/08/07/where-and-why-does-invest-ni-invest-in-ni/

Norsk Petroleum. (2016). *Norway's Petroleum History.* Retrieved August 23, 2016, from http://www.norskpetroleum.no/en/framework/norways-petroleum-history/

O'Dwyer, P. (2015, November 11). A Look Inside a Global Giant: Apple and their European Headquarters in Cork. *Irish Examiner.*

Reidy, P. (2017). *An Assessment of the Rationale Efficiency and Targeting of Supports in Enterprise Ireland* (Spending Review Series). IGEES Unit, Department of Public Expenditure and Reform.

Rowthorn, B., & Wayne, N. (1988). *Northern Ireland The Political Economy of Conflict.* Polity.

Schaltegger, S. (2002). A Framework for Ecopreneurship: Leading Bioneers and Environmental Managers to Ecopreneurship. *Greener Management International, 38*(Summer), 45–58.

Schumacher, E. F. (1973). *Small is Beautiful* (Abacus edition). Sphere Books.

Taylor, C. (2016, August 24). Microbrewery Beer Production Rose 550% Over Three Years. *Irish Times.*

Veblen, T. (2012). *The Theory of the Leisure Class.* Renaissance Classics.

Watson, D., Whelan, C. T., Williams, J., & Blackwell, S. (2005). *Mapping Poverty: National Regional and County Patterns* (Combat Poverty Agency research Series, No 37). Institute of Public Administration.

Wikipedia. (2016). *The Apprentice TV Series.* Retrieved July 5, 2016, from https://en.wikipedia.org/wiki/The_Apprentice_(TV_series)

CHAPTER 6

Counting the Republic

Introduction

Humans count. We estimate, calculate, measure and take decisions, small and large, based on the results. Throughout history, even in our mythological legends there are examples of this culture of counting. One of Ireland's epic myths, the Táin Bó Cúailnge, begins with a husband and wife, the queen and king of Connacht, Meabh and Ailill, counting their possessions to see who is the wealthiest. Their obsession leads to a bitter and pointless war that destroys lives and sets in motion the events that lead to the tragic last years of Cú Chulainn.

Our history is littered with examples of the growing importance of counting for economic reasons from the early Roman kings deciding they needed a census to the Norman Domesday Book in the 11th century and the conception of national accounting measures in the twentieth century that created the now ubiquitous measures of Gross National and Domestic product, GNP and GDP respectively.

Cicero writes in his Book of Laws on the complicated purpose of the census that had developed in ancient times. He states that the census categorises the citizens "according to their tribes", dividing them with "reference to their fortunes, ages and ranks", (Cicero, 1853, p. 464). The Domesday Book was commissioned by William the Conqueror in 1085 to assess the extent of land and resources his conquest had yielded him. His

R. Smyth, *The Invisible Republic*,
https://doi.org/10.1007/978-3-030-86734-8_6

other purpose was to have a gauge on what taxes he could levy on the population of his new kingdom (Domesday Book, 2017).

It was Simon Kuznets in 1937 who constructed the original formula for Gross Domestic Product (Econlib, 2017). GDP became the benchmark measure for economic activity across the developed world. It also became a measure of comparison between states. There have been many criticisms of the measure, particularly in recent years. Specifically in that the aggregate nature of the measure means it is blunt instrument for measuring the position of individuals in any economy. It does not measure individual wellbeing or distribution of income within an economy, even though this was an area Kuznet did focus on in his other research work.

In recent years there have been a range of evaluations on the limitations of GDP plus new alternative measures. Stiglitz, Zen and Fitoussi's report on economic progress and social wellbeing stands out in this field (Stiglitz et al., 2011) as does the annual UN Human Development Reports (UNDP, 2017). There is also now an annual World Happiness Report (World Happiness Report, 2019). These alternatives all point to serious flaws in the GDP and GNP measure, but both measures are still used across the world.

In Ireland this is even more of a problem as this method of economic growth is distorted by transfer pricing practices of a range of multinational firms from the financial, pharmaceutical, computing and online sectors. It leads to an overly inflated GDP figure which is not at any practical level a measure of economy activity in Ireland. In 2016 the GDP figure grew 26.3% (Burke Kennedy, 2016), (Kelpie, 2016). This distortion had been flagged up before by economists and a particularly excellent criticism of the measure was provided in 1998 by Denis O'Hearn in his Inside the Celtic Tiger book (O'Hearn, 1998). It is a key shortcoming in the attitude of government to counting that, for nearly two decades academics, ministers, statisticians, politicians and government after government had some knowledge about this problem and still did nothing to correct the measure. One conclusion to draw from this it that government and its institutions measure for reasons of political strategy not accuracy.

In 2017 the Central Statistics Office belatedly introduced a new measure—Gross National Income, which shows an economy just over two thirds the size of the economy measured by GDP (CSO, 2017b). While a more accurate measure of this form of economic activity on the island it still does not tackle any of the other limitations already discussed here.

There are many more aspects to counting in the world today from sports performances, economic indices, social studies as well as a growing research industry. And now in this digital era, this world of 'Big Data', new methods of measuring our lived existence can only hint at the power and impact of algorithmic influences on our daily decisions. Counting is political and always has been. Republicans need to liberate counting and we cannot be passive about how business and governments count, especially when this is supposedly done in our interests. These measures need an effective empowering transparency.

So can we measure freedom? Can we measure progress? To me it seems that we haven't given enough attention to how the activities of society are measured. It is completely wrong and at variance with the principles of individual freedom that so much is now known about societal interactions and that the governments and businesses who have the capacity to measure these interactions and also to influence them have little or no accountability on what they do with this aggregate information.

One of the great failures of the years after the war of independence and the civil war was that the new state was in many respects like the old. There were new managers and some new objectives of government but across substantial swathes of the administration it is hard to gauge now the depth of operational change in how society was run.

No great thought was given on what would be a tangible measure of our new found independence and freedom. This is not to claim that the new governments didn't try and grasp the chance for progress. Rural electrification, school building, housing schemes and the emerging semi-state sector showed successive governments grappling with the social and economic challenges of delivering a tangibly different experience of progress than that under the British occupation.

But I believe not enough thought or planning was given into a new set of measures that would calculate the level of social progress promised in the 1916 Proclamation or the 1919 Democratic Programme for Government. So now our economy, our social progress is measured by an array of inherited British and imposed EU and IMF/World Bank flawed measures. Some have an intrinsic usefulness and merit on their own, but they aggregate into a flawed picture of what Ireland is today.

Examples of Institutional Counting in Ireland Today

1. *The Housing Crisis*

We don't have enough new houses, there are too many vacant homes unused throughout the 26 Counties for examples, rents are high and increasing and there are less dwellings for rent than ever before. Oh and house prices are rising back towards Celtic Tiger madness levels. Finally we have a record number of homeless people on our streets.

So how do we measure this? First off is the already mentioned DAFT.ie who produce separate quarterly reports on rents and house prices. The January 2019 DAFT rental index showed an 11% increase in rents to the end of December 2018 (Daft.ie, 2019). The Residential Tenancies Board also produce quarterly reports. Their figures for December 2018 showed an increase in rents over the year with an average national monthly rent of €1134 in December 2018 compared to €1061 in December 2017 (RTB, 2019). Daft's competitor in house sales and letting is MyHome.ie who also compile measures for rental costs and house prices.

The CSO were once the only producer of property price data, and in 2016 revamped the methodology underpinning their index. Their January 2019 report showed that in the 12 months to the end of January property prices had risen 5.6%, but were 18.4% lower than their 2007 peak. But it is interesting that others have joined in measuring this social phenomenon (CSO, 2019a).

Property Industry Ireland, a sectoral association of employers group IBEC have also got into the business of publishing data on housing. Called the Property Watch Report in September 2016 they estimated that the number of finished new dwellings for 2016 will be 14,000. The Government target was 25,000!

One statistic that would be great to have annually would be the number of vacant dwellings in the state. This is captured by the census every five years. In July 2016 preliminary census reports from the CSO revealed that there were 259,563 vacant homes in the 26 Counties, Yep I was shocked too. It is a staggering figure and makes you wonder about the true causes of the housing crisis in Ireland? Greed and profit, that's what I thought too.

The housing crisis culminates in homelessness and over 10,000 people were without permanent dwellings in 2019. The Department of Housing, Planning and Community Development produces monthly figures. In February 2019 they estimated that there were 6480 adults homeless, 4304 in

Dublin, However you need to add in the 3784 dependents, children of these homeless people, 1707 families without a home (DHPCLG, 2019). It makes you wonder about the hundreds of thousands of vacant homes, but also about the thinking behind this measure and how it seems to be distorted to cloud the actual number of homeless people on Irish streets.

2. *Waiting for medical treatment*

Trolley Watch began in 2004. Yes we have had a healthcare crisis for that long. And if you are of my vintage you can probably still remember the 1986 Fianna Fail campaign promise to reverse Fine Gael/Labour policies with the slogan “Health cuts affect the old the sick and the handicapped”. So here we are over 30 years later and in mid-April 2019, 631 people were on trolleys in the 26 Counties (INMO, 2019). Run by the Irish Nurses and Midwives Organisation, Trolley Watch publishes weekly figures. It is interesting that it was workers in the sector, not their managers or government created this measure. It is actions like this that highlight the importance of more radical approaches to how we measure social and economic statistics.

However this is only one measure of the crisis in the health care system. Over 700,000 people were waiting for hospital treatment in January 2019 (Bowers, 2019). The National Treatment Purchase Fund produces monthly figures of the numbers of people waiting for hospital appointments and procedures.

3. *Wages and jobs*

The growing employment figures are an often repeated and relied statistic for the current hybrid Fine Gael government, but they inherited this measure and like many governments before them are unlikely to make any change to how employment and unemployment data is calculated. And yes as I write employment figures are rising. There are monthly Live Register figures showing the numbers signing on, and there is a Quarterly Labour Force Survey. Quarter 4, 2018 showed 2,281,300 people at work in the 26 Counties, up 50,500 on the same time in 2017 (CSO, 2019b).

What are these workers earning though? The monthly unemployment figures state that 128.800 people were unemployed at the end of December 2018. However the Live Register figures, also produced monthly show 232,366 people signing on and receiving a social welfare payment in March 2019. That’s more than a 100,000 people working part time and needing supplements to their wages.

Figures on earnings are produced quarterly by the CSO. The December 2018 figures showed an average weekly wage of €761.653s, that's €23.46 an hour. That weekly and hourly wage can vary greatly. For example those working in accommodation and food services earn an average €360.73 weekly compared to €1175.46 in the Information and Communication sector, (think Google, Facebook) (CSO, 2019c).

Then there are the annual poverty figures which are usually released in November. The 2017 figures, released in 2018 show 15.7% of the population at risk of poverty, with 18.8% suffering enforced deprivation. The households at risk of deprivation had an average annual household income of €12,521. The lowest 20% of earners had 8.3% of disposable income in 2017 compared to the highest 20% of earners having a 39.9% share of disposable income (CSO, 2017a).

The Low Wage Commission published its second annual report in July 2016, recommending a 10 cent an hour increase to €9.25, the ICTU had lobbied for an €11.50 minimum hourly wage by 2017.

On a related issue, New Zealand banned zero hour contracts in 2016. I wonder is there any chance this could happen in Ireland. If you are worrying about the take home packages of the 1% in Ireland, April is the key month when Irish public companies start their AGMs and we have weeks of revealing pay and remuneration packages.

In 2017 CRH chief executive Albert Manifold had a total package of €8.6 million, and according to the ICTU the average worker on €37,646 would take 230 years working to matching Manifold's salary (ICTU, 2018).

4. *68.5 million refugees*

Then there are those with absolutely nothing displaced and fleeing their country. Annually in June the UN Refugee Agency (UNHCR) publish their yearly report. In 2018 they reported there were 68.5 million people forcibly displaced around the world. 44,000 new refuges every day (UNHCR, 2018).

In November 2016 the Irish Refugee Protection Programme reported that 109 asylum seekers had arrived in Ireland with an additional 215 due to arrive by the end of that year. When we count it this way our government's contribution doesn't seem enough.

5. *The cost of schooling*

Eurostat figures released in December 2016 showed that Irish families were paying more than twice the EU average on education. Education accounts for 2.6% of Irish Household spending compared to an EU average of 1.1%. The children's charity and advocacy group Barnardos produce annual surveys on the cost of sending children to school. In 2018, they found that the cost of sending a child to junior infants in primary school was €360 and €765 for a secondary school child entering first year (Barnardos, 2018). Yet despite these costs you will still read of our free education system.

Counting Freedom

We can conclude that social and economic statistics have become significantly politicised. Maybe we should recognise that they always were and in the post-independence Ireland there are in many areas a distorted range of counting measures and methodologies, whether it is the simple questions of how do we measure poverty, unemployment and homelessness. To me the purpose of these measures is to formulate a policy to tackle the problem. But in Ireland and elsewhere too often the measures are about making the problem look smaller than it actually is.

There is also two other questions that need to be considered. They are things we don't' count but should, and things society does count, but you wonder why, do I really need to know this? Finally there is the question of the secret counting by government and business to either 'nudge' us or make us more willing to purchase, to make us more amenable to spend or use a particular technology.

What We Do and Don't Count

Government and developers will count house completions, or what they call 'dwellings'. But they don't tell us easily how many rooms these dwellings had, or the size of the spaces. In a society that gives lip service to the importance of education surely every child should have a space to study, especially when they get to secondary school? A space for a desk, a room of one's own. How many playing spaces are there in these new developments? How quiet are they? Do people have real privacy or is there noise from above and below or through the walls. But we don't count this. We don't count the quality of housing, and critically whether it is increasing or decreasing year on year.

We count workers as costs rather than the dynamic factor they are in any economic enterprise. This is the same across the public and private sectors. One small example of this are strikes and industrial action taken by workers. This is counted in Ireland by the Central Statistics Office, who measure days lost by industrial action. Why not count days worked, or workers in part time jobs who want full time work, or how many workers have pensions. That would be a social goal and a reason for counting: A government that has a target for pension reform and wants to ensure all its citizens have an adequate standard of living.

There is a culture of managerial capitalism, which too often had narrow one dimensional views of the firm. How profitable is the firm, are profits growing. There is little counting of how happy the workers are in this firm. How long is their commute to work, how is staff morale? The difficult things are not counted and then worse still they are discounted from the important measures of how successful or not the firm is.

A firm's share price can be considered and speculated on, this creates a focus on quarterly results and a wholly short term view of the firm, which is great if you are trading shares but who else really benefits from this measure? This is not to say that quarterly results can be ignored but there is no case for them being the driving force in a firm's strategy.

Counting on the island of Ireland is a serious issue. If we really want to underpin economic progress on the island we need to have agreed common measures on economic growth, unemployment, housing, prices, wages and other economic indices. At present these measures are still calculated almost wholly in isolation. One simple example of the myopia of this practice is the annual figures on the 'best universities in Ireland'. This measure is extracted from the annual rankings of universities around the world. Yet year after year Irish news media report on this and ignore Queens University and the University of Ulster. It might seem a small issue in the mountains of counting going on in an economy, but it highlights perfectly the failures of our counting processes. If we are failing on something as simple as this, what else are we getting wrong? What other distortions of measurement do we have in our societal counting?

The distortions in counting go beyond the economy, they permeate society. Think of the myriad ways across nearly all media, the creative economy, art and fashion that we frame our discussions in terms of a measure that validates in some way the activity. How many people watched a programme, how many social media followers does someone have, how many, how copies of a book were sold, how many listeners, readers, streamers were there. How much were they paid for their work?

One of the apt examples of this pseudo cult of measurement is found in the price of art. At one level we are often told of the importance of the creative process for us as individuals, for society, art is important. In all the cities I have been too, there is public art, art galleries, and exhibitions, but can we put a monetary value on this? Do we need to? In 2016, Edvard Munch's Girls on the bridge was sold for $54 million. Does this make the painting more valuable, more worth viewing? An untitled 1982 Basquiat painting sold in 2017 for $110.5 million. A New York Times article from the time tells us that "only 10 other works have broken the $100 million mark" and that Basquiat had joined the "rarefied $100 million club" (Pogrebin & Reyburn, 2017).

The perceived monetary value and the actual cost of something are worthwhile measures, but we often confuse the two when communicating with each other and as a society. Take the example of Leicester City football club, who play in the English Premier league. The year after a relegation battle they won the premiership in 2016. One of the ways used to interpret and discuss this feat is the costs of assembling the winning squad. They are the only club other than a small group of four to win this competition. The four were: Arsenal, Manchester United, Manchester City and Chelsea.

A 2016 Daily Telegraph article put the actual cost of assembling the squad at £45 million. Winning the Premier League increased the value of this team by 400% according to the paper (Telegraph, 2017). Each summer we witness growing record sales of professional soccer players. Are the current crop really more expert that they can be more valuable than previous generations? We don't know yet. What we do know is that millions more pounds has been invested in the sport because of the sales of TV broadcast rights. Does this make the players more valuable? The monetary value of them is a temporary transient measure at best.

This monetary fixation flows into other areas such as the net worth of a person, the flow of revenue they have generated, but this is presented in a way that the monetary value is an accurate gauge of their creative worth. A society that counts solely in monetary terms is creating a distorted partial picture of what actually is transpiring in that society. Celebrity prosperity should not be a gauge of what is worthwhile in society.

We don't want though to fall victim to the orthodoxy of the Soviet or Maoist planning policies that ultimately negatively impacted real growth in their economies, germinating instead a culture of false accounting, and a refusal to accurately reflect actual economic activity in their economies. We laugh at the news and propaganda coming from North Korea. It is an obvious distortion, but we have our own distortions here in how we count and the claims made from that.

For example in Ireland we have parallel but separate economies, consisting of those who work for multinational firms, those who work in the domestic economy or those in the public service. Their experience is very different as you move from sector to sector. They are all working in the Irish economy, getting paid, travelling to and from work. Yet their daily experience, their hours of work, their pension entitlements, their wages and salaries are all very different. Yet we just count them as workers. There are many more examples of this false accounting, but at a national and governmental level we can ignore these tiers in our economy and the resulting very different experiences of those who live and work in these parallel but different Irelands.

Algorithms, Nudging and Digital Counting

It is remarkable how remiss society and government is at accurate counting in so many areas. It is striking then how at the same time so much effort is put into digital counting by businesses and by government and also how successful and accurate this counting can be.

Google and Facebook have built profitable businesses from the accurate collection of digital information about their users, what they call their 'communities'. In the twentieth century audience research became a feature of mass media as companies sought to sell their content to the largest possible number of viewers, listeners and readers. The second reason for building this mass audience was to reach the largest number of purchasers so advertising could be linked into the audience interaction with the respective media content.

Alongside this another counting platform emerged through the social and statistical sciences which created the first repeatedly accurate attempts to measure opinion, and the opinion poll became part of public life. It sounds good at one level, a bottom up approach to find out more about the tastes, views and opinions of individuals and then aggregate this into findings about society. So yes we can usually accurately predict who can win an election and understand more often than not which type of media genres are more successful than others, but in this Pandora's box we didn't give enough attention to how the counting of opinion might create attempts to influence opinion, attitudes and values.

The British Government has a Behavioural Insights Team, who have a series of goals including, "enabling people to make better choices for themselves" (BIT, 2017). The Behavioural Insights Team's annual report explains the group's strategy. They believe that "By employing behavioural evidence and empirically-based research, BIT can help ensure that where possible we deliver policy aims by working with the way that people live their lives" (BIT, 2016). In the media the BIT team is often called the 'Nudge Unit', derived from the work of Richard Thaler and Cass Sunstein (Rutter, 2015) (Thaler & Sunstein, 2009).

What is fascinating and also worrying at the same time is the hidden elements of this counting. Government and businesses are counting and measuring our activities and in the case of government formulating policies and making interventions with little public oversight or discussion about this. Those involved would I think not see their work as problematic at a societal level. For example in a 2015 Guardian interview, David Halpern, chief executive of Behavioural Insights team, highlighted some of the unit's successes including signing up "an extra 100,000 organ donors a year", persuading "20% more people to consider switching energy provider", and doubling "the number of army applicants" (Rutter, 2015).

Halpern explains how they "would refuse to help a major drinks company improve sales, for example, but might help with a project to reduce sugar consumption" (Rutter, 2015). That their aims are noble is great, that they and many others have access to powerful tools of observation and can use these to influence behaviour is worrisome. The still unresolved questions about the US elections in 2016 are another example of the power of online social influence strategies, which begin by calculating and measuring behaviours of audiences and using this information to target people with online content, some of it often erroneous.

At a fundamental level this amounts for me to a form of coercion, and a very basic republican principle has been undermined.

Counting for Planning

A core reason that counting is important is the implications it has for how a society plans. This could be do with simple things like building roads, schools, houses, hospitals but it is also has an economic and social dimension. Effective efficient planning, fair and equitable planning policies are a visible manifestation of the republic delivering. I wonder how conscious we are of the impact of public service planning on our lives day to day and in the longer term. Are we aware of the millions of euro being spent daily to this end? The public services we have were created from the results of the state counting perceived need across a range of areas and then delivering the infrastructure to meet these societal needs.

On the darkest cold winter mornings there is for me no more welcome a sight than the distinctive lights of an approaching Bus Eireann coach. Most days I don't think too about the logistics of the journey, of all the workers involved in getting me to work, the drivers, mechanics, cleaners, administrators and managers who coordinate the work of getting 1300 buses on the road every day.

Across the island this year upwards of 2.9 million people are going to work each day. Many of them like me are dependent on public transport such as buses and trains, and Dublin's two Luas lines. Even those lucky enough to have a car might not think of the massive public investments that make it all happen.

Waiting for the bus, I can't ignore the sounds of the nearby Dublin Airport, landing and dispatching the first thousands of that day's passengers. In 2015, 27.1 million people passed through the airport, 31.5 million in 2018. The runways and terminals are run as a commercial business now, but it was state investment of taxpayers' money that made the airport possible. It was a green field when the state began to build and now it is a glittering profitable private sector jewel.

There is an ongoing debate about the airport company's plans for a third runway and no doubt in time a third terminal for the facility. There's that word planning in its narrowest sense, in isolation, focussed only on one place and conflicting with attempts to have the airport development seen in a wider context. One claim that the Dublin Airport Authority has made regarding the new runway is that 17,000 jobs are at stake (Kelpie, 2017). It is an interesting debate, local need versus the wider economy. However absent from this debate is the question of the island's airports as a piece of wider infrastructure. Is Dublin the correct site for infrastructure? How are we developing airports on the island as a whole? We aren't having this debate and in fact have moved the opposite direction by breaking the airports into individual units that have an element of pseudo competition between each other. This is where counting and planning lead to errors, and a form of economic myopia.

The bus crosses under the M50, the total cost of which I haven't been able to find out. Though considerable sums of public money have been invested in the project over the decades it took to get it from the drawing board in 1970 to final completion in 2010 when an extra €950 million was spent widening the motorway to six lanes along the entire route (IrishMotorwayInfo.com, 2017).

One example of the failure of planning comes in the lack of detail surrounding the M50 is the cross Liffey bridge which the Irish government had decided would be funded through a toll bridge, built by a private sector company. In 2010 the Department of Transport Secretary General admitted in a letter to the Public Accounts Committee that the department did not know how much it cost to build the M50 bridge, even though in 2008 it agreed to pay €600 million to National Toll Roads, the toll bridge operators (Ryan, 2010). NTR will earn €1.155 billion (Ryan, 2010) from the toll revenues on this bridge. An Irish Independent article from 2010 puts the cost of building the M50 bridge at €58 million (Brennan, 2010). Here is just one example of the financial costs of planning failures.

Along the M50's periphery you might notice the electricity switching stations, built again with your taxes that make sure the lights are always on and link the city to the power stations near and far.

You might notice the water towers, again a public sector investment, €2.7 million for each one. They are vital to maintain water pressure in a growing city. Some days I pass through Ballymun, rebuilt with €942 million of government money, private sector developers unwilling for years to take on the massive reconstruction needed to save this community. Further down the arterial road towards the city centre is Dublin City University, a state run, taxpayer initiative that has brought third level education permanently to the city's north side. Later I go past the Mater Hospital the massive public wards and theatres dwarfing the dependent private hospital by its side.

Here again another social planning fiasco. A large surface car park between the public and private hospitals was at one time the proposed site for a new national children's hospital. There has been an ongoing debate about location, size accessibility for patients, but still no new children's hospital. There has been a refusal to have a fully transparent planning discussion about medical services the state provides for children. In 2019, cost overruns at the new site of the children's hospital entered the news cycle again as the new hospital looks like being the most expensive medical facility in the world.

There are other examples of our public sector at work that involve substantial investments of resources and time. Across the island in 2017, 1,190,701 children attend primary and secondary schools, built and run mostly by the state. There are 243,450 people at universities and colleges again built by the state north and south.

We could go and list the hospitals, housing projects, economic development centres, ports, roads, parks, libraries and museums, all built and often run with public money, your money. Ireland as we know it couldn't function day to day without the infrastructure and services provided by the state, yet do we value enough the scale of what has been achieved to keep the lights on, to have the bus arrive on time.

We need to value our public sector, to protect the assets we have paid for and most importantly to ensure that those working in it have a fair wage, decent working conditions, the respect of their management and the gratitude of the public who use the services. We need to recognise the positive planning that went into delivering these services while also being critical of the limitations for a transparent and democratic discussion about how we plan for these services to be delivered.

The Republican Roots of the Irish Public Sector

So when I get on that bus every morning I see the service as a tangible manifestation of the thinking of Lalor, Wolfe Tone, the 1916 leaders and the first Sinn Fein government of 1919. It might seem silly but this is your bus, your public sector, your right to the sovereignty of the nation, your right to proper planning particularly of the public sector resources we often take for granted.

I see the public sector in Ireland rooted in the philosophies of the United Irishmen, the Fenians, the 1916 Proclamation and the 1919 Democratic Programme. The structures of the Irish public sector were partially formed and shaped in the twentieth century by the ideas and struggles of these people and groups. Its botches and fiascos in the intervening years can be attributed in part to a failure to remember the principles that drove the struggle for independence.

At a basic level this meant the creation of institutions and services for the people which were equal and just in their operation. It meant the building of a public service that would promote the welfare of all.

Wolfe Tone highlighted the evils he saw in the 1790s writing that "We have no national government; we are ruled by Englishmen, and thus servants of Englishmen, whose object is the interest of another country, whose instrument is corruption; whose strength is the weakness of Ireland".

Fintan Lalor wrote repeatedly of his thinking on the scope of an independent Irish government and administration and on the need for a radical reform of how Ireland was run. In an 1848 article in the Irish Felon, Lalor wrote his classic synopsis of this propounding "Ireland her own, and all therein, from the sod to the sky". Surely this also now means buses, broadband, hospital beds, classrooms!

This thinking is returned to in the Fenian proclamation of 1867 that asserts how, "We have suffered centuries of outrage, enforced poverty, and bitter misery. Our rights and liberties have been trampled on by an alien aristocracy, who treating us as foes, usurped our lands, and drew away from our unfortunate country all material riches" (O'Day & Stevenson, 1992, p. 76).

The proclamation asserts the Irish people as "the real owners of the soil" who "never lost the memory and hope of a national existence" (O'Day & Stevenson, 1992, p. 76). The 1916 proclamation declares, "the right of the people of Ireland to the ownership of Ireland" and "declares its resolve to pursue the happiness and prosperity of the whole nation and of all its parts" (O'Day & Stevenson, 1992, p. 76).

The 1919 Democratic Programme of the first Dail gives the first clear road map to actually bring the Irish public sector into being. It declares that, "the Nation's sovereignty extends not only to all men and women of the Nation, but to all its material possessions, the Nation's soil and all its resources, all the wealth and all the wealth-producing processes within the Nation" (Oireachtas, 1919).

Specifically the Programme, promises to "promote the development of the Nation's resources, to increase the productivity of its soil, to exploit its mineral deposits, peat bogs, and fisheries, its waterways and harbours, in the interests and for the benefit of the Irish people" (Oireachtas, 1919). It also commits to "adopt all measures necessary for the recreation and invigoration of our Industries, and to ensure their being developed on the most beneficial and progressive co-operative and industrial lines" (Oireachtas, 1919).

Perhaps the most crucial lines in the programme text is the declaration that "we desire our country to be ruled in accordance with the principles of Liberty, Equality, and Justice for all, which alone can secure permanence of Government in the willing adhesion of the people" (Oireachtas, 1919).

It is time to stop and think about the "right of the people to the ownership of Ireland", and how are we counting, how are we planning to deliver it and how that principle holds up in the Ireland of today. We collectively need to consider these principles when we look at the issues confronting how government and the institutions of state make planning decisions. This comes into consideration whether it was the issue in 2017 of bus drivers wages and the cherry picking of profitable routes for the private sector. It counts when we think about wage cuts being forced on public sector workers, or in an underfunded public hospital sector, with patients on trolleys, with hundreds of thousands of people waiting for an appointment, when we see another round of privatisation proposals. All of these issues are examples of the challenge of counting fairly.

Conclusion

When it comes to the related issues of counting, measuring and planning we need always to ask some simple questions. Who are we counting for? Have we counted everything including the externalities, the true costs, and the total impacts? When it comes to planning we need to ask again who we are planning for, is this about planning for the people, in a spirit of equality? Or is it about maximising a financial profit, or helping a vested interest. It is possible to achieve better, fairer and more accurate counting and measuring and better planning can be achieved from this. In the Ireland of today we haven't made it a principle of good government, which it must be.

References

Barnardos. (2018). *School Costs Survey 2018*. Retrieved April 17, 2019, from https://www.barnardos.ie/news/2018/august/barnardos-school-costs-survey-2018-take-action-and-demand-change

BIT. (2016). *The Behavioural Insights Team's Update Report 2015–16*. Behavioural Insight Ltd.

BIT. (2017). *Who We Are*. Retrieved July 7, 2017, from http://www.behaviouralinsights.co.uk/about-us/

Bowers, F. (2019, January 11). Reduction in Hospital Inpatient Waiting Lists—NTPF, RTE. Retrieved April 8, 2019, from https://www.rte.ie/news/health/2019/0111/1022706-public-patients-waiting-list/

Brennan, M. (2010). Private Firm to Reap €1.15bn Bonanza from M50 Toll Deal. *Irish Independent*, February 1.
Burke Kennedy, E. (2016, July 12). Handful of Multinationals Behind 26.3% Growth in GDP. *Irish Times.*
Central Statistics Office. (2017a). Survey on Income and Living Conditions. Retrieved July 5, 2017, from http://www.cso.ie/en/releasesandpublications/er/silc/surveyonincomeandlivingconditions2015/
Central Statistics Office. (2017b). *National Income and Expenditure Results 2016.* Retrieved July 17, 2017, from http://www.cso.ie/en/releasesandpublications/er/nie/niear2016/
Central Statistics Office. (2019a). *Residential Property Price Index.* Retrieved April 8, 2019, from https://www.cso.ie/en/releasesandpublications/ep/prppi/residentialpropertypriceindexjanuary2019/
Central Statistics Office. (2019b). *Labour Force Survey Quarter 4 2018.* Retrieved April 12, 2019, from https://www.cso.ie/en/statistics/labourmarket/labourforcesurvey/
Central Statistics Office. (2019c). *Earnings and Labour Costs Quarterly, Q3 2018 (Final) Q4 2018 (Preliminary Estimates).* Retrieved April 15, 2019, from https://www.cso.ie/en/statistics/earnings/earningsandlabourcosts/
Cicero, M. T. (1853). *The Treatises of M.T. Cicero: On the Nature of the Gods; On Divination; On Fate; On the Republic; On the Laws; and On Standing for the Consulship.* H G Bohn.
Daft.ie. (2019). *Irish Rental Price Report.* Retrieved February 20, 2019, from https://www.daft.ie/report/ronan-lyons-2018q4-rental
Department of Housing, Planning, Community and Local Government (DHPCLG). (2019). *Homelessness Report February 2019.* Retrieved August 22, 2019, from https://www.housing.gov.ie/sites/default/files/publications/files/homeless_report_-_february_2019.pdf
Domesday Book Online. (2017). *The Domesday Book Online.* Retrieved June 19, 2017, from http://www.domesdaybook.co.uk/index.html
Library of Economics and Liberty. (2017). *Simon Kuznets (1901–1985).* Retrieved June 21, 2017, from http://www.econlib.org/library/Enc/bios/Kuznets.html
ICTU. (2018). ICTU Report Shows that Executive Pay Continues to Climb. Retrieved April 16, 2019, from https://www.ictu.ie/press/2018/12/30/ictu-report-shows-that-executive-pay-continues-to/
INMO. (2019). *Trolley Watch.* Retrieved April 9, 2019, from https://www.inmo.ie/Trolley_Ward_Watch
Irish Motorway Info. (2017). National Primary Route 50. Retrieved July 14, 2017, from http://www.irishmotorwayinfo.com/inex/roads/m50/m50.html
Kelpie, C. (2016, July 13). 'Leprechaun Economics'—Ireland's 26pc Growth Spurt Laughed Off as 'Farcical'. *Irish Independent.* http://www.independent.

ie/business/irish/leprechaun-economics-irelands-26pc-growth-spurt-laughed-off-as-farcical-34879232.html

Kelpie, C. (2017, June 30). Airport Runway Rules Could Cost 17,000 Jobs, DAA Claims. *Irish Independent*.

O'Day, A., & Stevenson, J. (1992). *Irish Historical Documents since 1800*. Gill and Macmillan.

O'Hearn, D. (1998). *Inside the Celtic Tiger*. Pluto.

Oireachtas. (1919). *Democratic Programme*. Retrieved July 18, 2017, from http://oireachtasdebates.oireachtas.ie/debates%20authoring/debatesweb-pack.nsf/takes/dail1919012100016

Pogrebin, R., & Reyburn, S. (2017, May 18). A Basquiat Sells for 'Mind-Blowing' $110.5 Million at Auction. *New York Times.*.

RTB. (2019). *Residential Tenancies Board Rent Index*. Retrieved April 8, 2019, from https://onestopshop.rtb.ie/images/uploads/general/RTB_RI_Q4_2018_report_and_infographic.pdf

Rutter, T. (2015, July 23). The Rise of Nudge—The Unit Helping Politicians to Fathom Human Behaviour. *Guardian Newspaper*.

Ryan, C. (2010, August 3). Original Cost of M50 Toll Bridge Unknown. *Irish Examiner*.

Stiglitz, J., Zen, A., & Fitoussi, J. P. (2011). *Report by the Commission on the Measurement of Economic Progress and Social Wellbeing*. OECD.

Telegraph. (2017, May 4). How Leicester City's Premier League-Winning Squad Has Quadrupled in Value. *Daily Telegraph*.

Thaler, R., & Sunstein, C. R. (2009). *Nudge; Improving Decisions About Health, Wealth, and Happiness*. Penguin Books.

UNDP. (2017). *Human Development Index*. Retrieved June 21, 2017, from http://hdr.undp.org/en/content/human-development-index-hdi

UNHCR. (2018). *UNHCR Statistical Yearbook 2016*. Retrieved April 16, 2019, from https://www.unhcr.org/en-ie/statistics/country/5a8ee0387/unhcr-statistical-yearbook-2016-16th-edition.html

World Happiness Report. (2019). *World Happiness Report*. Retrieved April 8, 2019, from http://worldhappiness.report/

CHAPTER 7

Business Theologies

Introduction: Business Heresies

When was the point where business became bigger, more powerful and at times more effective than government or has it always been the case? How did business wrestle control of society's agenda away from democratically elected governments, given that, for nearly two centuries in Europe, citizen revolt, agitation and political struggle sacrificed so much to end monarchical and oligarchic aristocratic rule, only to have it recreated in contemporary society, where the business sector seem to be calling the shots in terms of many of the day's important decision making processes.

How did it happen that the business community became not just a dominant agenda setter in modern society but in parallel evolved into a protected species with unprecedented perks and privileges, creating an environment where business interests are pre-eminent. This is the case in not just Ireland but throughout the international arena of market based and industrialised economies.

The role of government today is often not just to facilitate an enterprise environment, they must actively work to nourish promote and effectively pander to the whims of enterprise. I don't how many times I have read news reports or had people moan first hand to me that one of the problems of the Six-County economy was the absence of any Fortune 500 firms located in the region, as if their very presence alone would be a soothing treatment for economic malfunction.

R. Smyth, *The Invisible Republic*,
https://doi.org/10.1007/978-3-030-86734-8_7

What is interesting about the pro business culture is that it is not always promoted in a rational manner. Supporting the business agenda has become a theology. Those who dare even remotely question the role of business in an economy are branded as heretics.

So let's get heretic for a moment. Why do we need firms and businesses? Are they an efficient method of managing economic resources in the short and long run? Businesses are interesting also because of their institutional nature, in that many of them, usually the most successful ones, outlive their workers and founders. So they become a way of transferring not just wealth from one generation to another but also a method and an ideological tool of economic organisation.

The motives for starting firms are dealt with in the chapters on entrepreneurs, what we want to talk about here is whether it is possible to explore the role that business should play in an economy and the impact they actually make.

Why We Might Need Firms

From a free market ideology point of view firms are looked on as the driver of economic growth, employment, innovation and wealth creation. They are the efficient solution to the problem of how best to harness scarce resources, matched with the creative input of their owners to meet the demands of consumers.

There are examples easy to hand that prove this is the case. For example if the state was to co-ordinate economic activity by either running firms themselves or nationalising what government deems to be important industries, a failure in planning, strategy or innovation could have massive consequences for the economy as a whole. However a small or even medium sized firm getting its strategies wrong and going bankrupt is less serious as firstly there are other firms who might not be shadowing the failing firm and secondly any error is contained within the firm and might not go viral into the economy as a whole.

For example the decision of the British government in the 1940s to begin a process of aggressive systematic nationalisation of industry was ultimately a total failure. Coal mining, ship building, car manufacture, electricity generation, gas, phones, steel foundries, ports, train and bus services all came under state control.

The result was that short term electoral needs to preserve total employment levels stifled innovation and development of these firms. It also lead to the firms' managers developing a culture where they could ignore market forces, domestically and internationally. Most importantly it meant a failure to spot the newly emerging industries in computing and telecommunications.

The British Government ended up owning, a range of state enterprises which were ever decreasing in importance and value, but increasingly costly to run. The knock on effect in the economy as a whole was that investment by the private sector in what we would now call "new economy" business lagged far behind that of other states as the dominance of the state in the economy as a whole provided an unnecessary comfort zone for the public and private sector that lead ultimately to a serious waste of resources.

Firms: A Short History

Firms as we know them today are essentially a product of the industrial revolution and were economic entities based around the newly mechanised industries. A mechanical plant such as a foundry, or a mill became a firm. It had owners, managers and workers. Essentially the firm was an efficient unit to co-ordinate the organisation of resources to a particular purpose, in this case usually producing, manufacturing and selling goods and services.

Then as the mechanisation technology developed so did the number of goods that could be produced and correspondingly the number of firms grew also.

Firms did exist before the industrial revolution, but most were small operations compared to the scale of modern companies. In fact what was emerging was a social unit of organisation that would become larger than villages, towns, regiments, armies and ultimately states. The other pre-existing economic unit was the farm/estate which seen in a modern context could have had numerous businesses contained within its operations.

In terms of how we understand firms today and the firms that existed before the industrial revolution there are two key aspects. The first is that firms were legal entities and this is still the case today. It is this legal existence that becomes crucial in our understanding of firms. This is important from a republican point of view because of the fact that by conferring a legal personality on firms we have also given them rights, rights that are in some circumstances greater than the rights we allow citizens!

The second factor is that most firms were small operations employing a few people, often no more than two or three. Today this is still the case and the vast majority of firms are small ones, yet a lot of media coverage and comment is about large firms who are much rarer breed than the common smaller species.

The big difference today is the emergence of the large firms, which are in proportion to the total economy a small employer but their relative size bestows on them great political and economic power beginning from the simple fact of the scale of economic resources they can direct to achieve any particular desired outcome.

In fact the dominant units of economic organisation in pre industrial revolution Europe were the large farms and agricultural estates owned by the aristocrats. The industrial revolution was a serious challenge for these economic entities which though still profitable and still needed were being surpassed by the new mechanised manufacturers and their associated industries. Agriculture mattered only in how it fitted into the new economy of the industrial revolution.

Agriculture had to accept its gradual demotion in the economic pecking order the same way old industry has had to move sideways today for the new economy firms. What was being transferred was an ability to wield economic and political power.

What also changed about firms were the products they were creating. They began to develop characteristics bundled into the concept we now call a brand along with the now familiar marketing and advertising strategies deployed by firms to promote these types of products. The twentieth century witnessed an explosion of brands and economic activity surrounding the development, investment and maintenance of brands, giving firms another asset to protect and if needs be to fight for!

Powers of Firms

Firms have evolved into not just an effective method of economic organisation. They are also a source of economic power and hence a political force. These powers can be exercised in many ways but for our arguments we outline four key areas. They are the exercising of economic power, political power, the imbalance in power between individuals and firms in terms of how firms deal with government and vice versa. Finally there is the context of the media power firms can exercise, or call upon to their defence.

Exercising Economic Power

The economic powers of large firms include tactics such as predatory pricing where companies have the ability to use price setting as a means to preclude market entry by rivals, or below cost selling which allows larger firms exploit economies of scale and drive out their smaller competitors.

Then there is the example of firms who control particularly important or valuable economic resources which they exploit to maximise their own profits. The cartelisation exposed in Europe's mobile phone companies who were deemed to be making exorbitant profits out of roaming charges is an example.

A particular unique example of this would be the OPEC states realising that they could set the price of oil in the 1970s, and this cartel is now into its fourth decade of successful price setting, their unique control of resources is the amount of total global oil production under their control.

A more recent related example of this is the battle between producers of goods like Unilever and Procter and Gamble, 'traditional' retailers like Walmart or Tesco and the growing power of online firms like Amazon who are entering the traditional retail arena. In 2017 Amazon purchased Whole Foods Markets for $13.7 billion laying down a significant marker of their market strategy (Bhattarai, 2017). Their battle for market share is removed from the consumer. In this case you are the prize, your disposable income and where will it be spent is the battleground. I wonder what Fourier would think of the quality and purpose of jobs in Amazon, Tesco or Walmart, not to mention one of the super production plants of Unilever or Procter and Gamble?

Firms like Amazon, Wal-Mart and Tesco with multiple sites across states have emerged as having an economic superiority over the actual manufacturers of the goods they sell.

Other economic powers of firms relate to standard economic behaviour like vertical and horizontal integration. Coca Cola and Pepsi own not just their own brands and bottling plants but also the very cold cabinets we the buyer take them from. Control of the cold cabinet means an absence of competitors' products in that refrigerator and a higher cost of market entry for any competitors who might be thinking of taking on these two drinks giants.

Disney along with their cinema output and resorts own ABC TV, ESPN, and have the media rights to Marvel Comics content, the Star Wars franchise and now the back catalogue of 20th Century Fox and its affiliates. Microsoft owns LinkedIn and Minecraft among a vast range of acquisitions over its corporate history.

This acquisition trail of companies is common across the tech industries, as larger firms swallow up smaller competitors or chase what they believe is valuable intellectual property. And so, even the still young Facebook owns Instagram, What's App and the virtual reality firm Oculus. In both the film and tech sectors small producers and micro firms find it difficult to get an independent avenue to market. In the tech sector most small entrants are in the area of smart phone apps, and must sell their product through the Apple or Google's android stores. This market points to critical issues in the emerging app industry, most of the products are initially free, meaning that for the creators there is initially a very low stream of income. They are entering an economic sector where they have to work for free and when they do get revenue, surrender a significant proportion of it back to Google and Apple.

Political Power

The political power of firms relates principally to focusing government policies and legislation on decisions that enhances a firm's profitability either by increasing revenue or by decreasing costs. For example in Ireland, this has focused on tax cuts for firms in terms of taxes on profits and payroll, which are among the lowest in the world. Firms are usually to be found making the running for more lax health and safety regulations, employment laws and environmental protection codes. The demand for fast track planning decisions for business is another example of this.

Other examples of these three factors at work would include the European wide opposition by firms to the working hour directive which set a 48 hour maximum length for the working week. Britain as a country demanded and received a complete derogation from what were then called the Social Chapter commitments of the Maastricht Treaty and can in the aftermath of Brexit retrench further on any social commitments.

In the case of employment law the opposition by Irish business organisations to a minimum wage which would have little if any effect on their profitability is way out of proportion to the potential costs of the directive.

The Fair Trade Example

There is another aspect to this power of firms and it is in their ability to promote and develop societal trends. Sunday opening, eating out, cooking less, using facial beauty products that are not tested on animals are all examples of societal trends promoted by business that have also made considerable profits for the firms concerned.

Right now there are two powerful examples of how business is reacting to social trends, it is in the areas of climate change and environmental protection plus fair trade. At one level the media have played a substantial role in highlighting issues of global warming and world poverty giving valuable column inches and broadcasting time to environmental and economic campaigners.

It was a development agency in the Netherlands who started a concerted campaign to promote fair trade issues (Fairtrade International, 2017). How did they do this? Was it through well meaning articles, public meetings, street campaigns and leafleting. Well yes, my own college days were filled with such activities and we regularly berated the hapless person who happened to be nibbling on a Kit Kat about the crimes of Nestle and baby milk. At the same time Nestle's profits grew and grew as they branched out into other coffees, foods and soft drinks, many of which we were ignorant about.

Perhaps the most ironic part of the Nestle boycott on my part was my brand switching to Maxwell House, part of what was the Kraft Group, who have been criticised for the high fat and salt content of many of their food products who then became part of the Altria Group which included the tobacco giant Phillip Morris, the people who gave us the Marlboro Man. Kraft is now part of a mega food group called Mondelez that includes Kraft brands, Cadburys, Heinz and Oreos (Mondelez, 2017).

But an activist called Max Havelaar, who was involved in a Dutch development agency called Solidaridad took another more important tack; they began to act like a firm and developed a series of fair trade brands and certification (Fairtrade International, 2017). They began to behave like a business. For the purpose of their campaign they were a business developing brands, promoting their products and shaping society at the same time. The growing market share for these goods has prompted food giants like Cadbury's to buy up the Green and Black chocolate range getting not just a fair trade product for the shelves but an organic one also. And in time they were bought by the already mentioned Kraft.

Fair trade is just one part of this process, an increasing number of businesses are stressing their environmental credentials, whether it is in better processes, surcharges for carbon emissions, or announcing new checks and practices for respecting the human rights of international workers who make part of the products. On the negative side it has led the creation of the term "greenwashing" where firms attempt to demonstrate and promote environmental credentials as a method to increase sales and profits (Merriam Webster, 2019).

Even though many other corporate giants in the food trade tried to introduce their own fair trade certification policies Fairtrade International won out. Now their logo adorns products in Starbucks, Nestle and many other international brands. It shows that maybe the most powerful tool in taking on a brand is another brand!

What this shows is the power of the firm to shape how society behaves, and influence what it values. The corollary of this is that the firm and the business community can also negatively impact on trends that it sees are against its interests. This is significant as it means that important decisions about how society acts are being taken outside the formal political process and as Margaret Thatcher was so fond of saying. You can't buck the market!

The Power of the Firm and the Individual

One overlooked aspect of the power of businesses is their relevant strength to that of their workers. Popular myth would characterise the period post World War II to before the Thatcher years as ones where well meaning firms were at the mercy of their workers, who would jeopardise the future of the very enterprises they work for just for some small workplace gain.

This fits neatly into one of the first examples given in this chapter, that of the British nationalisation project of the mid twentieth century. The failures of the nationalised industries is often laid at the door of workers and their restrictive work practices, which is at best a simplistic and wholly unfair interpretation of what actually happened. The Glasgow Media Group has done some excellent work on how the media portrayal of managers fell into the category of "reasonable men and responsible citizens" but not so for the workers (Philo et al., 1982). It is though an important part of the business theology which brands workers, who are in fact a vital factor and dynamic in any firm, as troublesome and potentially dangerous if not dealt with using extreme caution.

The reality of economic history is that firms have with only small exceptions had the upper hand over their workers. So how could this be true? Firstly firms usually have substantially more resources than their workers, individually and collectively. Secondly firms are legal entities and have rights as such. It could be argued that in some economies the rights of firms are superior to that of the individuals in the economy, even though we are quaintly informed time and time again that 'sovereignty rests with the people'.

The power of firms relative to individual workers is most visible in the context of the issue of pay. Workers' pay is a cost and must be restricted. Not just that, it is often the most important cost in how the firm ranks the things it must pay for. It is not uncommon for media coverage of firms' activities to talk about how much of a percentage a firm's labour costs are relative to the total costs incurred by the company. Even if the firm's process is labour intensive and costs would therefore be naturally high, this is not of consequence and we must marvel at how the firm copes with such a high wage bill.

For the individual worker the only way around this is to rise up the firm's management structure as other wage increases through union negotiation etc will not deliver real long term gains for the worker. The worker must submit to the company's hierarchy, its ideology and as you rise through the corporate ladder become a company tool in containing the wage costs of the workers below you. Failure to accomplish tasks like this will be an impediment to your future upward mobility. The emergence of hierarchies in the workplace is well documented. The example of what is now called Fordism is one pertinent example. Harry Braverman offers an interesting analysis of the effects of Fordism (Braverman, 1974/1998).

The short version is that Henry Ford had little time for trade unions and was viciously anti organised labour. He used the assembly line as a means to disempower workers, by breaking up the physical tasks of constructing automobiles into their simplest tasks meaning that he did not have to pay his workers the wages rates of skilled workers and that he was able to recalibrate his workforce with the number of unskilled manual workers vastly outnumbering the skilled. Ford's logic was that the unskilled workers would have little bargaining power, and no economic leverage as their lack of skills made them easily replaceable. This is not a unique stand alone example and the history of employer union relationships is filled with other comparable relevant examples.

A nineteenth and early twentieth century example of the power of firms was found in the operation of US mining companies. When opening new mines, these companies ensured that they owned the mine and all the surrounding resources, including shops and houses. This meant that the worker was not now just a price taker in terms of wages but also when buying food, clothes or even paying rent. In some cases workers were paid in company tokens that could only be exchanged in company stores.

More recently an Irish supermarket in the early 1990s attempted to introduce work place practices which in one store meant that there were over 200 part-time workers compared to 10 full time staff. Many of the workers were on what was then termed zero hour contracts, where in any given week they did not know what their hours of work would be. Workers were expected to wait by the phone for a daily call to work or not as the case may have been. Now in the twenty-first century the zero hour contract is even more prevalent, matched by the marginal working conditions of those in the so called 'gig economy'.

One of the most infamous US examples of the imbalance between workers and the firm that employs them was found in General Electric under the tenure of former CEO Jack Welch who implemented a "rank and yank" philosophy where what he deemed the underperforming workers were denied bonuses, moved within their organisation, some even being dismissed. In 2013 Welch called the practice "differentiation", maintaining that, "It's about making sure that all employees know where they stand" (Welch, 2013). The rank and yank philosophy became prevalent in the late twentieth century throughout corporate America.

The Irish and now international airline Ryanair's previous disputes with its pilots and other staff are other examples of this attempt to disempower workers and frustrate them from joining unions, while making them pay for training on the use of new planes bought by the company. Most interesting in the Ryanair example is their successful transference of a hard hitting and at times abusive attitude to their employees to their customer relations.

Despite the vast amount of negative media coverage generated by the firm especially in terms of the quality of its services the firm's profitability has grown and grown. Even those who verge on despising Ryanair still buy tickets because of the low prices knowing that, there will not just be exploited workers delivering that service, but also that the service itself might be substandard. I have seen the staunchest anti-capitalists crumble when contemplating the price of a holiday. It points up a crucial point about the role of firms and how they present themselves to the public.

A significant section of people cannot see any alternative to the firm as a provider of goods and services and even in this complaining consumer culture many people will put up with a lot of crap to have more euros or dollars in their pocket at the end of the day. I sometimes think it is this reality that empowers firms more than any other single factor. In recent years, Ryanair have made attempts at a PR 'niceness' but this is a thin veneer over the company's actual corporate philosophy. So the history of firm worker relations is one where except for the shortest of periods firms have had the upper hand and have been able to drive their own agendas forward at the expense of their workers.

An Environmental Example

Dealing with environmental waste is another best example of the political powers of a firm compared to that of ordinary people. In Ireland and across the EU member states agreed to fundamentally change the way waste is managed. The 1994 Packaging and Packaging Waste Directive meant that businesses were facing a substantially changed waste management environment. The directive has been updated several times since 1994 (European Commission, 2019).

The EU directives would make any company who generated more than 25 tonnes of packing annually completely responsible for the disposal of that waste. Consumers could in theory return any packaging to the shops from where it was bought. However there was a loophole whereby individual firms could forgo having to dispose of their waste if they joined a recognised recovery scheme. Membership of such schemes is costed in relation to the waste you produce.

In both Ireland and Britain these schemes were started by the business community's representative organisations. In Ireland it was the Irish Business and Employers Confederation who brought together the original members while the British CBI played a similar role in the formation of Valpak. So fees are being paid, memberships taken out and directives enforced—big deal! Most fascinating from an Irish perspective is that the Irish recycling company Repak, describes itself as a "not for profit company set up by Irish business and owned by its members" (Repak, 2019). 'Not for profit' are words not often heard in the market driven private sector. Wouldn't it be great if this principle clearly established and endorsed by the private sector in Ireland could be extended and promoted more widely as an economic principle? How many other not for profit businesses could be established?

What is important is where the ordinary customers have been left in all of this, they are the example of the contradiction, the inequality in how political power is exercised. In Ireland today, households are bombarded by television and radio advertisements, encouraging them to recycle and reuse. There are no such advertisements for firms, even though it is they rather than firms who have the actual power to reduce the amount of plastics and metals used in packaging their products.

Households who don't have this power are being levied with significantly increased service charges for waste disposal, being told that they have to change their habits while the firms that actually manufacture and sell them the goods are getting a different message from government and the EU.

At the same theme in Ireland, where recycling facilities are infrastructurally underdeveloped, government moved to change the law creating new fast track planning legislation for incinerators that bypasses local government. These incinerators are run by private business, the first of which has started operations in Dublin. They have not generated any local support and are opposed by communities wherever they are sited, but ultimately will be built while no fast track legislation for recycling has been introduced.

Part of the logic at work seems to be that there is only a weak and unpredictable income stream possible from the recycling, for example the recycled paper market is extremely volatile. However a waste burning facility has a much more predictable guaranteed income stream and it seems that it is this that can move governments to action.

The Privatisation Example

How firms influence governments and exercise political power is integrated into their world vision. Firms see the world in terms of costs and revenues. Costs are to be avoided and revenues exploited. The replication and use of these criteria by government to formulate policies for dealing with individuals and households can be wholly unsatisfactory and shows again how firms have different rights and influences over how decisions are made. The most important aspect being that government deals with business on terms decided by business, while households and individuals have incredible difficulties at times getting government to deal with them on their terms.

The drive towards privatisation of state utilities at a national and international level is an example of this process. Many of the businesses now being privatised such as telecommunications, transport, energy and other utilities show the private sector breaking new ground not because of government prohibitions being lifted but because the costs are now lower.

During the twentieth century the private sector in Britain, Europe and other developed states steadfastly refused to get into the emerging telecommunication and electricity supply services. The deterrent for them were the huge set up costs especially if government had decided that these services would be rolled out on the principle of universal access. The costs were too much of a deterrent. There was also the mitigating factor that many governments considered these to be vital services and wanted to keep them under state control.

However, something changed in the late twentieth century and the private sector got on board. In Britain this happened because the method of market entry meant being able to buy hugely expensive state infrastructure at bargain basement prices. It meant that costs had been substantially reduced while revenue could only increase.

In Ireland this process has been mirrored, but also compounded by two other factors. One was the refusal of the private sector to invest in the newly independent state in the early part of the twentieth century and their subsequent refusal to invest in renewing the infrastructure in the new century. The experience of the newly independent Irish economies in the 1920s is a good example of the behaviour of private sector firms and government and of the relationships that emerged and evolved between the two.

In the Six Counties, though there was now a new local parliament, the economy was still part of the British unit sharing the same currency, tax regime, economic policies etc. The local parliament though saw its role as aiding local business that supported its political hegemony. This led, as was the case in Britain, albeit for different political reasons, to increasing amounts of aid and other supports being diverted to businesses whose economic role was waning such as ship building and heavy engineering (Farrell, 1987).

In Britain, these practices were tied up in the increasingly complicated relationship between the trade union movement and government as well as an establishment belief that some businesses had to be maintained in the national interest. In the Six Counties the parliament supported businesses that had a political role in endorsing unionist power. It is ironic that most of these businesses are defunct today and the shipyards that built the Titanic were redeveloped as offices, a tourist amenity and a centre for film making.

In the 26 Counties, there was an entirely different relationship between the newly emerging political elite and the pre-existing economic one. The state, partitioned now from its north-eastern industrial base, was a mainly agricultural economy. The economy for the next century was never able to house or employ all of its citizens. It inherited a banking system and a transport infrastructure but found quickly that there was a lack of resources or funding to develop much needed infrastructure especially in the areas of electricity generation, phone services, education and health. The new Government also found a private sector that was often merely branches of a British parent and not concerned about the Irish economy and not politically linked in or supportive of the independence project. They would only be investing in the new economy in the context of low risk and quick returns.

Similarly the Irish business community was equally reticent and what followed was a unique economic project. Successive governments, beginning with Fianna Fail and continued by its successors, began to create new firms through the offices of various ministers and their departments.

In the context of electricity generation and the developing phone service, the state entered the market in the context of providing universal access to the power and phone networks. This meant considerable investment over the long term. The knock on effects would be hugely positive for the economy as a totality and the quality of living of households and communities especially in the context of electrification but not immediately profitable for the energy provider. However, in the short run political context, these flagship projects meant that it was also clearly visible to voters that the new regime was delivering real change.

However, the state's involvement in the economy and in running companies was much more widespread than this. The state ran an airline, a shipping company, a ferry service to Britain and then France. It set up insurance companies, separate banks for industrial development and agriculture, a horse breeding industry followed by one for greyhounds. As was the case in Britain and beyond the state took over the running of ports and public transport as well airports, developing along the way the world's first duty free shops.

In terms of energy, a national turf processing company was started and in agriculture a range of food processing concerns running from sugar production to soups. The drive towards privatising these firms has come partially from the impact of the Thatcher project and US Austrianist economic policies but also from within the EU.

The Semi State Principle

So why does, or did the Irish government own or hold shares in so many businesses. The simple answer is that no one else wanted to. As the state floundered in the years after partition the Irish and international private sector were reluctant, unwilling even, to invest in the new state.

And so successive Irish governments made investments on our behalf in electricity supply, gas networks, forests, insurance, banking, developing our bogs, ports, airports, telecommunications, horse and dog racing, ship building, and steel. It is a long list and there are still 29 semi-state companies on the government books according to www.gov.ie.

Sure enough when the businesses got profitable or corporate sharks scented difficult trading conditions—the business equivalent of blood in the water, there suddenly were suitors aplenty. This is where Aer Lingus found itself today, sold to IAG, yet the value of the airline's Heathrow landing slots alone had been independently put at €1.2 billion based on the value of slots negotiated by SAS.

Irish Life

Established in 1939 Irish Life is now part of Canadian financial group Great-West Lifeco. In 1939 18% of the company shares were held by the Irish Finance minister. In 1991, it was floated on the stock exchange. The state took nearly €602 million at the time. Since then the group went on a disastrous spate of acquisitions and mergers ending in the Irish Government taking over the Irish Life and Irish Permanent group in 2012 and pumping in €4 billion. Irish Life was sold in 2013 to Great West for €1.3 billion. For now the net cost to you the tax payer is still something north of €2 billion!

Greencore

Also sold off in 1991 was Suicre Eireann, now Greencore. The state got €210.65 million from the stock market floatation. In December 2018 the company reported profits of £104.6 million from a revenue of £1.498.5 billion (Kelly, 2018). Imagine if the Irish government had kept a shareholding like it has now in Aer Lingus. There would be steady dividend stream and some real long term payback to the Irish economy.

Irish Shipping and B&I

This firm was started in 1941 to secure transport of good and goods to the island during World War 2. The company grew in terms of fleet and tonnage transported. It was part of the consortium that started ferries from Rosslare to France, a business that is still profitable today.

In 1984, the then Fine Gael Labour coalition allowed the firm to go into liquidation. In 1992, the Fianna Fail PD coalition approved the sale of the government's shares in B&I ferries for €10.8 million

In the years since the volume of trade has massively increased through Irish ports. The wages and working conditions of many of the workers on those ships has deteriorated though.

Eircom

You like me have lost count of the owners and sales of Eircom since the €6.399 billion floatation of the firm in 1999. Then Eircom had debts of €540 million, by 2012, five owners later the firm had debts of €3.8 billion.

According to the 2016 State of the Internet index two-thirds of the 26 Counties has web speeds of 10Mbs, a rate the EU designates as substandard. The Irish Government is committed to spending €500 million to improve broadband access. If we owned Eircom still, this might be a very different story. Three years later, there is still no agreed broadband plan, and the price of any rollout is spiralling to billions of euro.

Oil and Gas Rights

It took an investment of €3.4 billion to develop the Corrib gas field off the west coast of Ireland. The scale of this investment we were supposed to believe was something the Irish Government could not afford. They are not even a shareholder in a business that can pump the gas equivalent of 9700 barrels of oil a day, and would be able to meet at 60% of Irish gas demand at the time of completion. The irony that the Norwegian Government through its Statoil company owns more of Irish natural fossil fuel resources than the Irish government should be lost on no one.

The Role of the Media

Much of our perception of business comes from how the media in its broadest sense portrays and characterises the sector. So what role do the media play in this scenario? Well our starting point must be to echo recognition of a point made by many other theorists and writers, particularly Antonio Gramsci. His theory of hegemony, which is that the media we think of as an independent organic life force, which exists to play some quasi institutional watchdog role in society, are actually not the benign guardians we see them as.

Gramsci writes on hegemony that, "Everything which influences or is able to influence public opinion belongs to it", and includes libraries, schools, associations and clubs to architecture, street layout and even their names". Gramsci describes these factors as the "trenches and fortifications of the dominant class", and that the press is the most "dynamic" element of that structure (Gramsci, 1971, pp. 375–3777).

Media companies use the firm structure as their method of organisation and the sector is in fact a place populated by firms who need to maximise revenues and minimise costs just like any corporate entity. The activities and development of the media sector and the companies that populate it have become a dominant part of the business sector today as new economy activity has become ever more focused on information, communication and creative type products. So how does that leave them placed when it comes to reporting fairly and critically on the activities of other firms? John Fiske when considering television culture introduced the idea of a cultural economy that has a social and semiotic power and that has the capacity to be critical of the financial economy (Fiske, 1987). While this may be true of some elements of film and TV content what is the state of play in the news media sectors?

Two trends become apparent, the first is that media reporting in Britain, Ireland and North America seems to begin with the logic that the free market system despite flaws is the best economic organisational structure available to humanity at this juncture. So any media reporting kicks off with would be free market critics put in a position of being guilty until proven innocent, or more likely being at best misguided well meaning utopians, but more likely crackpot tree hugging commies until proven even remotely rational.

It also means that, not only do the media not give much time to covering the views of those opposed to the market system, they actually devote considerable time to promoting free market ideologies and the cultural trappings that envelop this. How is this achieved? First by deciding that a firm's profits are the apex of a pyramid of business news followed by triumphant profiles of those who succeed. Then there is an ongoing parade of eulogies and celebritising of successful businesses and business people. We see how they live, their tips for success, clothing and diet choices. We are invited to ponder their reading choices and consider their views on too many aspects of public society.

Negative business news is often reported in the context of being a threat to profits and jobs, rather than maybe being considered as newsworthy in its own right. There has been though in recent years a substantial improvement in the level of critical coverage of business activity. This has happened in the context of news media developing greater understanding of their audience interests.

Audiences are consumers and as such they want to know the products they consume are not just good quality and value for money, but they also need to know whether or not the products are safe, environmentally friendly, and will not have any negative health side effects. In the case of transnational brands, we want to believe that the products are made under conditions where workers are not being exploited. This has improved media business coverage but has not eradicated the starting proposition that businesses are best. It is only in this limited sense of writing about consumer interests that any critical coverage of a firm's activities are entertained.

The final place where this institutional bias in the news media is found in reporting on industrial relations disputes and again the work of the Glasgow Media Group has shown up a bias against workers in how media report industrial relations issues.

Irish examples of the media imbalance would include the 1999 nurses strike where over the course of the three days of the dispute when nurses took to the picket line the Irish Times ran more than ten articles daily covering the dispute. However of these ten plus articles no more than one or two a day actually dealt with the reasons for the strike or the attempts to resolve the impasse. The majority of news coverage was to do with the effects of the strike on patients, who had been amply cared for. There were no deaths reported because of the dispute yet this was where the media focus remained.

In 2005, the Irish postal service was riven by a long running dispute between management and unions over rationalisation and changes in work practices. An Post workers had built up a system of institutionalised overtime which they were reluctant to end without substantially higher wages. The company was moving from profit to loss and back to profit again over a series of years, the domestic mail delivery service where the industrial relations problems started was in profit. It was the international mail delivery agreements particularly with Britain that were costing the state owned firm millions annually, yet the media focus was on the stubborn workers who perish the thought were threatening to block Christmas post deliveries. The workers had committed the heinous crime of trying to 'stop Santa'. Was it any wonder that with such negative media coverage the unions had to end their work to rule and rethink their strategy?

The 2005 Ice Hockey lock out in the USA is another example where it seemed the players were at fault for being too greedy and committed the unthinkable crime of denying fans a hockey season. The untold narrative that it is ok for firms to make a profits but not workers was lost on most of the media reporting on the dispute

My personal favourite is the New York Times opinion writer who surveyed the conviction of the late Kenneth Lay former CEO of Enron, declared that the problem with Enron and Worldcom was not the loss of jobs, pensions etc and the depth of the scandal but that "irresponsible capitalism" was giving business a bad name!

In contemporary Ireland the negative reporting of industrial relations continues. 'Troublesome teachers, militant strikers, demanding workers', any of this sound familiar? You have been reading, listening to or watching reporting on industrial relations disputes in the Irish economy during 2017.

In 2016 through to 2017 this included disputes involving, teachers, LUAS drivers, doctors, nurses, DART, Bus Ath Cliath and Bus Eireann drivers, City Jet, the Gardai, Bausch and Lomb, and Tesco workers.

You find in media coverage that unions have 'leaderships', 'executives', 'factions' and 'central committees' while employers are well, just employers. In a public sector strike ministers get a mention, usually on how 'inappropriate' it would be for them to get involved. Take a bow ministers Bruton, Harris, O'Sullivan and Ross.

Industrial disputes are nasty affairs with 'threats' and 'demands' made by workers while the public are portrayed as the losers as they deal with the loss of service when a work stoppage actually happens, which is rare by the way!

There were 71,647 strike days in 2016, involving 29,372 workers according to Central Statistics Office figures. This is less than 2.5 days lost work per employee, hardly a mass strike in an economy with 2,048,100 workers in 2016. The 2018 figures were the lowest since 2011.

So why do the news media write headlines like, "Secondary Schools plunged into chaos" or 'Traffic chaos looms as Dart drivers to vote on strike action", taken from the Irish Times and Independent in 2016.

Skewed industrial relations coverage in Ireland goes deeper. There were 35 articles in 2016s Irish Times coverage of the dispute between teachers and the Department of Education. In the headlines accompanying the articles there is not one quote or a teachers' union source named.

Even in the pull quotes within the articles there are no union sources quoted. We do get quotes from Education minister Jan O'Sullivan, who is replaced later in the year by Richard Bruton, who gets a pull quote as does Public Expenditure Minister Paschal Donohue and Education Department Secretary General Sean O Foghlu.

In the Irish Times teachers strike headlines union sources are never given equal prominence. The news media would claim they don't take sides, but they use hyped distorting language, focusing on the impact of strikes on the public rather than the working conditions that have led to industrial action in these isolated cases.

In the 2017 Mandate strike at Tesco, newspapers were wholly unable to call out Tesco, a profitable company in Ireland, for seeking to pay a section of their workers less wages after more than 20 years working for the company. They had no problem though taking the money for multiple days of two full pages of advertisements from Tesco during the strike! Is that really balanced and fair reporting?

Is There an Alternative to Firms?

So do we really want to countenance moving beyond the firm? It is an all encompassing part of society and has become one of the bedrocks of how societies organise themselves. With over 348,000 firms in Ireland, can they really be that terrible, that malevolent (CSO, 2016; NI Business Info, 2017)?

It is true that some firms have a lot of power and can threaten and often succeed in bypassing and undermining or simply directing government decisions onto their own agendas, but is this not really the behaviour of a small minority of firms, are we really implying that the whole body economic is corrupt?

I suppose it depends on whether you see the firm as a feature of society, a naturally occurring phenomenon or a parasite, an infestation. To continue an environmental analysis, it seems that the world has evolved as a place where the firm has no natural predators. It has emerged as the top rung of society's food chain. Government, its only possible predator has become a partner, a collaborator and at times a willing enabler to the dominance of the firm.

Even on an international level powerful organisations like the EU, the IMF, OECD, and the WTO all take a relatively benign attitude towards the firm and in some cases like in the USA, China and the Russian Federation, firms are integral to the political strategies of these superpowers.

For example the USA's ability to move financial might across frontiers comes not just from government spending but from the decisions US firms take to invest or not in particular regions. Ireland is a key example of this and in particular the 26 County economy, which is dominated by US Foreign Direct Investment (FDI). Examples include the presence of firms like Apple, Coke, Dell, Facebook, GE, Google, Intel, IBM, Microsoft, and Pfizer. At the same time, the Six Counties does not have even one Fortune 500 firm with operations or any presence there. One economy is often deemed a modern miracle and the other a basket case.

In China over the first decade of the noughties a series of firms there attempted acquisitions into the key US markets particularly in the context of oil and consumer electronics. In both cases economic nationalism played a huge part in terms of the US repulsing Chinese acquisitions and in the attempt of the Chinese private sector to make an impact in the US marketplace. Also over the last decade the Russian Government has moved to take strategic holdings in a range of energy and resource firms as energy nationalism becomes a growing feature of the international economy.

Perhaps the best example of economic nationalism came in the spat in 2006 between George Bush and the US Congress over the purchase of key US ports by a firm owned by the Government of the United Arab Emirates. Bush ended up defending Dubai Ports World proposed acquisition of the US ports. But at the end of the day a key US company could not be owned by another government.

So with firms so core a feature of society, what is the secret of their success, how have firms managed to create a society that not only nourishes and enhances their stature but also acts swiftly to see off any potential threats?

Despite the conclusion that firms have evolved as a key element of modern society it seems that it isn't a position of security and this is where the concept of business theologies comes from. Firms are far from secure on their throne and in fact there is a constant patrolling of the political and economic landscape for any threat to the business ascendancy.

Sinn Fein, the Media and Business

From a Sinn Fein point of view they have often felt the wrath of the business community. Perhaps the most common example and condemnation they have hurled at them is the contention that party policies are "Marxist", which I have realised over the years is a code for the most serious, most grave offence in the business theologian's charter. They are to borrow a Christian analysis the 'Doubting Thomas'; They are the twenty-first century Luther, questioning the infallibility of business.

Tying any of the commentators down to the specifics on the Marxian threat is difficult. Common proofs of Sinn Fein's Marxist madness include their support for a state bank, opposition to privatisation and party spending proposals.

State Banks

The formation of a state bank was a plank in Sinn Fein's policy strategy and for many republicans is a symbolic icon of what a people's government could be, and of the dynamic positive role it could play in economic life. For a long time all the elements of creating such a bank force existed including the 26-County state's credit corporations for industry and agriculture as well as the extensive branch network of An Post, the ESB too were technically in the consumer credit market. There were also other state owned financial sector firms such as the Irish Life, the massive insurance firm.

Pulling these elements together could it was argued create a vibrant retail and commercial financial services bank. This was a position held by not just Sinn Fein but by the Labour Party too at one time. Labour's entry into government in 1993 saw them baulk at the state bank hurdle going instead for a softer focus in terms of delivering on its left leaning agenda. Sinn Fein was at that time the only Leinster House resident in the Marxian mad house. There were no other left wing socialist parties in Leinster House and those that are there now support a "public banking and finance system" (Solidarity, 2017).

Today the ACC, ICC and Irish Life have been privatised while An Post's branch network has been eroded somewhat with the remainder still an asset much sought after by the private sector. The banking sector collapsed in 2008, and not surprisingly was nationalised overnight and in the years afterwards refinanced, refloated and let back into the wild with only cosmetic changes to how they operate. A massive opportunity to reform, to democratise the finance function in business and society and how we deal with money was lost.

Irish banks in the 1990s and noughties became the envy of Europe with returns on equity double the EU average, the larger banks enjoy a position of operating on both sides of the border enjoying substantial benefits of a two currency island levying cross border transactions and also controlling clearing bank payments which yields them dominance in the retail markets. Over the last two decades years financial regulators in both markets have begun to focus on the restrictive and anti competitive practices that permeate the Irish bank market. This has only evolved on a small scale, and in many respects today the Irish banking sector is merely a little chastened. Some open Saturdays and have more soft focus advertising, but that is about all the reform we have seen in the financial sector.

From a republican viewpoint, we have to ask why banks exist, what role do they play in the economy now, and is this the role they should have. When the Great Recession emerged in 2008, the banks were powerless and collapsed. It was government who took a shareholding, who created NAMA, it was the government, flawed and ineffectual as they were at the time who became the lender of last resort.

Republicans believe that banks are a consequence of economic activity. It is this factor that makes republicans propose that the role and power of banks should be harnessed more effectively to make a greater contribution to underpinning positive economic activities, enhancing the performance of households and firms who make banking a feasible business in the first place.

Retail and business banking today is just one side of the financial sector. These institutions have morphed into another abstract financial business of speculative trading in just about anything from stocks and shares to currencies, commodities and on and on. The financial sector has become a massive online betting business, albeit one with a more sophisticated technology to calculate odds. However, its purpose is not to support actual economic activity. It is rarely an actual investor in this activity. The financial sector seeks only to profit as quickly as possible from its speculative investments.

Finding anyone other than republicans and small parties of the left to support the idea of nationalising banks is difficult, if not impossible, yet in a financial crisis it became the only course of action. It was the larger parties of the right who made it happen, literally at the stroke of a pen, though they kept no minutes of the meetings that led to this decision!

It is possible to find though people who believe that bank charges are exploitatively high, that borrowing costs could be lower, especially for mortgages, small loans and credit cards. There are those who believe that banks should be more willing to invest in business, be more flexible when it came to supporting new business start-ups, especially micro enterprises and social economy firms. You will find those who believe banks should be an economic actor promoting regional development through their branch network, and most importantly believe that all of this is possible without banks making a loss. These are the tasks Sinn Fein saw for a third force state bank so the national bank project when teased out is not such a crazy idea after all.

Sinn Fein and Privatisation

Irish republicans have opposed privatisation in all its forms, whether it is the sell off of state assets and infrastructure, the development of public private partnerships, private finance initiatives or the privatisation of state services.

The reasons for doing this are often presented as some undeveloped unproven love of big government and an all encompassing state complete with gulags and re-education centres for those not buying into the revolutionary ethos. As the years go by, especially since the embryonic days of the peace process and the resulting Good Friday Agreement, I have realised that the social political and financial establishment of Ireland had an enduring insecurity in their own position. At a primal level they fear the overthrow of the state by republicans. Sometimes, even now, I see signs that the establishment still has this fear. And so they often see republican opposition to privatisation as a proof of this desire to overthrow their institutions and replace them with some soviet like clone.

The actual reasons for opposing privatisation are rooted in practical analysis based on ensuring economic efficiencies, long term cost control and the experience of the specific failures of privatisation. Take the nearest example of Britain's privatisation programme where a minority were enriched, the working conditions of workers deteriorated as did the level of service to the public. Most importantly so did the level of safety, as shown by the collapse and renationalisation of Rail Track after a series of deadly accidents on its network. The new entity is now known as Network Rail.

The attacks on Sinn Féin and other parties on the left for not supporting the privatisation agenda are still ongoing, yet the reality is that there has been a collapse in the privatisation argument in Europe and beyond, privatisation has brought profits for some but not real economic progress. The experience of firms like Jarvis in the 1990s and noughties, who became a PFI giant only to be unable to deliver on time or with the promised quality and is now effectively a shell of the company it was, is not an isolated one, but an example of a serious deficiency in how the privatisation programme has been implemented.

What has been repeatedly proven is that governments do not necessarily have to build infrastructure, but they do need to carefully manage the process. For example in Ireland through the early noughties over €3 million was spent daily on road building, paid for by the Irish Government, but built by private sector construction, to a public need criterion, and now run after completion by the National Roads Authority who also coordinate the maintenance of the infrastructure.

Also proven is that the private sector is not good at running infrastructure. They often can only see things in the context of the next quarter and their share price which is exactly the wrong emphasis for developing long term investment projects that all of society can benefit from. They are though good at building it when someone else is paying. One of the problems of the presentation of the market economy is the constant assumption that economic assets should produce supernormal profits, when in fact in the long run, the free market economic theory suggests that this is not the case. The return on investment will decrease. Ideally, we want a situation where the infrastructure the government invests in yields revenue and that this revenue would cover over time all of the costs of building the infrastructure in the first place, and maybe even an economic return on the investment. In terms of transport, housing and communications infrastructure, this is a feasible proposal. However, it only works if the investment and the assets created are considered in the long term.

Public Spending

Sinn Fein has in the 26 Counties made budget submissions year after year, as well as election manifestos outlining its plans for spending and investment. For the first few post peace process years the media resolutely refused to even comment on Sinn Fein's economic plans, but as the party's electoral strength grew election after election the media focus on the party began to consider its economic policies, only to dismiss them as either utopian or too costly.

The irony of this was not lost on Irish republicans especially in the 2002 election where the then Fianna Fail/Progressive Democrat coalition increased public sector spending by 23% in the first six months of the year, and made serious promises in the run up to the June election to spend billions more if returned to government.

Predictably the post election spending proposals never materialised, particularly as the economy was undergoing a minor economic crisis of falling demand internationally as the global and domestic economy tried to adjust to the post 9-11 and foot and mouth crises.

That didn't stop some in the media attacking the naivety of the Sinn Féin policies that proposed substantial increases in the sums invested in state infrastructure and services, such as healthcare, education, public transport, information and communications technologies and most importantly indigenous business addressing particularly the deficiencies in innovation and research and development.

I mention these areas as in each case either the government has acted on the need to increase spending or other economic commentators have marked up the deficiencies in current government strategy, perhaps the best example is the lack of broadband availability around the island which has a history parallel to the privatisation of Telecom Eireann in 1999. In Ireland today we still cannot house all of our citizens, we still don't have enough schools, hospital beds, transport infrastructure.

In the run up to the 2007 election, Sinn Fein were again deemed to have the wrong economic policies as Fianna Fail, Fine Gael, Labour and the Progressive Democrats fell over each other to offer another round of tax cuts. Within a year the Great Recession had engulfed the economy, taxes rose repeatedly, the needed infrastructure projects long fingered again, but for the business and banking sectors, there were debt write offs and no tax hikes. This is the ever repeating core inequality in economies throughout the world. Workers and taxpayers have to take the strain when businesses fail, and they also do not profit fairly when business succeeds. They lose in both sides of this relationship.

Back to the Question of an Alternative to Firms

The Size Problem

Accepted economic theory tells us that the more numerous firms are the more competitive a market can be, leading to greater quantities of goods and services produced for lower prices. If this is true, surely it is in the interest of an economy to have as diverse a business community as possible and as aggressive and dynamic as it can be and not a market dominated by a number of small firms.

The problem with many markets today is that there are a handful of heavily concentrated firms dominating each sector, This is the case in key areas like retail, the drinks industry, tobacco, petrol, telecommunications, computing hardware, online media and the list could go on. The problems of oligopoly and cartelisation are dealt with in the chapters on markets and socialism. In this chapter I want to focus on the issues in a different way.

If we accept the proposal that firms are a good idea, a good vehicle for allowing society organise itself, can we hold onto the positive without suffering some of the negative impacts firms can have. One way of doing this is to address the size problem. Firms that become oligopolistic are bad for society when it leads to higher prices for consumers, supernormal profits and the exercise of an undue influence on government policy and decision making. There is also the problem of where oligopolies merge in the Business to Business (B2B) markets which allows firms have an even greater impact on what other firms do or don't do and disempowers the final customer, the citizen voter, even more.

Oligopoly and Size in Retail Markets

One pertinent example of this is the retail market, which in Ireland like many other markets is in a state of change where despite new entrants the overall market is still evolving into one of an ever dwindling number of firms controlling ever larger units of output.

At the micro level independent grocers and newsagents have been almost entirely subsumed into larger groups. It might seem on one hand that an increasing amount of outlets are emerging and this is true as new Spars' and Centra and other symbol group brands pop up on city, town and suburban streets, but there is a striking uniformity about them especially in terms of the goods they are selling. In the previous decade it was the Starbucks invasion into the coffee shop sector.

All of the firms in the market promise low prices and this seems like a good idea. However, can low prices in retail stores be bad for consumers, for workers, for low income and poor households, for the economy and for the environment? According to a growing number of unions, environmentalists, charities and small businesses the answer is yes. In March 2006, the Office of Fair Trading (OFT) in Britain began a full scale inquiry into the competitive practices of the big four retailers, while in Ireland new changes to competition law is putting that retail sector on the same footing as the now suspect British market. It reported in 2009 and one of the key findings was concern with the power retail giants had in the purchasing markets leading to a phenomenon called 'below cost selling' (Competition and Markets Authority, 2009/2016).

As Britain was investigating sharp business practices among its retailers, it was opposite day in Ireland. An amendment to the Competition Act signed into law in March 2006 removed a 19-year Dublin Government ban on below cost selling. The major retailers could run a loss, lowering prices below competitive levels, driving smaller shops who can't absorb these types of losses out of business.

In Britain below cost selling had been legal. In 2006, there were still 39,000 independent retailers, but their numbers were falling all the time. John Fingleton then OFT chairperson estimated in 2006 that 5% of small shopkeepers had gone out of business in the past five years. In 2016, a PWC report found that The PwC and Local Data Company report found that "2,656 outlets closed on Britain's high streets in the first half of the year. This was a rate of 15 stores a day" (Ruddick, 2016).

What's Wrong with Below Cost Selling?

In 2006 the OFT in Britain has a range of concerns about competitive practices in the British retail market. They include:

1. *Buying power.* The big four used their huge purchasing power to secure lower prices from their suppliers who recoup these losses by selling to the small grocers at a higher price, this is cutting the margins of the independent corner shops who are not part of a big retail group. The small shops are carrying the costs of the big retailers.
2. *Below cost selling.* The OFT had identified 2708 products being sold below cost, this accounts for 3% of total sales, while 7% of drink sales are being sold below cost.
3. *Predatory pricing.* In Britain the big four retailers were accused of aggressively cutting prices to drive local independent supermarkets out of business leaving the neighbouring big supermarket with a local monopoly on food sales in particular areas.
4. *Land hoarding.* The big retailers have built up substantial land banks in Britain to prevent competitors from building supermarkets. The OFT identified 468 such sites, and 75 sites which had been resold with binding clauses prevent the new owners from building retail food units.

More than a decade later Tesco has been challenged by new market entrants in Ireland and Britain, principally the retailers Aldi and Lidl, and changing consumer practices of smaller but more frequent shopping trips has eroded the dominance of the larger retailers' super stores, but it has not changed oligopolistic practices in the sector. Across the sector the staff are low paid, many part time. Suppliers are under constant pressure to lower margins and so one group of companies is still in a position to exploit others, which is very far away from any conception of what a free market should look like.

Just as there are interdependencies for the individual in their market decisions the same can be said of businesses. They too have a chain of links with suppliers onto to the final consumer. It is interesting that we hear so little about suppliers to these businesses when it comes to trumpeting the successes of market based economic systems. Is it because there is market failure here too? Part of the theology of the business community has been the protection of a flawed system that protects the larger companies at the expense of the smaller ones.

Co-Operatives and Alliances

A question not asked often enough is, 'what is the firm for?' And what role do we want it to play in society. At a basic level the firm is an efficient method of organising and co-ordinating resources to achieve a particular outcome, usually the production of goods and services. But why are so many of our firms based on either a key 'owner' or a group of profit and dividend driven shareholders and not co-operative based. In Ireland the growth of co-operative businesses was a key method for the agriculture sector to grow in the nineteenth and twentieth century, yet despite this success the firms, one after another, morphed into international shareholder driven concerns as the companies sought to continue to grow outside of their original economic mission.

The collaborative nature of computer and digital communication products would seem to suggest that a co-operative structure would be the most effective mechanism to harness and share the collective intellectual property of the workers in these labour intensive businesses. However, this is wholly not the case. These companies pander to a co-operative work ethos but are usually driven by a key 'visionary' who ends up the billionaire owner despite depending on so many others to complete the vision in a product or service. The Irish Cooperative Society (ICOS) has over 150,000 members, yet the core of its business is still related to agriculture and related economic activity in the rural economy (ICOS, 2016, 2017). Why is it that the types of firm we have in our economy have so uniform a structure? Why don't we have more diversity in the nature of the firm?

Innovation and Responding to Social Change

Also important is the fact that society understands that and trusts the firm to be able to perform certain tasks. It has also developed a view that the firm can achieve and complete these tasks better than any other method. It distrusts alternatives to this status quo. Firms are an accepted part of societal organisation and are a reflection often of the values and needs of a society at any given time. Right now, there is the welcome sight in Ireland of a range of new food producers and retailers, responding to a societal demand for better quality food and it is clear that individuals have responded to this by forming companies to supply these products and services.

There is an ongoing churn in the structure and activity of firms as society changes. For example when I was a child, we had bread and milk deliveries to the door as well as an insurance man who came around once a fortnight collecting policy premiums. Having such a delivery service today seems inconceivable but the array of fast food and other deliveries was considered madness then.

As the demand for the bread and milkman disappeared so did the jobs, some took redundancy, early retirement, some ended up unemployed. Some started new businesses, many of that generation did not. The reasons for this were possibly because of the massive structural change and decline in market based economies in Europe at the time, also the lack of credit to fund a new venture and maybe also because of the lack of business and entrepreneurial skills. The structural unemployment they were enduring was prevalent at the time and meant that it was hard to find new jobs.

The Value of Firms

So as a control and co-ordination mechanism the ebb and flow, the growth and decline of firms plays a role in steering society through periods of economic change. However, it seems that in order to accommodate this positive element we have to put up with an awful lot of other nonsense from firms and the business community. The ability of firms individually to anticipate economic change has been misconstrued, falsified in a belief that the business community is some form of oracle able to predict economic change. In return, we are subject to its every whim. The fact is that like any institution who becomes focused on its future survival, on preserving its longevity at all costs, firms are often in danger in losing touch with their very reason for existence.

It seems that the self-appointed business community in Ireland, Britain and beyond suffer deeply from this delusion about their role in society and their importance

References

Bhattarai, A. (2017). FTC Clears Amazon.com Purchase of Whole Foods. *Washington Post*, 23 August.

Braverman, H. (1974/1998). *Labor and Monopoly Capital: The Degradation of Work in the Twentieth Century*. Monthly Review Press.

Central Statistics Office. (2016). *Business Demography.* Retrieved September 4, 2017, from http://www.cso.ie/en/releasesandpublications/er/bd/businessdemography2014/
Competition and Markets Authority. (2009/2016). *Groceries (Supply Chain Practices) Market Investigation Order.* Retrieved September 8, 2017, from https://www.gov.uk/government/publications/groceries-supply-chain-practices-market-investigation-order
European Commission. (2019). *Packaging and Packaging Waste.* Retrieved April 20, 2019, from http://ec.europa.eu/environment/waste/packaging/index_en.htm
Fairtrade International. (2017). *History of Fairtrade.* Retrieved August 30, 2017, from https://www.fairtrade.net/about-fairtrade/history-of-fairtrade.html
Farrell, M. (1987). *Northern Ireland: The Orange State* (2nd ed.). Pluto Press.
Fiske, J. (1987). *Television Culture: Studies in Communication.* Methuen Publishing.
Gramsci, A. (1971). The Concept of Ideology. In *Selections From the Prison Notebooks of Antonio Gramsci.* International Publishers.
ICOS. (2016). *Our Members.* Retrieved August 23, 2016, from http://www.icos.ie/members/introduction-2/
ICOS. (2017). *Who we are.* Retrieved September 9, 2017, from http://icos.ie/about/who-we-are/
Kelly, L. (2018). Greencore Operating Profit Grows 1.7pc as Company Focuses on Core UK Market. *Irish Independent*, 4 December. Retrieved April 23, 2019, from https://www.independent.ie/business/irish/greencore-operating-profit-grows-1-7pc-as-company-focuses-on-core-uk-market-37593428.html
Merriam Webster. (2019). *Greenwashing.* Retrieved April 20, 2019, from https://www.merriam-webster.com/dictionary/greenwashing#h1
Mondelez. (2017). *2017 Fact sheet.* Retrieved August 30, 2017, from http://www.mondelezinternational.com/~/media/MondelezCorporate/Uploads/downloads/mondelez_intl_fact_sheet.pdf
NI Business Info. (2017). Northern Ireland Companies Directory. Retrieved September 4, 2017, from https://www.nibusinessinfo.co.uk/content/northern-ireland-companies-directory
Philo, G., Beharrell, P., & Hewitt, J. (1982). Reasonable Men and Responsible Citizens. In *Really Bad News.* The Glasgow Media Group. Littlehampton Book Services Ltd.
Repak. (2019). *Company Overview.* Retrieved April 20, 2019, from https://repak.ie/about-us/company-overview/
Ruddick, G. (2016). Britain's High Streets Under Strain as 15 Shops Close Every Day. *Guardian*, 25 October.
Solidarity. (2017). *Anti Austerity Alliance Budget Statement 2017.* Retrieved September 7, 2017, from http://antiausterityalliance.ie/2016/10/aaa-budget-statement-from-corporate-tax-haven-to-socialistgreen-economy/
Welch, J. (2013). Jack Welch: 'Rank-and-Yank'? That's Not How It's Done. *Wall Street Journal*, 14 November.

CHAPTER 8

Conclusions

The society we live in today is far from any ideal envisaged by republicans whether they be United Irishmen, Young Irelanders, Fenians, Volunteers or today's Sinn Fein activists. Indeed for anyone on the left, socialist, environmentalist, anarchist or other this is a place far from any utopia any of us would have planned to be in.

For those who claim to favour free markets or a market lead approach this society is too a failure. We have not created a free market system. What has been created is an increasingly dense chain of oligopolies and cartels spreading internationally, perhaps not at the pace envisaged by Marx and Engels more than 150 years ago when they wrote the Communist Manifesto, but progressing none the less.

For those who believe in the power of social democracy and the potential of good government it is again a clearly far from ideal world we find ourselves in. For the individual citizen who sees themselves as a sovereign person removed and at odds from the turbulent demands of modern society they too are in a difficult place.

The perceived freedom of many individuals is at best elusive, dependent on their ability to amass income and wealth as nothing else seems to be quite as potent in charting a course through modern society. Many people in contemporary society are often victims of simply standing still in a social and economic environment that is rapidly changing. They have work skills that are no longer marketable, or they live on below average incomes dependent on the state to deliver adequate services such as housing,

R. Smyth, *The Invisible Republic*,
https://doi.org/10.1007/978-3-030-86734-8_8

transport or healthcare. These people can end up ill and virtually imprisoned in old age because of government policy failures to supply basic social services. Their corner shop closes, a new mall opens, but it is accessible only by private transport. They have houses built before modern insulation standards and cannot afford current high fuel costs. We could go on with more examples, but the core point is that repeatedly we can demonstrate that the individual is not free in society today.

Are we not free in the consumption choices we make? The framework of income and consumption that is often given most prominence in the media and political discourse is one based not just on the short term, but on the income and consumption patterns of young healthy high-income workers. These middle class young professionals working and living in Irish society today are often enjoying standards of living that are unsustainable in the long term. They will not be living this way in their retirement years, or if illness or some unforeseen crisis or shock strikes the economy. In fact focusing on the young double income household consumer as the norm is seriously deceiving. It is not representative of aggregate societal spending. It elevates that sector's consumption as a model for the rest of society to follow. It promotes often reckless and usually unplanned spending to a prominence it does not merit.

When the Great Recession of 2008 began, unemployment began to rise, and debt levels of tens of thousands of households became unmanageable, there was a noticeable shift in the consumption patterns of society. Growing vegetables, home cooking, and book sharing became fashionable. The years of reckless and spurious consumption now forgotten as people brought their own water bottles and lunches to work, if they still had a job. The point here is that our consumption patterns are often driven by external economic factors. Add in the power of mass advertising and the resulting 'cultural norm' and you have a societal consumption pattern where the individual person making a spending decision has the least impact. What if we could move to a society where the individual had better quality information about their choices? What if the individual had more control over their choices. What impact would this have?

Economic Coercion

The society we live in often creates an illusion that it is through consumption of goods and services that an individual exercises freedom or demonstrates how good a society is or can be. Other views on this world illusion is best explained by writers like Eric Fromm in his book *The Sane Society* (Fromm, 1955) or the contribution of Robert Putnam (2001) in *Bowling Alone*. But the prevailing view is one where the ability to accumulate resources becomes paramount in determining or measuring success. For example a common attitude in debt relief and global poverty campaigns seems to be that the world's poor are being deprived participation in a society like ours. The gap in wealth between the underdeveloped world and the richest nations is one that must be bridged so these underprivileged people have to opportunity to live and consume like us. It is an incredible arrogance when you think about it.

The reality of the modern consumer driven world is that the ordinary person is in a place where their choices are continually constrained and channelled. The individual today is expected to not just uphold the laws of society and adhere to social norms, they are also being asked to participate in a very particular way.

You work, you earn an income, you spend that income and that is the exercise of your freedom. If you want to change that exercise of choice there are limits in the options open to you. You can only recalibrate your income-consumption choices. Do you return to study, or take another job, move to another region, start a new business or sell an existing one. The message is simple—If you want to make wider choices, or impact on the wider environment, get a higher income.

Surely the exercise of freedom should be more than a relationship between income and consumption choice? Well how more complex can that exercise of rights be? For republicans freedom is not just about a demarcation of rights, it also about the effective guarantee and active promoting of them. It should also be about what society does to not just stop the erosion or breaching of rights, but more importantly should be about the promotion of a good society and vitally ensuring the absence of coercion.

From a republican point of view the absence of coercion is not being delivered in the contemporary economic environment. There is in fact coercion everywhere. Examples include the fact that most often the individual worker or purchaser is a price taker where market structures are generating supernormal profits at your expense, where the actual choice of goods is limited and constrained, where the costs of dealing with the negative effects of economic activity are not being shared equally. One glaring externality issue is the failure to count the costs of dealing with the negative environmental costs of manufacturing, production and ongoing consumption of goods and services like petrol and electricity. When governments eventually act it only levies more taxes on the end users who are the least able to act on the environmental problems. The coercion of the end user to carry the cost of other more powerful groups' mistakes is prevalent in the modern economy.

Then there is the fact that in the 26 Counties, relatively high day to day living costs such as expensive property prices, child care and health insurance mean that only one out of every three workers has an occupational pension and the majority of workers will be dependent on the state pension in future years (Reddan, 2017).

Other examples of this include the failure to clean up pollution or the levying of environmental taxes that don't lead to any real behaviour modification. Coercion happens also in the issue of access, such as who has not just the ability but also the means to start a business venture or expand the one they are in.

Illusion of Consumption Freedom

It is interesting to note that in the development of economic structures considerable wealth and power is surrendered to those who control conduits of economic activity. Banks, especially those with a retail arm have a major say in the flow of currency, the money we use day to day and on what your credit rating will be, the limit on your credit card etc. The retail sector can seriously impact on what you eat and wear, the telecommunications and ICT firms influence your entertainment choices, such as how you spend your leisure or how your child plays, all of these things are being impacted on.

Even the simple act of going to the cinema, it is a combination of not just having the resources to attend but making your choice under a barrage of advertisements on television and at the cinema itself not to mention the billboard ads and endless media coverage in reviews and interviews.

A personal example of these forces at work was during the launch period of Jurassic Park in 1993, a hugely lavish film with high box office takings. Because of work commitments I couldn't attend during the peak of advertising and hype about the film. When I did have more time and the film was still in the cinema, the advertising cycle over, I found that my appetite for dinosaurs didn't need to be sated. So if I had gone what factors were driving my choice? I have since survived all the sequels and reboots!

This raises a question as to how my choices are actually made. My fear is that the consumption-income related choices of the modern individual is a complex maze that effectively imprisons the person in a life, or way of life that is not of their own choosing, where it is increasingly difficult to pick out their own essence, their own unique personality. They are assailed on one side by advertising, the fashions and trends of society all mixing with the ever changing cultural and social norms as well as the concept of a changing standard of living and the complicated spending patterns associated with that.

Take for example the expanding need of humans for wardrobe space. My grandparents' clothes fitted comfortably in a two door wardrobe and a chest of drawers. Yet we all, male and female, with so much more wardrobe and storage space today, will declare with ease that we have nothing to wear! Yet when we buy something, it is often a temporary salving of perceived need that over time needs to be satiated repeatedly. We are no better off, but be sure a string of others are remarkably more profitable as a result, beginning with the shop we spent our money, the credit card company we ran the debt up with and so on. But we can also be sure that the assistant in the shop, the farmer who grew the cotton, the dyers and machinists who put together the garment that for the moment filled the gap in our conscious need for happiness are no better off than us the buyer, so why did we buy it and why do we feel the need to buy and buy again. The trend towards the privatised nature of consumption has been a feature recognised by many writers and commentators particularly in the last century by Raymond Williams amongst others.

Another example of this individualistic consumption is the rate of increasing car ownership and the range of complimentary goods on offer. The amount of resources put into automobile manufacture and ancillary goods is an example of the privatised consumption of leisure and possibly wrong goods being produced.

The car envelops the driver and his or her passengers upon whom the right to travel alongside has been conferred. The driver is in the moment king of this travelling castle, totally in charge. The driver makes the music choices, sets air conditioning, deciding where to go, by what route and how fast. It sounds great, a feat of liberation except that most of us use a car to travel to and from work, the shops or schools etc. There is no doubt that cars are handy for those who have them but when confronted by the gridlock which is the physical manifestation of these individual choices there clearly is a problem. We are sitting, usually relatively placidly in vehicles designed for open and empty roads, but we are only inching to our chosen destinations.

If efficient and comfortable travel is the objective, well surely it would be in all our interests to pool the car resources in some sharing exercise to ease the gridlock. An even more challenging scenario would be to wonder what if we pooled the investments that would have been made in cars into an alternative transport system. The aims and objectives of this alternative were the same as private car, which seems to be travel on demand, could it be possible?

Private car use is in urban life an example of the consumer driven cosseting the modern person lives through. We are always at one remove, one step from each other even though in urban life humans live so close to each other. We are so much a part of each other's lives, yet we like defined gaps, borders between our gardens, partitions between our desks and most of all a lot of metal and glass dividing us up in our daily commuting misery. This false individualism is disempowering people and is coercive in that there are few alternatives to living this way.

Wrong Career Choice

We are surrounded by goods that maybe should not exist or in a better world would not exist, and we are equally surrounded by other important choices that should not exist in terms of the occupations and career choices we make.

Take the example of a young drug dealer, emerging as part of a milieu where third level education is not seen as the norm, and in a growing economy it may be possible to get employment easily albeit low paying, but where conspicuous and expensive consumption in the wider society is the standard, his earnings will never meet ambition.

He, as it usually is a he, starts doing errands, getting involved in the logistics of drug supply, building up to small deals, maybe through his own drug consumption and a growing relationship with his drug vendor. He then decides to build enough money to buy a larger stake and sell more of the product, this is not that surprising a choice as many other businesses deemed legitimate operate on the same basis.

Along the way his increased income is spent on clothes, entertainment, vehicles, weapons and a loud life of thumping music, a flash Lexus and ostentatious spending, all tinged with an edge of violence, casual drug taking, the pressure of work and a dubious but demanding customer network, dependent on an unstable product supply chain. The drug entrepreneur usually over extends himself as his business grows, or ends up in dispute with the regulatory authorities and is incarcerated, or falls out with his competitors in disputes that can be about logistical business issues but just as likely to be about girlfriends, the idea of "respect" etc and end up dead. To the overeducated middle class this seems like a fairly high risk choice, yet in the midst of the lower cost and local authority housing areas of Ireland it seems like an attractive set of lifestyle choices, despite the possible short life span and terminal endings.

But are the middle classes so different in the choices they take. It was the same when I attended college and even today, when I meet third level students, I was and still am struck by the amount of people who had invested time, money and immense amounts of emotional energy in academic pursuits in which truthfully they were not interested in. It was the status, power and financial gain possible from the positions on offer after graduation that attracted them.

So I went to college with and now occasionally meet friends who were miserable when studying and are miserable in the workplace, making misery also up to a point for the clients and co-workers they interact with.

Their only solace is the money, the relatively high financial remuneration they receive, which allows them divert their angst into consumer purchases, more clothes, better drugs, legal and not so, nicer cars and more luxurious holiday homes. So we are back into the cycle of consumption as the best determinant in how we exercise freedom.

Wrong Economy

Hayek deals with the concept of the wrong economy, producing the wrong goods in his writings on the "catallaxy of competition". Marx introduced the idea of alienation while Weber gave us the concepts of status and power, and taken together these diverse thinkers echo our opening point that for many on the right or left there is something wrong with our current societal structures.

Enlightenment thinkers like Hobbes and Rousseau forged the idea of a human leaving a state of nature to form a social contract that would constitute their basis for entering and participating in society. It is clear today that some semblance of this social contract still exists. The state in the European Union makes a series of guarantees in term of protections and services it provides and it in turn expects payment in the form of tax revenue and general compliance with the laws it creates. But, I still contend there is a substantial imbalance between a human's desire for freedom and an actual ability to exercise it.

What is clear is that we don't know at any level what a free economy would look like, how people would live, what they would invest their time and abilities in. We don't really know what goods and services humans would choose to produce, what we really need or want to consume. This is a crucial point and too often discussions about economic issues are clouded by the intense loudness of the short term economic problems that beset society rather than taking a long term strategic view also that could lead to avoiding the short term problems arising in the first place.

Solution of Good Government

So what are the solutions, what options are open to us? Well one simple answer is in creating good government. Across the world the absence of good government is frightening. It is more common to find the striking proof of bad government where decision making is driven by anti democratic vested interests or short term electoral cycle decision making. The debacle of the US Trump administration and the British Conservatives Brexit fiasco are just two of the latest instalments in the giant encyclopaedia of bad government.

Other examples of bad government include tax cuts to aid the wealthy that have no real underlying justification except the appeasing of an economic elite, deregulation that leads to chaos like the financial sector driven Great Recession in 2008, or the lack of effective regulation, where Britain's leaking, accident prone and overly costly nuclear industry would be a relevant example of many others you could choose.

A good government that was really committed to a market economy would make sure that the markets were accessible and efficient and not dominated by oligopolies, cartels or vested interests. They would seek to renew the social contract, getting an empowered public debate that might yield agreement on how to justly redistribute resources across society, that could efficiently and effectively invest in the infrastructure and services needed to deliver that fair society.

Another solution is to start to actively question why we do things. Too often in social, political and indeed economic life we take a lot of features, structures and institutions in life as a given. We accept societal relationships, supposed economic axioms, social theorems as true without ever questioning them. One reason for this already outlined is that those who do question are often deemed deviant, heretics or just spoil sports who need to be ignored by the soft normal well rounded, comfortable middle.

Examples of things we should question in terms of economic structures from a republican point of view include asking why do we tax, which taxes are useful, which are not. How, if we think markets have a role to play in society, do we keep them competitive? How do we stop oligopoly? Are there some businesses that need not exist in a better world like advertising or the arms industry and that is only beginning with the As?

The Markets Made Me Do It

These questions are rarely if ever asked. Governments in parliamentary democracies are caught in a strange environment pincered between a hectoring opposition and a pseudo questioning media, often with all three groups having the most malformed grasp of public opinion and interests. All three are locked into supposed roles they believe they must play, such as pretending to be deadly protagonists with an impartial media referee being just the starting point of these ill formed understandings. In Ireland media broadcast regulations create a twisted atmosphere as this 'performative toughness' dominates political broadcast journalism (Leonhardt, 2019).

What has happened in the twentieth and twenty-first centuries is that governments have been tricked, or maybe even coerced, into believing that markets and the businesses that constitute them can efficiently perform important administrative functions. In many states and regions, laws have been changed to reflect this belief. There has to be competition, there has to be supposedly competitive market solutions to how goods and services are supplied, and it is illegal not to have these. At first glance, markets seem to offer a lot of solutions to government, plus the great get out of jail clause of 'the markets made me do it'. This personalisation of market systems promotes the idea of markets being somehow an organic living entity. This viewpoint was popularised in a quote attributed to Margaret Thatcher where she said, "You can't buck the market". It became the war cry of the early Thatcher years. Is this true? Can we not shape and direct markets? One way of thinking about this question is to ask how competitive many of these newly legislated market sectors are. In example after example you will find from power generation, to communications and even refuse collection, the so-called 'free market' legislation has actually created a powerful legal oligopoly. In this more likely scenario, the true value of a free market has been lost to excess profits of the suppliers of goods and services.

You could write a book on the issues of electoral systems and party structures, and how they impact on the form of a government a state has. A good start on the flaws of the party system is found in Madison's 1787 Federalist Paper No 10. The warnings here about the power of frivolous factions are one of the many warning bells about the healthy functioning of democracies today, but more on that later.

However, the focus here needs to be narrowed onto the question of good government and policy making in relation to economic and fiscal policies in particular. There is in any time period competing definitions or theories on what is or isn't good for the economy. Over my own lifetime I have witnessed the decline in Keynesian demand led macro policies, the ascendancy of Monetarism and Austrianism leading to the embedding of Neo-Liberal thinking in both domestic and international economic structures. And as I mentioned above this economic ideology has also become the basis of a significant amount of public law.

I also experienced the periods of economic growth of the late 1960s and early 1970s followed by the depression and desolation of the 1980s and particularly the trauma of a whole generation being gripped by the malaise of stagflation and the wholesale dismantling of huge sectors of the economy. There was in my mind at the time an astonishing lack of understanding of how the economy worked, how it fitted together, especially in the mainstream media where the successful entrepreneurs, economists and investment bankers of the day were worshipped as some form of voodoo masters, modern alchemists.

At the same time, in the 1980s, there was the growing individualism characteristic of the time. Michael Douglas in the film Wall Street parodied this playing the lines of Gordon Gekko's "Greed is good", "Lunch is for wimps" and other euphemisms of the time. Then as the economy internationally returned to growth, accommodating the shake out of deflation, the restructuring of activities as some manufacturing and other processes moved out of developed economies, while the new computer and information sectors grew in strength the language of economics began to change again.

Though there has not been a return to the Keynesian nationalisation programmes of the pre and especially post WWII era, and though there is still an ongoing dismantling of state resources and services through privatisation, this generation of economic policy initiatives is not full of the fervour of earlier periods.

The Neo-Liberal philosophy is still the dominant economic rationale. Now that it is enshrined in government legislation and a range of legal constraints it is being articulated in a way that often denies its existence as if its proponents are only too willing to bask in its benefits without promoting the brand identity. In practice, this has meant growing wage inequality, weaker social and employment protections and tougher more demanding working conditions. The new super enterprises of this generation, such as Google, Apple, Facebook, Microsoft and Amazon characterise the reality of aspects of the widening inequalities of the contemporary labour market. Their workers can range from high paid associates to minimum wage precarious shop floor employees under constant surveillance to meet targets.

Democracy Has Been Kidnapped

We have repeatedly returned to the question of governments and the electoral systems that create them, and never in a good way. It was Thomas Friedman, a writer, social commentator and New York Times opinion writer who in July 2006 coined the term "The Kidnapping of Democracy". It was the title of an article he wrote disparaging the electoral successes of what he describes as "Islamist parties" in Iran, Lebanon and Palestine. His criticism was that these parties were using their achievements in the electoral contests as a means to take control of the political process and then undermine the institutions to which they were elected in the first place by dragging their states into a regional conflict. I wonder what he thinks now over a decade later of the Trump election or the British Brexit fiasco?

While I don't agree with his analysis that Hamas, Hezbollah and Iranian conservative parties had kidnapped the democratic process, I did find the general idea compelling. Democracy has been kidnapped but not by Hamas, there are a lot more powerful electoral highwaymen out there. In fact when you think about an electoral system that cannot accommodate different and extreme points of view within a given society then what sort of electoral system is it anyway?

But back to the kidnappers. Money, middle class, middle aged white men seem to me to be the kidnappers of democracy aided by PR, marketing and advertising campaigns that sacrifice truth and debate to a slogan.

Now in the aftermath of the 2016 US presidential election it seems that online media has also become a kidnapper.

I often wonder who was it that initiated the notion that an electoral system or an electorate had to be ruled by a large but soft middle or centre faction who don't really have a firm or fixed view about anything. Anthony Downs's 1959 book *An Economic Theory of Democracy* must shoulder a lot of the blame as it lead to a widespread promotion of Duncan Black's 1948 work on rationales for group decision making. The success of Downs's work lead to the development of a technocratic approach to the electoral process, and this suited the mass political parties without firm ideological positions that were emerging in many European electoral systems at the time, and was a major factor in the modern dominance of a supposed political centre in political life.

The common currency across these parties is solely a desire to have and retain power, which means finding a way to exercise influence and control resources that favours your interests subject to the sole constraint of how the voting public think you are doing in representing their needs. It is here that the seeds of declining voter participation in political parties and actual voting are sown. Parties of the middle succeed on the failure of marginal, political isolated voters to turn up at the polling booth. It suits them that some voters feel powerless and disenfranchised. Maybe you wonder why you hear repeatedly people say that political parties, candidates are all the same. It is often sadly too true.

Maybe now we are on the trail of the real kidnappers of democracy. The idea of commanding the middle ground electorally leads to the politics of acceptable parties, of acceptable political debates and contests. It is leads to the fallacy of the acceptable 'party of government' argument. Voters cannot actually vote by belief or ideology. They have to vote in favour a 'party of government'. Think of the political contortions the Labour Party in Britain had to subject itself in the 1980s and 1990s to get re-elected. It wasn't just some name and bland rule changes, the process involved a hunting down, a flushing out of any hint of radical ideas or principles. Then duly cleansed and sanitised and with a media seal of approval New Labour were ready for power and the middle ground fell to them.

Next it was the Conservatives who were subjected to similar contortions, cleansing and redesigning of their political branding. During this period the important questions of Conservative ideology remained unanswered. Issues such as Britain's role in Europe, its participation in the Euro, the Conservatives understanding of the effects of mass privatisation programme of the 1980s on the economy and British society were all left not dealt with. Because the middle ground cannot effectively debate or decide on these issues.

Instead of dealing with these questions the Conservatives selected a new leader in David Cameron, a new logo and a new image as it attempted to paper over the ideological chasms in the party offering the cure all of being in government as the solution. Cameron could win elections but he lost the ideological debate and now Britain stands on the verge of an ill thought out Brexit.

While it may be true that in any given era the electorate likes to map out and establish a middle ground as a method of navigating through any particular time period it is also true that such a policy suits our posse of kidnappers. Democracy has been stolen not by radicals or fringe political groups, but by money, marketing methods, elements of the news media and most chillingly by powerful factions of vested interests, who could be described as the real extremists in that it is their needs, their interests that come first. There is a long queue of kidnappers before we get round to the so called political extremists in this story. So if you want to destabilise the electoral system, get in line, your turn won't be coming soon.

It is no accident that money is central to the kidnapping process. This book began with a discussion about money and rights and here we are again talking about money. You cannot successfully contest an election without lots of it. It never ceases to amaze me the perception created in the media and fuelled by other political parties that Sinn Fein are the richest party in Ireland, that the party coffers are awash with Yankee dollars, nestling in the bunkers vacated by the IRA guns. Worse still Sinn Fein are cheating in electoral campaigns by being able to "unleash" their army of activists, to knock on doors, push leaflets into mail boxes and stick up posters, while the larger parties have to often pay people to do these tasks.

The bottom line behind all of this is an argument that Sinn Fein bought the electoral successes achieved by the party, it wasn't won on the logic of their argument or compelling policies, it was won because Sinn Fein had more money or more feet on the street. The money spent by the larger parties who have substantially bigger budgets than Sinn Fein is somehow "purer" money, the real truth is that Sinn Fein's community activism, their activists based membership is an unacceptable method of campaigning because it bypasses money and the establishment media who relish their gatekeeper roles.

Even in Ireland and Britain where political advertising in the broadcast media is not allowed substantial sums are still needed for the leaflets to every door, the posters on lamp posts, the banners, the hiring of cars, buses, function rooms. If you have serious money you can buy the billboards, the newspaper, magazine advertisements and the now ubiquitous social media posts.

The 2012 Obama Romney presidential election campaign involved the two candidates spending $1,997.7 billion on their contest (*New York Times*, 2012). According to Bloomberg the candidates' spend in 2016 fell to $1.5 billion, with Clinton's spending doubling that of Trump (Bloomberg, 2016). Trump's spend was helped by having his own private jet, a prebuilt media brand over 30 years in the making, and a massive news media interest in his campaign. None of these resources are available to ordinary citizens attempting to enter the electoral world. Democracy has a lot of kidnappers!

It seems that the modern electoral process cannot work without money and media coverage. Trump excepted the more successful you are at fundraising the better is your electoral performance. Political party and electoral candidate funding is hampering the democratic process.

That modern electoral contests can seemingly not exist without massive financial spend is problematic enough, but when you add in the use of marketing methodologies and advertising techniques into the electoral process the problem becomes critical. Political marketing means you can buy in the expertise to hone your political message and sell yourself or your party.

The news media are also a key enabler in the kidnapping process. They increasingly see politics as a cheap form of entertainment, a reality TV show, where the contestants carry most of the costs. The media's role is merely to report, comment and adjudicate on the race. They don't have to write a script. There is an audience, the actors and sets come free. The key point here is that we can't expect democracy to save us, the political market is open to the same sources of exploitation and abuse as the market system. If we can't have a functioning market system why would you expect to have a working political one?

Final Themes

If there were core themes to be taken from this book they would be these.

Question Everything

1. Question everything, don't take my word for it, and question all rationale, all so called truths beginning with the ones in this text. Always be a heretic, no matter who you are dealing with. There can be no better method of learning than the words why? Too often people, parties and institutions err towards supposedly sacred, theological justifications for actions. The world I live is filled with supposed relationships, and structures that in fact do not exist. This puts a responsibility on you, the reader, to find out the answer to your questions, to investigate, read and think.

Make Government work

2. Let governments do the tasks for which we elected them. Governments need to be let govern, they need to be answerable to their voters, to the citizens, but not slaves to the electoral cycle or the mantra of business. Unfortunately, in the world today business has found a niche between enabling wholesale profiteering and exploitation of government funding and policies, occasionally throwing small crumbs to the electorate. Voters have largely bought into this reality that business comes first and that this benefits the wider society. How could they not, after all this is the status quo endorsed by the news media and an array of vested interests, including politicians themselves, and of course the shrill never ending drum beat of the business community's needs and demands.

Recognise Conflicting Tendencies

3. There are I believe four tendencies that characterise how we as humans live and interact with each other, they are:
   (i). The desire to be free and find expression for that freedom in the economic choices we make.
   (ii). A sense of sympathy, fair play and justice that leads to the concepts of fraternity and equality that underpin the republican vision. It means that, yes freedom is rooted in the individual and

their inalienable rights, but the citizen's experience of that freedom can be enhanced and amplified by playing a role in ensuring the collective wellbeing of the society they constitute or the communities they live and work in.

(iii). Then opposing this is the tendency of those who develop economic or political advantage and seek to have this institutionalised and perpetuated in society. It seems that there are those for whom wealth as we understand it today is an end in itself. It is the core failing of market capitalism that it creates economic structures that yield control of the conduits of economic activity to a few private individuals or groups. It ignores the fact that these conduits and structures only exist because of the collective aggregate endeavours of a mass of individuals.

This is a fundamental point, the economy is the sum of its parts and nobody except an elected parliament or assembly should seek control over these processes and relationships.

In the twenty-first century, these conduits of economic power are institutions such as the banking system, the control of important infrastructure and the concentration of ownership of property especially in retail and commercial settings. It is the oligopolies and cartels in these sectors that most often dominate our consumer choices. Added to this list is the growing power of tech companies. This includes firstly those who create the equipment or operating systems like Apple, Google, Huawei, Microsoft or Samsung. Then there are the firms who control and own platforms like Facebook, Twitter and Snap.

(iv). This third tendency leads to the fourth where those who control economic society begin to seek political endorsement for their economic hegemony. They then most dangerously propose a philosophical ideological rationale for the inequalities they create and perpetuate, which in many cases transcends into a theology of power and control.

How these tendencies have interacted, how the tensions between them have played out is crucial to our understanding of economic structures and societal behaviour.

For example, the current raft of market regulations and corresponding regulatory institutions creates an illusion that oligopoly and cartelisation is containable and controllable. Yet a quick look around the economy shows that this is just not so. Take as one example the struggle to regulate the emerging tech and social media based oligopolies. If we are struggling to control these new businesses what conclusions can we draw about the existing range of regulations in other industries and economic sectors.

The Problem of Complexity

Terms that are used too often in this text are where I repeatedly write about economic activity as a web, or a complex maze of individual choices. I use these terms because there is often a contradiction at the centre of political and media economic comment. There are economists, journalists and politicians who tell republicans that our policies are too simplistic, we don't understand the complexity of the economy, yet the very same people will turn this logic on its head when it comes to the own hobby horses and agendas.

It is a simple argument that begins with claiming 'my positive agenda is complex, your agenda is simplistic' and so on. However, the real complexity is in how the millions of individual choices made daily by people have all sorts of short and longer term consequences.

Also crucially important is the context in which they are happening. For example centuries of focusing on wealth and resource accumulation must I believe have an impact on the resource choices of individuals and households. At one level there is the evidence of ever greater levels of accumulation being achieved and the generally accepted idea that this is a good thing, despite the obvious environmental problems such ongoing accumulation is creating.

Then there is the question of the aggregate power of these individual choices and actions and how this aggregate affects the individual, the household or the community they live in. We can see the aggregate at work in terms of how people and societies live, but there is still incomplete understanding of how the flows of individual choices build into a macroeconomic outcome.

Finally, there are those who are seeking to amplify and enhance certain aspects of the visible measurable aggregate. This could happen for two reasons, they are to enhance the common good or for private profit or gain. A common good example would be a government seeing the positive transformative power of education invests more public monies in this area. A private gain example would be the builder who sees the public desire for more dwellings and builds up large land banks, slowly building houses to the price artificially high by restricting supply.

Competitive, Collaborative Creative?

Underpinning these questions is the issue of what motives underpin an individual as an economic actor. We are as humans uniquely competitive and collaborative in our efforts at work, in our private lives. We need each other and yet we want to create and achieve individually. This is the nub the republican ideal outlined here seeks to tackle. Individuals want and need to be free, yet at the same time we have ties, sympathies and a fraternal links beyond ourselves into families, workplaces and communities. Individual freedom can only succeed if it works at these multiple levels and the inherent interdependencies in our economic and social activities are understood and accepted.

Searching for Solutions

Republicans want to close these avenues of advantage and prevent the economic institutionalisation that abuses personal freedoms exploiting both individuals and the communities they are part of. We want a solution, but believe that it will involve substantial change, not just reform or restructuring, not tinkering or refining. Such a change begins not with a policy shift or a new programme for government, though these would be important areas for action. It begins with an acceptance of the reality of economic life in the modern world. This means accepting or trying to begin to understand the complex maze of activities and choices that are being made by people within the economy. It means understanding also the forces that are impacting on that web especially those that are seeking means to amplify their impact. Government policy is such a force, as are the strategies and vested interests of divergent economic actors, whether they be large companies, groups of businesses or indeed large states or regional economic unions like the EU and the USA. In recent years social media and other online platforms have gate crashed this group and are a significant force in influencing economic decision making.

It means trying to grasp the shifting tides of consumer behaviour, the stormy seas of competing, then cohabiting then competing strategies that often characterise human endeavour. It means recognising that the only thing worse than an over powerful economic actor bent on exploitation and profiteering is a government bent on exploitation or strategising out of ignorance and weak will.

Helping the Invisible Republic Become Real

In the opening chapter we talked of an invisible republic, where despite the economic and political constraints of the time there were enduring positive bonds between people. And that as the years go by, as governments rise and fall, as trends emerge take shape and spin us momentarily, then dissipating, the core trends of the invisible republic would endure and re-emerge.

My argument was that we as a people still wanted to do things better, we still believed everyone should have a fair go, and that we would best be served by being partners in a fraternal society. In the intervening chapters we outlined some of the helps and hindrances to that invisible republic.

We showed the forces of coercion and tyranny at work and tried to lay out the basis for a new set of solutions rooted in the concept of recognising true relationships. We wanted to challenge the theologies of failed economic policies and institutionalised exploitation and coercion that blight society today.

In the introduction I summarised the core conclusions of this text and here they are again borrowing an idea from the opening pages of Wittgenstein's Tractatus Logico-Philosophicus (Wittgenstein 2001). I sincerely believe that we need in this century be able to explain our key ideas simply and clearly, and that is what I have tried to do here. We need to recover the republic but the first step is to recover ourselves and then offer a hand to the person next to us. We are each other.

The Principles of Socialist Republicanism in the Twenty-first Century

1. Individual freedom entails living in a state absent from coercion and exploitation.
2. We cannot be free as individuals unless we can exercise economic and political choices.

3. Republican freedom is conditional on a recognition of social interdependencies and the guarantees of equality of opportunity, access and treatment for citizens.
4. Money is not a neutral benign entity. Too often money is used to enslave and exploit. The renting of money resources should be entirely under the remit of a democratically formed government.
5. Markets will always tend towards oligopolies that seek to profit from their dominance and this is the rationale for market regulation.
6. To underpin the principles of social justice some goods should not be for sale, should not be able to be purchased. The provision and distribution of these goods should be regulated by society's democratically formed institutions.
7. Entrepreneurship is an exercise of republican freedom
8. We can only understand our society if we measure its activities, processes and outcomes accurately and comprehensively not just in terms of money.
9. Business cannot enjoy rights on a par with an individual citizen. The person is sovereign.

References

Bloomberg. (2016). *Tracking the 2016 Presidential Money Race.* Retrieved September 10 2017, from https://www.bloomberg.com/politics/graphics/2016-presidential-campaign-fundraising/

Fromm, E. (1955). *The Sane Society.* Henry Holt and Company.

Leonhardt, D. (2019). *A Plea to NBC,* June 25. Retrieved June 25, 2019, from https://mail.google.com/mail/u/0/#inbox/FMfcgxwChSGQDWSgvcSKMGqsCWzrnSGV

New York Times. (2012). The 2012 Money Race: Compare the Candidates. Retrieved September 10, 2017, from https://www.nytimes.com/elections/2012/campaign-finance.html?mcubz=0

Putnam, D. R. (2001). *Bowling Alone: The Collapse and Revival of American Community.* Simon and Schuster.

Reddan, F. (2017, February 16). Just One in Three Private Sector Workers Have a Pension. *Irish Times.*

Wittgenstein, L. (2001). *Tractatus Logico-Philosophicus.* Routledge.

Index

R. Smyth, *The Invisible Republic*,
https://doi.org/10.1007/978-3-030-86734-8

R

S

T

V

W

The manufacturer's authorised representative in the EU is Springer Nature Customer Service Centre GmbH, Europaplatz 3, 69115 Heidelberg, Germany. If you have any concerns regarding our products, please contact ProductSafety@springernature.com

Printed and bound by CPI Group (UK) Ltd, Croydon, CR0 4YY

30/09/2026

02225704-0002